AFRICA

*We Owe It to Our Ancestors,
Our Children, and Ourselves*

Michael Ba Banutu-Gomez

Hamilton Books

A member of

The Rowman & Littlefield Publishing Group

Lanham · Boulder · New York · Toronto · Oxford

The Prophet of Islam, Mohammad, tells us, "Let not those of you who possess grace and abundance swear against giving to those who have fled Allah's way. Do you not love that Allah should forgive you? Allah is Forgiving and Merciful." *The Holy Qu'ran*: Surah XXIV, verse 22.

CHRIST JESUS of Nazareth advised his followers, "Love your enemies, do good to those who hate you and lend, hoping for nothing in return. Condemn not, and you shall not be condemned: forgive and you shall be forgiven." St. Luke, Chapter 6, verses 27, 35 & 37.

Teacher Bahá 'u'lláh wrote, "Set your faces toward unity. Gather together and root out whatever is the source of contention amongst you."

This book is dedicated to my family and to those who love and care about Africa's success.

Contents

Preface

Africa: We Owe It to Our Ancestors, Our Children, and Ourselves is an essential resource for students, scholars and practitioners in the fields of Managing International Business, Managing in Developing Countries, Development Studies, Policy Studies, International Relations, Organization and Management Science, Earth Systems Science, as well as the disciplines of economics, sociology, political science, anthropology, and psychology. I urge people to buy this book, read it, and put the ideas into proactive action, from the roots to the tips.

I was born in Bakalar village, North Bank Division in the Gambia, West Africa. My parents were of the Manjako ethnic group from Guinea-Bissau, West Africa. I was born into a family that eventually included three older brothers, three older sisters, a younger sister and three younger brothers. My father taught me the value of hard work when I went with the farmers' association to work members' fields. I learned to see myself as a member of a community, which depended on each of its members to work for the common good. When someone was sick, the people in my age group worked their fields, made bricks, and fed their livestock. I learned that unity creates a successful community. My mother never let me forget the value of education because she did not want me to depend on rainfall for my living. I was sent to live with a family in another village so I could walk to St. Michael's elementary school, two miles away.

My brother Sampierre enrolled me in the Boy Scouts, which taught me to respect myself and to treat all people equally. I became a responsible person by doing tasks assigned to me and by valuing faith in God. Scouting taught me to do *first* what one has been assigned to do; afterward is the time to complain or offer suggestions. After primary school, I moved to the city of Serrekunda to live with the principal of St. Theresa's secondary school while completing my secondary education. I enjoyed service projects, which gave me the opportunity to listen to elders who told us about their lives and gave us advice. Our troop helped build a Mosque and cleaned and mowed both Christian and Muslim graveyards. In the Young Farmers' Club, proceeds from all of the crops we grew were used to pay for the lunches of poor students. This made me sensitive to opportunities to help others. I joined St. Theresa's Senior Choir and sang in their fundraising concerts to earn money to renovate our church. We also paid for poor people's burials out of our fundraising money.

Acknowledgments

The author would like to thank his wife, Shandra Banutu-Gomez, daughter, Nyima Francine Banutu-Gomez, and friends for their support and encouragement while writing this book. I particularly would like to thank my research assistant, Amanda R. Wingate, and Marcy Thorner, The Grammar Guru, for help in the editing process.

I hope that this book will contribute in some way to the education and service delivery skills of future dedicated individuals and professionals who care about Africa's success in the 21st century.

Introduction: A Child of the Land

In Africa, my home, the land is great. I want to be at home, to feel the cool breeze of nature. The wind smells so good. That is why African people are proud of where they came from. They see African society as good because they feel a sense of belonging to the society, the community. The community embraces everyone, so everyone feels that they are a part of a collective identity. Peace abounds in the community, because everyone feels at one with the community. I can remember going to the land, our farm, when my father, my mother, and everybody in the family went. We walked the entire way to my parents' farmlands, all of us together. We walked along the single lane dirt road past tall grasses and trees. On the way, we stopped to greet people who were already in their fields. My African culture taught me to say hello to all we passed regardless of whether we knew them or not. Also, we always said, "*barran*" which means "good work" in Manjako, my native language.

When we walked to our lands early in the morning, deer, bush pigs, squirrels, and rabbits often scampered across the road in front of us, or a snake glided silently in front of us while monkeys in trees sat quietly peeking at us and hooting in low tones to each other about us. People work together on the farm, everyone helping: children fetch water and give it to those tilling the ground and take care of their younger sisters and brothers while Mom and Dad work the land. As a young boy, some of my responsibilities on our lands included driving away monkeys who tried to dig up our peanut crop and scaring away pigeons that wanted to eat the peanut, sorghum, and millet seeds we had planted. I had to also watch out for squirrels that wanted our peanut seeds. All us children would go to the far side of the field closer to the bush where the wild animals usually emerged to raid our fields. We took with us our hunting dogs. Every day, I ran into the bush when our dogs chased monkeys and squirrels that were near the fields.

If my dogs trapped a monkey in a tree, I ran to tell my parents. We all got sticks and threw them up into the tree while we screamed threateningly at the monkey, who was so distracted it jumped down from the tree in an effort to escape us. By the time he had reached another tree, our dogs had him by the neck. We carried the dead monkey back to the field and roasted him for the dogs. Our dogs never touched a baby monkey. If they caught one, they would drop it and chase after its parents, which came when the baby cried.

Everyone in the family sees themselves contributing to the whole family. At noon, the children walked back to the houses with an old person to feed and water to our goats and sheep and move them to another field to graze. In the evening, the young children left their families still working in our fields to feed and water the goats and sheep and lead them to their sheds for the night. By these practices, a sense of responsibility was instilled in me from a very early age. I was proud of the responsibilities that my parents gave me. They were very supportive of all of their children and showed us how proud they were of how well we helped our family.

This is Africa. This is the land all Africans must love, the place where culture and life started. I love Africa. I never ever thought of anything for which I needed to ask my parents because they constantly were thinking of what we needed and asked us what we wanted after we had finished our assigned tasks.

When rain falls in Africa, everyone is happy. Children, adults, elders, everyone in the community loves rainfall. People rejoice when rain falls; because of nature, we have our food. Nature waters all the plants, trees, and crops, and gives us water to drink. It gives us showers. Everything looks so beautiful, so green. When I was child, we went outside to play when the rain came. We ran around and played soccer. I remember Africa in those days. Africa is a place to enjoy; a land of cultures, a land of pride, and of beloved Mother Nature. We must remember the days when we got up early to go to the farms to take sheep, cows, goats, or pigs to the fields to enjoy the green grass. I can see children running around. I can see little kids jumping and falling to the ground, smiling and laughing so loud. In the village there are no strangers; we fear no one because we know everyone in the community. At night, when stars were everywhere, children, elders, and everyone stay out. Children ran around; adults walked around. We played hide and seek and other exciting games, skipping down the streets. People did not depend on electricity, they depended on nature. God made light. It was great. I remember visiting friends, screaming in the streets. Because of the moon, we could see everywhere we went. The night was full of happiness and joy. After dinner, we young children cleared the table and then everyone gathered on the verandah in front of our house to listen to our parents or another older person tell true stories and folk tales that taught lessons about responsibility, history, and culture. When it was stuffy and hot inside the house, we took our mats and slept outside in the yard around the house, enjoying the cool breeze that touched our bodies as we slept. No one ever bothered us as we slept there until the sun rose. To me, this is freedom. I can find freedom in

Africa. This is because we all eat out of the same bowl at meals. This creates unity.

I was born in Bakalar village, North Bank Division in the Gambia, West Africa.

My parents were of the Manjako ethnic group from Guinea-Bissau, West Africa. I was born into a family that eventually included three older brothers, three older sisters, a younger sister, and four younger brothers. My father taught me the value of hard work when I went with the farmers' association to work members' fields. I learned to see myself as a member of a community, which depended on each of its members to work for the common good. When someone was sick, the people in my age group worked their fields, made bricks, and fed their livestock. I learned that unity creates a successful community. My mother never let me forget the value of education because she did not want me to depend on rainfall for my living. I was sent to live with a family in another village so I could walk to St. Michael's elementary school, two miles away.

My brother Sampierre enrolled me in the Boy Scouts, which taught me to respect myself and to treat all people equally. I became a responsible person by doing tasks assigned to me and by valuing faith in God. Scouting taught me to do *first* what one has been assigned to do; afterward is the time to complain or offer suggestions. After primary school, I moved to the city of Serrekunda to live with the principal of St. Theresa's secondary school while completing my secondary education. I enjoyed service projects, which gave me the opportunity to listen to elders who told us about their lives and gave us advice. Our troop helped build a Mosque and cleaned and mowed both Christian and Muslim graveyards. In the Young Farmers' Club, all the crops we grew were sold to pay for the lunches of poor students. This made me sensitive to opportunities to help others. I joined St. Theresa's Senior Choir and sang in their fundraising concerts to earn money to renovate our church. We also paid for poor people's burials out of our choir fund. I learned that it is my responsibility to share in the efforts to meet my community's needs. I joined the Serrekunda Youth Group and built houses and cleaned city property.

One day, I heard Ousman Jallow, the former minister of water resources, on the radio. He admonished us to refrain from criticizing our government unless we exercised our right to vote. Neneh Gomez encouraged women as well as men to unite and vote: "Women should not sit back but join men and express their views at political rallies. Both males and females are required to change society so men must respect the views of women." Upon graduation from secondary school, I entered The Gambia Teachers College and also worked as a volunteer assistant organizing commissioner at the Gambian National Scout Headquarters. As president of the Young Christian Students Association at my college, I surveyed three villages in each of the five divisions of The Gambia to collect data on poverty. I was interviewed on Gambian National Radio to discuss the findings of my survey. As the assistant director of the Culture and Drama Club at my college, I enjoyed visiting villages of different tribes in my country, to invite oral historians and musicians to perform at the orientation party we sponsored every September for new students. My experience of different tribal cultures made me realize that each person comes from a unique ethnic and cultural background and that one must learn about, respect, appreciate, and maintain other cultures if one wants to work successfully with other people. After I graduated from teachers' college, I taught sixth grade for one year, and then the Minister of Education requested me to accept a paid position as a Scout Commissioner in the Department of Youth and Sports. The following year, I flew to America to become an international Scout counselor.

My objective is to prepare myself to serve as an effective, responsive, and creative leader in private and public organizations and in government. I am working to strengthen commitment to community mechanisms by the application of principles of community development, which have guided traditional African social structures over the centuries. I want to work to reduce the level of violence in the world by motivating people to feel a responsibility to the community in which they live, study, and work. It is necessary to help people develop a more positive sense of their identity as a member of a community. We must be willing to give up the current emphasis on "I" for more of an emphasis on "we." I want to help all people take measures that can lead to the unity of the human race and eradicate fear between individuals and groups, regardless of race, religion, social or economic class, gender, or sexual preference. I would like to help bring about changes in agencies, institutions, companies, and governments that will lead to the creation of missions to support and maintain diverse cultures and develop policies that nurture the success of people of every race, culture, and ethnic background.

Chapter 1

The Traditional African Community

Music and Traditional Communication

We had telephones in Africa long before the arrival of Europeans. Our telephones were our talking drums, which were understood by the people in the community and interpreted by the elders. Whenever there was a disaster in a village, someone went to the drum and hit it. People far away who heard the sound listened carefully. If children were playing, they asked the children to be quiet because they knew something important was happening. Everyone was quiet, and then they listened to the elders for instruction after they had interpreted the meaning of the message. We made the drums without spending a lot of money. Why do we have to move away from our cultural traditions and inflict pain upon ourselves? Let's go back and evaluate what we had and value what our traditional culture can produce in Africa.

A celebration is a time when people rejoice for what they were able to plant and harvest from their land, a time to sit down and reflect upon one's actions. It is a time to think back on the hardships of life and forward to the future with joy. Any celebration is a time for sharing joy and happiness. Among traditional believers, Christians or Muslims, everyone joins the community in celebration. People laugh, play traditional drums, and sing. The happiness in the community is obvious to all who pause to appreciate it.

Music is so important in Africa that even on the farm, musicians are hired to sing and play drums as positive motivation for people working on the farm. The musicians tell those working on the farm about their great-grandparents, about the greatness of their ancestors, what the family values and what is unique about each family. A musician that keeps the traditions of oral history is not seen as a bum, as someone who does not want to work, but as someone with a special skill that can benefit the whole community. In the traditional view, musicians must be respected because music is the key to happiness. Music is the key to understanding that oneself, to learning about one's own generation, and the parents' generations and those before them. It is the key to understanding the ethnic group, the family, and the community.

Music helps Africans appreciate each person's skills in the community. People working on the farms use music as a key motivator; it gives them inspiration and power.

Through the experience of music, Africans look back to their past and express hope for their future. Music helps Africans to become more creative. It develops their physical, mental, aesthetic, and leadership skills. Each age group in the community enjoys its own kind of music. As one grows older and attains higher status in the society, the music one enjoys changes. This reminds younger people of the value of older people and to respect them. The tune and even the type of musical instruments used changes with the age group that is listening.

Music goes hand in hand with African spirituality. Africans regard music as a method they can use to make a connection with their ancestors and God. Music allows us to express our deepest emotions using a unique God-given gift that is present in each individual. Music helps each family to know about its founders. Music helps ensure the success of individual Africans by helping them socialize with each other. Music assists Africans to work together as communities and to plan strategically and embark upon community projects as a single social unit. African music is an ancient language, developed long before Europeans came to that continent. This language can only be understood and translated by people who have been taught its special skills.

Almost all African gatherings include music, especially rituals, in which Africans gather to pray to ask forgiveness from their ancestors and nature. Whenever naming ceremonies are planned, musicians are asked to come and play. The musicians rejoice with the people and create an air of excitement. The skills of the musicians are considered to be unique and are highly valued. Music plays an essential role in helping to maintain traditional African commitment to community mechanisms because it brings people together as human beings and is a way of supporting traditional culture. Traditional musicians pass on their skills to their children so that the traditional occupation of musician will stay within the family. Because of what they can offer their society by using their skills, musician's families are remembered for generations. For the children of musicians, producing music is a unique skill, a gift, which is harnessed and shaped by their parents. These children are taught that when they continue this tradition in their family, the founder (ancestor) of their family will be proud to see them sharing this gift with their community.

Music fulfills the role of a watchdog in the community: whenever something happens, people use music to communicate secretly with each other. For example, when a thief breaks into someone's house in the community it would necessitate secret communications. Also, music helps to relieve any stress that Africans feel. It allows them to distance themselves psychologically from their problems. Even on the farms, musicians tap into the positive energy of people working on the farm to empower and encourage them. Music is so powerful in African society that all Africans can state proudly,

> Yes, our ancestors have left us something that is unique and valuable; something that can benefit all generations, something that can positively shape our behavior, something that can create a human being who is whole; a person who can be proud of what they can do, see the product of their creativity and share it with other human beings to benefit them.

Traditional music is not easy to perform. African musicians take time to practice and carry out oral research. To find out more information about each family in the community, they go to the elders, the oldest people in the community. They use this information to prepare musical oral histories, which are ready to perform at any important occasion. They come out on those occasions and recite these histories with excitement, courage, and dignity. The sound of their voices and the movements of their hands creating the tunes on the drums express immense pride. Music is one of the most important keys to the empowerment of people in African society.

Not everyone in African society can become a musician. It is a talent given by God to a few individuals. Africans believe that these people have been chosen by God to serve the community through the use of their musical skills. We believe that they can help us reconnect in our hearts with our ancestors and with God. Musicians have received this special talent from God; it requires courage, stamina, and hard work to express itself, and a spirit of cooperation and self-awareness to the community. It promotes African culture and brings together the past and the present.

Musicianship is a unique talent that enables us to become alive with our whole body, mind, and soul and to unify with our environment.

Music is a very important aspect of African culture. When there has been a death, musicians come to call on the ancestors to take the soul of the dead person to join them. The musicians honor the dead person as someone who was valuable in their community, who was loved, and whom people want to remember with pride. With their music, the musicians say, "This person was someone special in the community and should be recognized and praised for what they have done in their lifetime." Whenever someone is a lost, in the town or in the woods, the townsfolk contact a traditional musician to use their talking drums to communicate throughout the community and from among villages. The sounds of the drums send the message and a description of the person who is lost and details about where they were last seen. Usually, it is not difficult to relocate the lost person because the information is circulated beyond the confines of the local community to people living in other nearby areas. In this regard, traditional African music helps people to work together, communicate easily, and solve their problems. Traditional African musicians use materials at hand to create their musical instruments. They have no need to import them from elsewhere. The musicians find the supplies they in their nearby environment.

I believe that moving away from traditional music and traditional African musical instruments is costly to Africans. When we copy Western music and use European instruments, we sell ourselves out in order to please them. In economic terms, the price of importing Western music is too high for Africans to maintain. What should we do, as Africans, to maintain traditional African music and musical instruments and support traditional African musicians? This effort would provide self-employment for people with special musical talents in Africa. When we Africans turn away from our traditional instruments and music, we negate all of our ancient societal norms and values, which operate hand in hand to support the role of African traditional music in our culture. We forget about our ancestors. We grow up not knowing our history, our respon- sibility to care for our natural environment, and how to socialize our children properly.

If we desire to use European musical instruments to perform Western music, we must copy Western musical education, content, and form. Why not revolutionize traditional African musical instruments and musical forms to allow them to be more responsive to the needs of present generation Africans? Africa does not need a carbon copy of what the West has done. We should follow the example of our ancestors and build upon it. We should be proud of what they were able to do in creating our culture, what they have given us, what they have shared with us, and what they have left for us on the earth. What conflicts are we creating among ourselves when we move away from our traditional African forms of music and musical instruments? What pain are we inflicting on the younger generation? What confusion are we creating in our African society? Do we need this type of confusion at this time? Some of the things that our traditional musicians have been doing and using may not be useful now, but that does not mean that we have to throw away everything! In the future, we need to be creative and invent new African musical forms, which can help us satisfy the social needs that traditional African music has fulfilled for millennia. It is time to look for musicians who are ready for Africa's twentieth century, but, we can- not do it unless we first look to our mother, the past, and reconnect her musical birth-cord to our present-day musical forms. Only then can a live birth of the future of authentic African music take place.

If Africans continue to say that music is so important to our culture, then why is our traditional music being neglected? If this is really true, then we should know what music meant to our parents, and to our ethnic group, from one generation to the next, until our present day. If this is really true, we would value our traditional musicians, their musical instruments, and their musical forms more than we value Western music. If we do not, we should ask ourselves this question: "Why do we serve and support other cultures more than we serve and support our own culture?" Let us stop brainwashing ourselves by highly valuing Western culture and its music, both popular and classical. Our traditional music made our ancestors powerful and gave them dignity in their society. Traditional

African musical performance is a skill that cannot be completely understood by anyone brought up in a Western culture. Its value and power can only be understood and released by Africans who believe in it and pass it on from one generation to the next. If human life as a separate species first appeared somewhere on the continent that we now call Africa, then the roots of all music originate in it also. Our traditional oral musical historians tell us that human civilization also originated on the continent of Africa.

Yes, indeed, to be proud of traditional music is to be proud of one's African ethnicity, proud of one's ancestors, proud of one's continent and its natural environment. We need to listen to our traditional musicians. They will continue to tell us how important it is to be proud of who we are, what we have been given by the community, society, and family, and to be proud to pass this on to one's children as well. We need to realize that because Africans have been moving away from an interest in traditional music, they have begun to face more poverty because what we are moving toward is not deeply rooted in our culture. Because we are adopting ways of life that are not deeply rooted in our culture, we are abusing ourselves, which carries a high price both socially and economically. This trend is causing our societies and economies to crumble because the foundation, our culture, is being eroded. This is happening all over Africa. We must be willing to assess ourselves and examine why certain aspects of our traditional African culture, such as our traditional musicians, are important and necessary to believe in, promote, and maintain.

When one loses one's traditional culture, one becomes psychologically frail and too weak to fight the external forces that constantly seek to exploit oneself and one's society. We fail to have a sense of direction because we have lost sight of our culture. Culture is the foundation of all social interactions for human beings. We can truly call our unique African culture our own. In this culture we invest our pride, our belief, and our conviction from one generation to another.

African music creates a community that can grow and socially evolve together, competent in the fight to resist the encroachment of poverty and able to alleviate the unavoidable suffering and pain that its members experience in their lives.

Death

In Africa, children get up early in the morning. Before they greet grandparents, fathers, and mothers, they brush their teeth and wash their faces. Children feel that they are a part of everyone, and in order for the family to communicate, they must greet each other. Families and elders mean a lot to an African child, and even death has a presence there. When someone dies in the community, people pay a visit—from children to adults—in the family. They mourn together because they feel part of the pain that faces the family. They take time to work on the widow's land. It shows the family that in the community there is oneness. Death is not the end of life. Those who are dead will guide those who are alive because those who died are closer to God. God is the one who called them. No one can resist God's call because it is so powerful. God creates us and is the one who can take our life away.

To prepare for death, elders buy traditionally woven cloth to be used to wrap them for burial. They choose the colors they want and talk to their families about what they want for their burial. They know when they are going to die. When one is sick, relatives are invited to visit and to talk every day to say goodbye. The visitors then ask those who are about to depart to ask the ancestors for their blessings and to extend their greetings to the ancestors whom they soon will be joining. In preparing for death, sometimes, people who know they are dying will request that a cow, sheep, or pig be slaughtered during the funeral celebration. If this will be a hardship for the family, the dying person will give permission for their memorial celebration to be delayed for one year to allow for enough preparation time. In the community, when the elders find out that a young child will die, they invite the age group of that child to visit. They allow people to talk with the sick child. This educates the other children to be aware of the fact that people come to the earth through the power of God and that God can call them back. What that means is that people are alive but at the same time, they can die and go to another world.

I knew this when I was a child. I knew that I would die one day because I was educated about death when I was a child. I was told that if people were to live forever, this world would be too full of people. Life comes and goes. People go to another part of our universe when they die. Their bodies turn into dust but their spirits remain alive through the power of God. For this reason, I did not feel that death was a threat but rather a part of life. I have seen people my own age die, people younger than me and people older than me die in my community. I am proud that my parents and community prepared me to know that nothing will live forever.

A child's death creates much pain in the community and society because the child has not had a chance to enjoy life nor contribute to the community and society. When a child dies, the whole community cries and mourns. Even calling that child's name becomes taboo. People avoid naming another child with the name of the one who died. If they did, they would open the wound that the death of that child caused in the family and community. A child's death is celebrated only once. When a child dies, their age group makes a contribution to the family. An older person's death may be celebrated twice because this person has contributed to the family and the community. The living can reflect on the role that person played in the community. For this reason, Africans are very proud to celebrate an elder's death.

Africans hold memorial celebrations because they want the community to remember their relatives who have died. A memorial celebration is a time for family and the community to get in touch with their ancestors. The surviving family members also want to show the person who has died that he or she is still a part of the family and community. The memorial celebration and rituals are performed to show this person that the family and community think of them with pride and that they appreciate the positive things he or she did for them. It is thought that this relative will be able to bring all of the ancestors who have been gone for years, decades, or even centuries to join in the celebration, to visit the family, and give their blessings. Even though we cannot see them, we feel that they are enjoying the celebration as much as we are enjoying it.

Usually, the memorial celebration is planned a year in advance so that family members and friends, who may be in other countries, can be informed and can attend or send their contributions. They come to enjoy the celebration and even though they know they may cry, it is part of life to feel this way. I speak for my ethnic group, the Manjakos, in saying that this is so important to African life that Africans believe that if they do not hold a memorial ceremony for a parent, they will not have blessings in their life. One cannot prosper under these circumstances because one's ancestors will not be proud and they will not forgive. That is not to say that one must steal or perform illegal acts to get money for this celebration.

Each year, we buy palm wine or get water and pour it on the ground and ask the ancestors to give us a good crop yield so that we might have money to celebrate and good health so that we can produce much to help the family prosper. If this is not possible, the celebration is postponed and the elders gather together to ask the ancestors to wait for another year.

This is a very important celebration for Africans. I think we should continue to hold memorial celebrations because it helps us feel connected to our ancestors and gives us the stamina to work for a good life until we enter the next world. It reminds us that someday we will join our ancestors and see our parents and relatives who have died. For this reason, thinking about ancestors becomes part of our daily life. It is great to think that one day one will see ancestors whom one has never even met before! We look forward to that day of our death. We call ancestors *baluum*. These ancestors who have died come occasionally to visit us. It is believed that if we do not hold a memorial celebration for parents who have died, their will curses will confer bad fortune because their age group, which is with them in the other world, will laugh at them and tell them that they have left nothing good on earth because their earthly family is so useless! "See, they are not proud of you, what you have done for them and what you have given them," they say. "That is why they didn't celebrate your death." Even though no one has ever seen this happen, no one wants their parents to suffer such shame. Because we wants our own death ceremony to be great, we set an example for children to follow by holding a memorial celebration for their grandparents. It is believed that if one neglects to hold a memorial celebration for a relative who has died, someone in the family will become sick and will not recover unless an apology is offered to that relative. This is why people are very careful not to neglect a memorial celebration. Someone who fails to plan and then hold a memorial celebration for a parent and then has a poor crop yield is blamed for their own misfortune. People in the community feel that such behavior is a threat to the whole community. It is a threat because people believe in it. It will be difficult to convince them that the poor crop yield has nothing to do with neglecting to have a memorial celebration for a deceased parent. Once Africans believe in traditions, it is very difficult to change their minds.

Memorial celebrations are very important because they bring the whole community together. Members of the extended family who now live in other countries often come back for the celebration. It is like a family and community reunion. People have to be very careful about what they do on earth because they know that one day they, too, are going to go, to die. How well a memorial ceremony and celebration is attended shows how well that person is respected for all the positive things they did for the community. These celebrations are also very important because they promote awareness of the culture and help foster pride in the society.

The memorial celebration is an opportunity for us to communicate with our ancestors and those who have recently died. This communication is very important in our lives, and provides a time for us to show our love and respect for our ancestors. It is a time for us to pave a positive path for all of us to join together and rejoice in the world to come. I hope and believe that one day, when I die, I will see my parents, ancestors, and relatives, and we will all be together in another world. I believe that when someone dies, the spirit goes to this other world. A family that holds a memorial celebration and then has a year of good health and a good crop yield believes that their dead relative asked the ancestors to request blessings for that family. God has answered their prayers. God has given them good health. This is so important that forgetting about it would lead to disaster and bring destruction to the family as well as the community. This kind of death celebration encourages cooperation and creates unity within the community.

Traditional Religion and Its Future

I feel that traditional African religion is great because we believe in God. We believe in only one God. Our ancestors were created by God and have been called by God to answer to Him. Because we were created by God and will be called to be with Him someday, like our ancestors, we will gather together to make sacrifices and ask our ancestors to pray to God because they are closer to Him—not because they *are* God; we know they are not God: we believe that they are *with* God. We believe that they will always be around for us if we need them and will come when we are sick. We feel that they can take pain and sickness away from us. This is a fundamental belief. This is traditional African religion. God made religion for all humanity. God is *one*.

Traditional religion is very important in Africa, where religion brings people together. Religion forms a community. Religion encourages people to appreciate each other. Religion bonds people together in a society and encourages them to show love to everyone in their community. Religion helps Africans to share the norms, values, and morality of their culture. Traditional African religion gives individuals the freedom to consider what they intend to do and to decide freely whether it is destructive to themselves or their community.

Religion presents the individual with the important choices that they must make in life. Traditional religion is important in Africa because it bridges the temporal gap between the ancestors and their descendants who are living. Religion brings Africans together as a family to reflect on their ancestors and to pray to them to ask God to give them guidance. Traditional African religion allows people to have hope for the future of their society. Traditional religion makes Africans feel prestige and pride in the culture and to embrace their roles in the community. It encourages us to respect our ancestors by telling us to gather together to remember them and to ask them to ask God for blessings for us.

Traditional African religion helps us to form a better community. It encourages people to work together on common social issues and problems in their society because it is a commitment to community mechanism. People love and respect each other and gather together in peace, even though they are faced with difficulty and poverty. This is because they have hope that their ancestors, who have gone to be with God but who come back to visit, will one day rescue them by the power of God's will. Traditional religion makes people seriously consider their intended actions and their consequences in the community. Traditional religion eliminates any "strangerness" in the African community because it brings people together to rejoice in one Supreme Being.

My ethnic group, the Manjako tribe, practices traditional religion. They believe that there is only one God and that their ancestors are not gods but instead are closer to God than we are. Because we know that we too will have to answer God's call someday, we also know that we are only temporarily in this world of the living.

Traditional religion encourages us to think about helping others in our community because it tells us that we depend on each other. No human being is better than any other because we are all created by *Nasibati*, which in Manjako means God. Traditional religion helps people to become responsible. It elucidates our role in the society and what is expected of each of us. It thus helps us to become obedient and to understand what we need to do to become better humans in our community. Traditional religion teaches us to become accountable for our actions and to be ready to look out for everyone in the community. This eliminates "strangerness" and builds a sense of community. It builds communities that care about human beings and provide role models.

Traditional religion guides us toward our final destination. As Africans, we know we will die and because of that, we know we must prepare for our future now and here. We must do that so that our destination, which is death, will become a positive experience for us. Traditional religion guides us to avoid evil deeds and to become constructive in our society. It helps us to value our culture and to maintain the norms of our society. Traditional religion encourages us as Africans to be proud of our ancestors, our communities, our skills, and ourselves. It helps us to have faith in God. It tells us to set a good example for others to follow so that our society will be safe, loving, and caring.

Traditional religion helps us to know our roots, to feel personal power, and to have the energy to serve our society. It serves as a path to enlightenment and toward an awakening to one's unique culture. It brings us together as a community that cares about its society and values human life. Traditional religion creates connectedness among individuals in the community and society. It also serves as a forum in which people's frustrations can be healed though the power of God and our ancestors. It plays an important role in the lives of Africans because it is a way to meet other people who are different. It forces us to see other people as essential parts of our own personal lives and not to see ourselves as independent of everyone else. Traditional African religion creates an atmosphere of "we-ness" rather than a focus on "I" because it is a community-based philosophy. It serves as a control mechanism in the community and the society. It helps us to avoid an immoral life and to make us aware of our own morality. It helps each of us to have a positive state of mind and helps to maintain the positive mental equilibrium of the community and the society.

Traditional African religion helps to socialize young people to become good citizens who are responsible, hardworking, and dedicated to their community. It gives us role models that we can emulate and to whom we can always to for advice. It gives us strength of purpose in whatever we decide to do in our communities. This faith holds us together as a family and as a community and is the glue that holds our society together. It teaches us about our capacity for spirituality and helps us whenever we are in danger; it is where we turn when we face difficulty. It calls on all human beings to gather together to serve one God. Traditional religion gives us the strength to do the tasks of our daily lives. It gives us the motivation to work hard and to think about the good of our family, our community, our society, and all humans around us as well as our environment.

Traditional African religion helps us to feel connected to the natural world and to love and appreciate it. It helps us to value our language because it is the language we use to communicate with God, our ancestors, and nature. It teaches us to view all people in the same way, regardless of the color of their skin. Traditional religion serves as a guide to behavior for all people who live in African communities and society because we are all on a journey in which the destination must be prepared for before it is reached. It mobilizes adults and molds the lives of young people in our communities.

Traditional religion gives us self-esteem and dignity. It serves to empower our spiritual life. It is the essential and integral foundation of African life because it links us with our ancestors and thus it has no historical beginning or end. For this reason, it keeps us in touch with the founders of our ethnic group or tribe and connects one generation with the next. Traditional religion takes us from this world to another world that is the home of all of our ancestors. When we practice traditional religion, we are at one with God and the founders of our tribe. It promotes cooperation in our communities and encourages a healthy fear of God. We believe that if we sin, not only will God punish us, but also that our ancestors will be angry with us, especially if we fail to remember them in our gatherings. Traditional religion brings us in touch with *nasibati*, the Supreme

Being, the creator of the world and of our ancestors; the most powerful force in the universe, the source of all good things. If we believe in and adore *nasibati*, we can ask for forgiveness directly from God because God is around anywhere we are; *nasibati* sees and hears everyone.

The spread of Western materialism has adversely affected traditional African beliefs and practice. As African people adopt Western materialism, they become more concerned with the material goods that they can gain for themselves and for their immediate families instead of being concerned with the needs and wealth of their communities. This has a negative effect on traditional African religion because it is a community-based social structure, not an individually based religion. Traditional African religion is concerned with the needs of all individuals, as a group, in the community. In the past, a member of a community held sacred a specific place that they believed was God's chosen place of prayer. A person to whom God had spoken had identified this place as sacred.

When Africans began attending Western-type schools, they were told that people who consider a particular place as holy are actually worshipping the devil. Now, people who still keep these beliefs and practices are seen as backward and primitive.

Traditional African religion cannot be practiced as an individual. Religious practice must be performed as a group, a community. Prayer and worship must be done together. People, as a community, go to the sacred place where they believe God wants them to pray when someone is sick and needs healing from God. For this reason, traditional African religion engenders a true commitment to community mechanism.

When a community suffers several tragedies in the same year, people go there as groups to bring some of their livestock to sacrifice and to ask God for forgiveness and for future blessings. When crops dry up or there is a severe lack of rain, a community may go to its sacred place to perform sacrifices and to pray. Traditionally people belief that by sacrificing livestock, God will bless the community and their wish will come true. It is hoped that after the sacrifice, evil will disappear and the community will be more peaceful by God's blessing. When Western missionaries discovered that the parents of their students continued to perform these traditional African religious practices, they sent the children home and would not let them return to school unless the parents agreed not to involve their children in the family's traditional African religious practices. Otherwise, that child would be ridiculed in the school and ostracized as a member of a "pagan" family.

At this time, there has yet to be dialog between traditional African believers and African intellectuals. Africans need to look at how traditional African religion supports and maintains a healthy African culture and society. Religion is the storehouse of essential values upon which every culture and society is built. To rob a people of their traditional religion is to perform a cultural rape that leaves their society an empty shell that is only a shadow of a real society. Traditional African religion requires young people to view their parents' friends as additional parents and all elders of their community as their grandparents whom they must respect and emulate. By bringing everyone together in a community, traditional African religion socializes the young to become useful members of their society.

Elders and Their Vanishing Roles

Age is important in Africa because one is valued and respected in society according to one's age and performance as an example to those younger. Age is a sign of dignity, prestige, respect, and status in the society. Someone who has gray hair is in a special class: a class of respect, of consultation, of advisement, of positive example. Such people will have the respect of the community and be supported and valued. Young children will learn from them and follow in their footsteps. This is why, even after death, one is still remembered. In old age, one is aware of one's responsibilities. One begins to question oneself about one's role in society and performs responsibilities according to how age according to society's expectations. This wisdom passes from one generation to the next.

Elders are people who are loving, caring, and appreciated by other people in the community, especially the young people because the elders are the ones who should set a positive example for the younger generation to follow throughout their life career. Elders in the community are looked upon for guidance and support, as well as training.

They are the ones to whom people should feel free to turn if there is any difficulty in the community. Elders in the community are role models. They are leaders. They are parents, uncles, aunts, and grandparents. They provide everything that children need in the society throughout their lives. Elders are the ones in the community who are responsible to mold the lives of the children of the community. They are the people to whom we should look as people whom we should emulate in our lives. Elders do not put us in danger and who are concerned with our progress and influence our future lives. They play an important role in society because they are there for every child, not just for their own biological children or their own related family, but also for everyone who lives in the community.

Elders intervene when there is a conflict in the society or the community. They also intervene when children or teenagers have problems, even if they are not their close relatives. As long as children live in the community, they are answerable to the elders, so elders take up this responsibility as something that is very important to them. They value and embrace it because it gives them the opportunity to apply their positive skills to raise good citizens. Elders try to bring the society together to forge a positive bond between the younger and older generations. Elders give direction to people in the community in a way that reflects on their past experience and applies it to the experience of the younger generation to show them their role in society. The elders' roles are very important in African society because their actions are very important. What they do will reflect their morality and how people value them in the community. Elders are teachers who are informally trained and who pass on unique skills to the younger generation. Their actions connect people in such a way that the society can be controlled. In this way, culture, morality, pride, and shame can exist within each human being in the society.

Elders are important not only in the community but also in the family because they work very hard to support their family. They are either employed in Western-type urban institutions or have traditional jobs such as farming in which they produce crops to support their families. Elders play an important role in the family because they take time to be with their family to be a good example to them so that the children will feel secure and will not become destructive. The failure of a child shows a failure in the social life of the whole family and community. Elders try their very best to know every child in the community and to be willing to help them on their way and give them advice whenever they feel that what the children are doing is destructive to themselves, their parents, or their community. They look out for everyone in the society so each person can become a better human being. Elders play an important role in the family because they try to know all the friends of their children and accept them and love and care about their children's friends and welcome them into the home. Elders in the family, as well as the community, want to know with whom their children fall in love so that they will know the family of the boy- or girl-friend so that they can build more relationships. Elders feel honored and respected when their children bring their loved ones to meet their family and introduce them to their parents. Failure to do so is disrespectful to the elders in the family and in the community.

In Africa, elders are advocates for children in the community. They can be agents of social change. Whenever elders meet with their age group, not only do they discuss issues that affect them but also issues that effect the younger generation and the problems that they face. They discuss how they might work with the children to help solve the problems. In our African society, elders are the allies of the children. Elders spread their arms and embrace everyone in the community. In Africa, in our society, elders are community organizers. They organize people of their own age as well as the younger generation around social issues that are affecting the community. They come out to challenge people about issues that are impacting society. The positive energy they put into it will motivate the younger generation to follow in their footsteps. The role of elders in African society is very important because if they fail to mobilize and socialize the younger generation, they will eventually end up with a society that is full of social problems, that has no values, morality, or freedom, and a society full of confusion with no hope for the future.

In Africa, elders play an important role in the family, especially when their children are in school. Even though they may not have been in school, they are always concerned about what one is doing in school, especially as regards homework. They will always ask whether homework has been done not. If one needs assistance, the elder will call on someone in the community who has had more education to assist. This is their responsibility in the family. They ensure that the children go to school, have food to eat, clothing to wear, and a place to live. Elders play an important role in the family as well as the community, especially, in what happens to their children. If a girl becomes pregnant, the parents always ask who is the father of the child. They communicate with the father's parents so that the boy can take up his responsibility to the child so the burden is not only on the mother. This is just one of the roles that elders play in African society because they feel that if they neglect this role there might be a lot of out-of-wedlock children in the community. If that happens, it will encourage children to have children without a place for them in the society. They know that if this is allowed to continue, it will lead to violence, lack of respect, and loss of dignity within the community. Elders will no longer be valued and respected in this community because it will mean that they have failed to perform their role in the family, community, and society.

In African society, elders can be seen as positive mentors in the community. Old age is important in Africa because the older one is, the more they are respected and valued in the community. With age comes the move toward the highest class in society with more responsibility. Elders know that old age brings respect, dignity, responsibility, hard work, and dedication as well as love of community. In Africa, elders play an important role in the family because they are the ones responsible for educating the children about their culture, traditions, and the norms of the society. In the family, elders are responsible for telling the children about the history of their ethnic group, particularly what is unique about their family. They tell them about their great-grandparents. They try to find time in the evening to sit down on the verandah to give the children a traditional oral history lesson about their community and their society.

Elders are very important because whenever there is a conflict between them and the younger generation, they always try to find ways to solve it. Failure to do so results in failure to perform their role as elders in the society, which is shameful to them because they would be seen as doing something wrong to their society. It is the role of the elders to make things work out in a positive way for the community. Elders in African society do not dress like younger people. They act their age as elders. They dress in a way that shows a high standard of prestige and dignity so that competition between elders and the younger generation will not exist. They dress in a way that shows they know their role in society and the expectations of them, which are held by people in the community. In Africa, it is insulting to meet an elder and tell them that they look younger. The elder will feel humiliated. In fact, if one tells an elder that they look younger, they may even call their children so that you will see that they are not young and that they do not want the compliment of being young. Telling an elder that they look young means, to them, that you are trying to devalue and take away their responsibility and role in the community. This is because they will think that their behavior and appearance does not comply with the high level that is expected of an elder. They will feel insulted and bitter about the intended compliment of looking young.

In Africa, elders have the right to seize and take a child away from someone who is beating the child, if they think that it is unfair treatment. They have the right to take a child away from its parents. They have the right to discipline the child in the view of the whole community. They may choose to intervene to solve a problem between children and their parents. In Africa, elders intervene when couples experience trouble. They intervene to help solve the problems because a problem in a family affects the whole community. The problem does not belong to the couple alone but to all the people in the community.

The only way for elders to continue to be heeded in Africa is to find ways to include elders in the workings of formal organizations such as schools. For example, in schools they should be invited to give lectures about their past, recent changes, and suggestions for the future. Teachers should encourage their students to engage older people in open dialog about things that are positively and negatively affecting African society. Most urban young people ignore any older person unless they have had formal education. I recommend that leaders of urban youth groups invite elders, both school-educated and self-educated, to come to speak to these groups to discuss matters of interest to both. Elders also need to have an opportunity to hear the concerns of urban youth. Those who administer urban schools and youth groups should arrange for urban youth to stay for a period of time with a rural family that has children of the same age. This will give urban youth an opportunity to experience and learn traditional African social practices. This activity may help them feel connected enough with their African culture to want to value and maintain it in their adult life and even desire to teach it to their own children. If adult Africans in urban areas listen to and value what elders have to offer, then elders will be motivated to share their knowledge, skills, values, and culture with urban youth. Urban elders are ignored because urban young people and adults are not prepared to listen to them. They learn from the media that they have the individual freedom to do as they like and that they do not have to listen to anyone. When an elder wants to say something to a child in the city, sometimes children pretend that they do not understand what the elder is saying, even if they understand the local language because they do not want to have to respect and cooperate with what the elder wants them to do. A response requires the child to talk in a respectful and deferential manner, and this is what the child is trying to avoid.

Exposure to materialistic values that are communicated by Western media prompts young African people in urban areas to relate to elders in this way. In urban areas, crime proliferates because young people value material goods so much that they will do whatever it takes to get them. Because elders are ignored, "strangerness" in the urban neighborhoods grows because social ties are weak. This allows crime to flourish in urban areas. Materialism encourages young people to judge a person more positively if that person can gain wealth by getting others to do their work for them. This inculcates the value of laziness, which in urban young people feeds an attraction for a life of easy money through criminal activity such as drug dealing, theft, and prostitution. These lifestyles increase the spread of diseases that jeopardize entire populations of African nations. Relying on a distorted view obtained from the media, urban African young people feel it is their right to have children out of wedlock if they choose. This increases the level of poverty for urban children because the father often is unemployed. This behavior threatens African nations because most African governments are not prepared to deal with problems of urban overpopulation.

African governments need to develop public policy that includes and utilizes elders to serve as consultants to young people in schools, community organizations, and other formal institutions in urban and rural areas. When elders have an opportunity to interact positively with young people in rural and urban areas, I believe elders will be able to come up with valuable ways to assist the next generation to create a better African society. When this happens, African young people will be more prepared to understand the concerns of elders and begin again to view them as valid role models. Also, African young people will then begin to see that the traditional African teachings that elders are trying to pass on to them will enable them to become more productive human beings. African governments should assist all schools, public, private, and religious, at all levels to develop curricula that stress the value of these traditional teachings and demand that it be implemented as soon as possible. I believe that this will help young Africans to value the traditional knowledge that their culture can offer them, and they will again respect, listen to, and value the contributions of elders in their communities and society. This also will allow all Africans to have an opportunity to evaluate their traditional culture and maintain the aspects of it that are the foundation of a strong African society, instead of neglecting, ignoring, and rejecting it while they emulate the materialistic images from Western media.

I recommend that groups of elders adopt local groups of youth to establish joint community projects that will solve community problems and benefit their town, thus improving their nation. Also, elders should invite young people to their meetings to help youth learn how to design a valuable role for each young person to play in the implementation of solutions to community problems. In this way, elders and youth can become involved in a mentoring process that utilizes the concerns and wisdom of elders and the energy and idealism of youth, thus strengthening important social ties that are now being destroyed.

When Africans begin taking on Western-style behavior patterns, they have a tendency to assume that this will level traditional African social hierarchy and thus equalize (or modernize) African society. I believe that this is a myth because in any human society, someone must always be in charge. When one encourages belief in this myth, one is actually creating more conflict and confusion within one's society. In any society, belief in this myth nurtures the growth of the related myth of individual freedom. Then, an artificial social environment of individual freedom begins to dictate its demands to the community resulting in the suppression of traditional community freedoms such as trust among all community members. The weakening of this essential trust enables crime to proliferate. I believe that one way to counteract the tendency to believe in these dangerous myths is for African governments, national institutions, and local groups of elders to sponsor open public discussions about these two myths so as to create an awareness of their disadvantages and how they can negatively affect the social and economic development of African nations. Africans must be aware that their culture is extremely valuable. Why else would Western anthropologists come to Africa to study our cultures? We, as Africans, must realize that our culture is our strength and by neglecting and rejecting it, we are like the giant Samson who allowed Delilah to cut his hair when he was sleeping making him weak until his hair grew back.

When elders are no longer welcome to perform their traditional role in African society, the strong social institution of African marriage, which previously withstood many difficulties, is weakened. When there is inevitable conflict between husband and wife, elders are no longer available to assist in the resolution of it, and there is thus an increase in domestic and child abuse and divorce. When Africans push away elders, they become vulnerable to suffering from the same social problems found in Western countries where, often by the time the law intervenes, people and children have been hurt or even murdered. Elders should be included in helping parents to bring up their children by visiting families with children and sharing in the supervision of children who come to stay with them. This creates a network of emotional and financial support for mothers, fathers, and children. In African children, this develops a sense of caring and love for the elders, which allows them to remain open to the words of elders as they mature. Elders who do this continue to feel valuable to their families and communities. People who are busy and loved live longer because they want to be well enough to participate in helping their communities to become better places for their descendants to live. When elders are not allowed to perform this traditional role of assisting families, people will not have shame about what they do wrong because they feel they have the right to do it if they chose to.

This encourages the growth of "strangerness" in a community because people know that an elder regarding what they are doing that is bad will not challenge them. In fact, right and wrong, good and bad are abolished and what is left is only the self-interest of individual right. Then, the word *God* becomes taboo. In any society, when God is taboo, humans are imprisoned within their skin and all that they are left with is whatever they can guard around them. All semblance of community has withered. When another human approaches us, our reaction is to be suspicious and defensive, so communities and societies are overrun by violence. No longer a means to build essential social ties, a smile is interpreted as a trick to deceive and a touch is felt as a violation, whereas traditionally a smile means peaceful intentions and a touch communicates an appreciation for all that is human. In any society, when the meanings of these two basic human behaviors have been corrupted, that society cannot progress because it will remain divided. In my opinion, when a society does this, it commits the most serious crime because it deprives its children of a peaceful environment in which to grow up.

Traditional Medicine

In Africa, we had our own doctors long before the Europeans came, so, let us not forget about our traditional medicine. The roots of trees and the leaves of plants were used before colonial masters brought European medicine. These were helpful in curing a lot of the diseases that came with the Europeans. The traditional approaches not only cured diseases but set broken bones. Traditional medicine people treated any bone that was broken. Why do we want to turn away from them? Why do we want to be blind to our own culture and native technology? Let us look at it in a more objective, critical way. It is important to keep this knowledge; otherwise, we will lose the richness of our native intelligence and the power of the African culture will disappear. We must be aware that we are being turned away from our traditional culture.

Traditional healers are very important in the lives of Africans. They are our doctors. We believe that they are given the power to heal by God and guidance in what they do by the ancestors and the spirit of nature. They have the power to cure diseases that we have in our communities. They have been given the power to heal people and can see far beyond ordinary vision. Their knowledge and skills cannot be explained to or by an ordinary person or by any Western theory or philosophy. Traditional healers are given respect in the community and people even fear them; if they wanted to, they could cast a spell that would cause destructive things to happen in the future. Africans believe in these healers because long before Europeans came to Africa, they were performing as doctors in our society and curing diseases and healing fractures. They have always had the role of healing people who are sick. Without traditional healers, all people in Africa would have been dead by now from disease.

Traditional healers treat headache, stomach, and chest pain, and help couples that are unable to have babies. They can also predict the future. They can predict when the community will have a disaster and can tell when a person will die. The knowledge and skills of the healer are usually passed on from one generation to another, to the son or daughter. Whoever the healer trusts most will maintain this professional occupation, for the family, in the future. Ancestors are of great importance to the ancestors of the healer, to maintain this occupation within the family because it is a valuable skill, which has been given to them, and they pass it down. The family will be respected and valued for maintaining this skill for the benefit of the whole community.

Traditional doctors use different means to heal people. They use herbs, roots, the help of ancestors' spirits, and their psychic power to cure people. People who get sick in an African community are taken to a traditional doctor and after certain rituals have been performed and treatment has been given, the pain will be cured. It's the same as being seen by the doctor in the hospital, in that the patient feels trust in the care provided. Medications are also part of traditional healing. These traditional doctors perform a role identical to a modern doctor, but the role of the traditional doctor far exceed the role performed by a modern doctor because it involves the community. The family will be part of the treatment and the patient will not be left alone, which creates a sense of power, support, and understanding. One does not go by oneself to receive treatment from a traditional doctor; the family goes along because they know that successful treatment plans must include the community. For many healers, this job is the only one they hold but for some, they perform this role when there is a need and they farm to support their family and do not depend on illness as the main source of their income.

Some traditional healers perform their services for free for some people. I remember hearing about a man who became sick in the 1970s. He went to the hospital where they prescribed different medications for him, but his illness got worse and worse. His parents decided that it was necessary for him to be taken to the local traditional healer. This was unusual because this person was born and raised in the city, not in a rural village. The traditional healer determined what was wrong with him, treated him effectively, and he became well. Previously, it was believed that this person was going to die. Now this person is a headmaster at a missionary school.

Another incident that I witnessed when I was a child involved a friend that I used to like to go out and wrestle with. He wrestled one day with one of our friends, and he suffered a broken arm. Because this happened in a village, he was taken to a traditional healer who treats fractured bones. This was in the village of Bakindik, in northern Gambia. The traditional healer performed his ritual, and the fractured arm was healed within seven days. Growing up in this society, when one witnesses a healing ritual, the power to treat and heal those who are sick in the community is obvious to the observer. These are only a few of the things that I have witnessed. My experiences of them are endless because I grew up in a village and I also lived in the city.

There are some illnesses that occur in African communities that must be treated by traditional doctors; they cannot be cured successfully by Western medicine. My father treated sick people. He used roots to treat people who had eye problems, whether it was conjunctivitis (pink eye) or a serious condition that required an operation. Such an illness required treatment for seven days. The longest treatment lasted fourteen days, and a full cure was the result. I, myself, know the treatment and can perform it because my father took me to the tree and showed me how to obtain what he used. I know how to find that particular tree and get the roots needed to treat a person who has an eye problem. Performing traditional healing is a way to express love of culture and to show pride in the skills that the family has maintained from one generation to the next. It also helps in the building of a better community because it improves the over health of the people and thus strengthens society. It also helps to eliminate poverty and demonstrate compassion toward those who are sick because the treatment may be given to those who are not even from the immediate community. People come from far away, traveling from one country to another to seek treatment from traditional healers. This builds a network of caring humanity and understanding across cultures and ethnic groups.

Traditional healers care about people. Sometimes they provide treatment in the patients' own home, especially if the patient or a member of their family can easily administer the treatment. Later, they may stop by to see the patient's progress. Traditional healers are very important to the overall well being of African society. Long before Europeans came, these healers were performing their medical responsibilities. If they had not been successful, many sick people would have died. Their successes have included many illness that cannot as yet be understood or treated by Western doctors but are easily cured by traditional healers. They understand the African community, its culture, and the mind of an African person, all of which must be considered when treating an African. This will allow the sick person to feel secure because the African person functions within their community. They have been socialized as a member of a community and so must be treated in a way that takes this into account. The sick person's friends must be involved because they need psychological support to feel empowered to improve their condition. If one does not consider this in trying to treat a medical condition in any African, the effect will be to disempower that person.

Consider this: Europeans did not settle Africa. Traditional medicine has successfully served Africans with medical problems since the beginning of human life on this earth. God gave Africans the natural intelligence to develop our native medical technology and philosophy. Western doctors and medical researchers will never understand it unless they become interested in becoming more diversified in their methods and theories and are willing to learn from Africans. When this happens, there will be the possibility that they can work together with Africans to create a strong health system throughout Africa. Yes, Africans are ready to admit that some of our treatments may not work for everyone, but is that not unlike an American who tries Tylenol™ for a headache and then switches to aspirin? So much of the effectiveness of a treatment depends on the faith that a patient has in it. Africans are used to trying the treatments of several traditional healers until they obtain relief. The patient is not forced to continue with a particular traditional healer, who will often refer patients to another who can treat the problem more effectively. We need to re-evaluate our traditional medical practices. We need to conduct research to see what are the best ways to solve various problems in our society. This may involve incorporating Western medical theories and treatments. We need to do a thorough investigation of all of our traditional medications and treatments. Rather than looking down upon traditional healers and rejecting their methods, we must appreciate and respect them in order to learn from and understand their medical philosophy and technology. How would Westerns feel if Africans came to them and said, "Your health system is wrong and should be discarded?" It is easier to condemn than to be open to learning something new. It is easier for Western doctors to condemn African traditional healers than to strive to understand their practices. Western doctors do not want to believe that their knowledge is limited and that Africans may be using something valuable that they have not discovered or considered.

Africans are very proud of their traditional healers who treat not only humans but also livestock animals and crops. Each traditional healer specializes in skills that have been passed on to them. Those who perform what Westerners call an *informal profession* are very important to the future of Africa. Traditional healers are not magicians. Africans are able to differentiate between a magician and a traditional healer. Some traditional healers ask patients not to pay them until they are well or else to pay a deposit at the first visit and then arrange to pay the balance of the cost of treatment when the treatment is fully effective and the patient is satisfied with the cure. They accept the money but they are genuinely interested in the overall health condition of the patient. Why is it that Westerners want their children to become professionals? Why should Africans not want their children to become professional traditional healers? Discouraging African children from becoming traditional healers is damaging to their self-esteem and leads to the disintegration of African culture and society. An African's life is not complete without valuing the norms and values of culture and society. Traditional healing cannot be separated from other social institutions of African culture and society. It is an integral part of our culture and maintains the equilibrium of the African psyche. It is an honor to be able to become a traditional healer and to come from a family that maintains that traditional occupation.

Traditional African healers involve their patients' entire families in treatment because they adhere to a holistic philosophy of healing. A person consists of both a body and a psyche in one whole. Africans believe their soul is connected to the souls of their ancestors, God, the natural environment (nature), living relatives, and the souls their friends and fellow community members. When Western medical professionals seek to treat ill Africans while ignoring the holistic nature of the African psyche, they often fail because they tell sick Africans the treatment and medicine will cure their body. In contrast, traditional African healers, when treating a sick person, always pray over them, asking the ancestors and God to help in healing their patient. They tell family members of the sick person to get a goat, pig, chicken, or sheep to sacrifice to the spirits of the ancestors, nature, and God, and to cook and serve it to everyone, so in this way, they encourage family, friends and community members to pray with and over the sick person. They also provide their patients with preparations made from plants that are known to cure specific illnesses. Because Africans do not see their bodies as separate from their minds, nor their self as an entity separate from their ancestors and family and community members, it is important to respond to illness by finding treatments that include physical, psychological, social, and spiritual components.

Wellness, for an African, means health in terms of all aspects of a human being: physical, psychological, social, and spiritual. I have personally known many Africans who received treatment from a Western doctor and did not get well until they were treated by a traditional African healer. I believe this occurred because the human mind is the most powerful agent in the healing process. Western medicine is just now coming around to realizing that the level of a person's mental health can enhance or suppress the healing process in their body. For this reason, the treatment a sick person receives must be congruent with their beliefs regarding what and who they are, in terms of their culture, in order to be successful. Leaders of African governments should help Africans and Westerners to understand the important role played by traditional African healers in maintaining the physical and mental health of all Africans.

I believe it is important for African governments to support and maintain traditional African healers because if Africans do not have access to them, African societies will become like Western societies such that the sick person is isolated in a hospital, hospice, or nursing home, and thus is disconnected from their community. Africans will succumb to the various neuroses, such as phobias, paranoia, and stress syndromes that plague Westerners. These Africans will become dependent on feeding their bodies with synthetic powders and pills, and still, they will not feel better. Because Africans will always feel that their lives are missing something, African societies will begin to exhibit a high rate of suicide, similar to that seen in Western societies where holistic treatment, which includes social, psychological, and spiritual components, as well as the physical, is rare.

Africans have had access to holistic treatment for centuries. Even up to as recently as the early 1990s, Westerners were still calling traditional African healers witch doctors. Now, many Western medical researchers travel to Africa to learn about the plants that these so-called witch doctors use and to study how they treat people using holistic methods. There is great interest in the West in obtaining new drugs and medicines based on chemicals found in the plants used by traditional African healers, as well as trying to discover how they effect cures in a fraction of the time it takes Western medicine to work. I believe that now is the time for all Africans to work to bring the issue of supporting and maintaining traditional African healers to the top of the list of important things that must be addressed by African government and community leaders, along with all African medical professionals.

Improving Health Systems in Africa

In contrast to traditionally trained African healing professionals, all our Western-trained doctors and nurses behave in ways that communicate that they see themselves as somehow superior to the rest of us, their patients. For this reason, they rarely take time to listen to their patients' medical complaints to develop a positive relationship with them as a healer. Modern African doctors fail to realize that not having the patience to listen to their patients limits their ability to diagnose and treat Africans effectively. Our modern doctors miss opportunities to view the patient as part of a whole that includes their family and community because their training originates in another culture. Another issue is that most modern African doctors come straight to their practice at a clinic from graduation without taking time to work under the supervision of an experienced medical professional. In Africa, most patients fear doctors and nurses because of the way many of them humiliate their patients. They do this because they are not trained to see their patients as human, but instead, as a place where disease resides or a battlefield where a doctor's skills can be proven inadequate. After experiencing humiliation, many Africans decide never again to go to a doctor for medical treatment. The humiliation increases if one is from the rural areas in the provinces.

Many African doctors steal medicine from government hospitals where they work and smuggle them to their own private clinics. There they sell them to Africans who do not notice that they are expired. Expired medicines are used widely in Africa because African governments import them from Western drug manufacturers who send salesmen looking for markets for expired medicine that they have produced. The money spent on expired medicine should be spent on creating African pharmaceutical companies. I have seen medications that had expired several years previously brought home by friends and neighbors who could not read. Even those who can read do not question what their doctor has given them. An example is my friend who returned home to our homeland in 1997. She went to the hospital for a medical problem and received medicine for it. When she returned to her village and happened to glance at her medicine, she immediately discarded it because it had expired in 1994, three years before. If medicine is marked with an expiration date, it should not be used because people should not be used for experiments. Often, medication that has not expired mysteriously disappears when expired medicine becomes available.

African governments have yet to set up health system evaluation programs in which Africans have an opportunity to learn their rights as patients. An evaluation of the health systems in various African countries would create a sense of responsibility among our leaders for the health care of our people. The evaluation process will give us an opportunity to become innovative in developing new ways to improve our healthcare systems. It is important to evaluate the type of medical equipment available to determine whether it is too old or outdated to perform needed functions safely. The evaluation process can help healthcare professionals establish a two-way feedback channel in which patients and citizens communicate with them regarding suggestions for improving the healthcare system that serves the medical needs of the people. Another communication channel that can be established by this evaluation process involves positive interaction between healthcare professionals, government health officials, and policy-makers. I believe that it will very helpful for African governments to have access to information flowing through these type of communication channels because it will allow them to see more clearly the medical needs of their people and also to provide the specific types training to all medical professsionals. I am convinced that when African governments begin to take the healthcare of their people seriously and consider it to be their highest priority, they will help create the self-sustainability of our continent.

Traditional Occupations

Palm Tree Tapping

The Manjako ethnic group traditional occupation is palm tree tapper. From one generation to the next, Manjakos maintain the occupation of palm tree tapper.

It is hard work to tap a palm tree. One might wonder why Manjakos maintain the traditional occupation of palm tree tapper. What is the philosophy behind palm tree tapping? Why do they continue to engage in palm tree tapping from one generation to the next? Palm tree tapping is not an easy job; it is a huge task. Every person who embarks on performing the traditional occupation of palm tree tapping must make a commitment to carry out all of the specific tasks involved in accomplishing it successfully, to their self, their family, and to their community.

To tap palm trees, the Manjakos use the following equipment: *Kanda-bo, Patee-bee, Kahyo-he, Karah-fe, Ee-kub*, and *Oo-bayla*. This equipment is used for palm tree fruit harvesting, as well as palm tree tapping. Before the palm tree is tapped, the tapper checks to make sure that the tree is not sick and is strong enough to survive being tapped; then, the palm tree must be shaved. When the palm tree looks beautiful, it attracts the tapper to it. The tapper needs great strength and skill, as well as knowledge and intelligence, to tap the palm tree. Because it is a very challenging traditional professional occupation, performing confers status in the community. For a Manjako man to ask for and be given a woman in marriage, he should know how to climb a palm tree.

A Manjako palm tree tapper's training begins when he is elementary school age. The learning process can take place in different ways. It is learned with the help of fathers, uncles, older brothers, or friends in the community or age group.

One may go into the bush and challenge one's peers to see who can climb the highest up a palm tree until one develops enough confidence to climb to the top of any palm tree. Sometimes, older people use fire to help teach youngsters how to climb palm trees. It is not uncommon for children to climb half way to the top, then be too scared to climb all the way to the top. The older person will light a fire under so that the child will be challenged to go up higher to avoid the heat from the fire. Looking down reveals the fire below, and it is clear that the older person will not put out the fire until the child goes up to the top. This is the usual teaching method. Every Manjako family wants to make sure their male children are able to climb palm trees because it helps to obtain praise for their male children from the community. Also, it allows them to marry and create extended families, as well as have a profession with which to provide an income for their family. There were no modern schools in West Africa until Europeans came. Until then, this was the only profession that Manjakos knew. It was a profession of which we were proud and that brought stability to our families. In this Manjako traditional occupation, females also have a role to play.

After the palm trees have been shaved, they are left for one week before they are tapped. What do people get out of tapping a palm tree? They get what we Manjakos call *Poot Po-Fahtch* or palm wine. Palm wine is used on various occasions. It can be used during periods of sadness in the family or community or during periods of happiness. Some occasions when it is used include naming ceremonies, marriage, death, burial, and feasts, whether traditional or Western style, for Christian or traditional African religions. People drink wine made from palm trees to have fun and enjoy. It makes them happy, but more importantly, it brings together the community. Drinking wine also builds sharing and understanding among the people of different ethnic groups who may be at such celebrations.

Palm wine tapping is done twice a day: in the early morning from five to eight A.M. and also, in the early evening from five to eight P.M. When people go in the morning to tap palm trees, they empty the bottles that have been used and are filled with palm tree sap. Sometimes, there will be as much as five liters to empty in the morning. Some people find it convenient to empty their bottles in the evening only. They may have up to ten liters each day. Tappers not only use palm wine for family occasions, but they also sell it for an income for their families.

My people use palm wine as a method by which to communicate with their ancestors. They do this by pouring palm wine on the ground before they drink it. Palm wine tappers are called *Bayu* in the Manjako language. After they empty the tapping bottles, they keep the wine a place called *Pi-Naak*, where the tappers relax and talk with other *Bayu* and customers come to buy palm wine. *Pi-Naak* is a place where people gather to talk and sometimes *Bayu* may give palm wine for free.

This is a way my people share what they have with their community.

Also, among the Manjako, there are people called *Bati-Bala*. These may be *Bayu* or they may be people who specialize in palm tree fruit harvesting.

They climb palm trees, whether shaved or not, and harvest the palm fruits when they are ripe by cutting off and dropping the palm fruits on the ground. When the fruits reach the ground, the women, called *Ba-Chemp*, gather and pile up the fruits where they can be seen and then taken for the next stage of processing. People harvest palm tree fruits early in the morning. The men climb the palm trees and the women gather up the fruit.

Everyone in the family has a role to play in this traditional profession. After the men have cut a lot of fruit, the women gather them up and before they take the fruits to be cooked to produce red palm oil. The children join in extracting the fruits from the *Oo-Nang*, the head of the palm fruit. Because everyone in the family can contribute a needed skill, division of labor is used in this family team project.

Red palm oil is used to cook sauce for food. It is also used as massage oil for adults, children, and babies. Everyone in the community buys red palm oil because it is very healthy for the body, and they love to eat food with sauce made out of it. Palm fruit prepared by the women is used to make *Oo-Nahg*, a sauce, instead of red palm oil, which is eaten with meat, rice, fish, and vegetables. *Oo-Poom*, also prepared using palm fruits, can be burned like a candle. It is especially used in rural areas. Processing palm fruit also produces *Ih-Rugh*, a by-product that can be used to kindle cooking fires even when it has rained. Palm kernels are used to produce a very healthy vegetable oil for frying food. Palm tree fronds are used as brooms. Palm tree branches are used to create fences for gardens. *"Oo-Chi-Dagh*, the woody stem that remains after the palm fruits are extracted, are used as fertilizer and is an ingredient in soap. Old palm tree trunks are split and used as a roofing material and to make doors for houses. They are used for many applications in construction, such as bridge building and canoes for water transportation. Palm kernel oil is an ingredient in margarine and dishwashing detergent.

Creating all of these products using palm trees makes a varied and interesting traditional professional career for people of the Manjako ethnic group. The economy of many African societies depends upon the processing of raw natural materials by many different traditional occupation professionals. We have a wealth of natural raw materials we can use to feed our economy. We need to create more markets for products that can be made from palm. African scientists need to provide traditional occupational professionals with technology that can increase their productivity and also introduce new products that can be made from these raw natural materials.

As a Manjako young person, I tapped palm trees and produced palm wine. I harvested palm trees to obtain palm fruits. I learned to do this by watching my father, and I observed my mother cooking with red palm oil. I saw her produce soap and palm kernel oil. Because my parents worked hard at their traditional occupations, they were able to afford to send me to school. Ethnic groups that practice this traditional occupation can usually support their families. Why should we neglect our traditional occupations when they provide us with so many useful and healthy products made from inexpensive, readily available natural raw materials? Instead of using national resources to purchase foreign-made goods for import, African governments should invest in technology that can develop and support local decentralized village industries. Because these natural raw materials are virtually free in our environment, we need to wake up and see how we can benefit from them by networking in the marketplace on a national and global level.

I believe that palm trees should continue to play an important role in the economy of West African nations. If Africa is to become self-sustaining, it needs to develop industries that utilize palm tree raw materials to create products that can be exported. For example, the spirits created by distilling palm wine can be used as a beverage, fuel, or antiseptic. Any African leader who bans palm tree tapping does not realize the size of the contribution that this traditional occupation makes to a national economy. This kind of leader does not understand the role that maintaining traditional occupations can play in creating a self-sustainable Africa. I have seen this traditional occupation performed by my ethnic group in my natal community, Bakalar Village in the North Bank Division of The Gambia, and I want to see it continue forever and ever. The traditional occupation of palm tree tapping, harvesting, and processing creates jobs for people who have not been to school. It creates self-employment and thus, self-sufficiency, as well as a valued role for these people in their communities.

Blacksmithing

The traditional occupation of my family is blacksmithing. Blacksmiths have an important role to play in the African community because they manufacture the tools that people use to work their farms. Their skills are available to help maintain their society. African leaders should support traditional occupations so that Africans will not depend on outsiders from the West for manufactured goods such as farm tools and end up paying high prices for imports. Among the people of my ethnic group, the Manjako, blacksmiths hold a position of respect and dignity in their communities. I grew up in a blacksmith's family. My father was a blacksmith. He held a position of power in his community. People came to him for advice because they considered him to be very smart. He produced farming and building tools and equipment such as hoes, cutlasses, and knives, implements for shaving palm trees and tapping a palm tree. A blacksmith is a traditional scientist who knows which metals to mix together to create a different metal. My father was proud of his skills. In the past, African leaders turned to blacksmiths to produce weapons with which to fight wars, including spears and arrows. Also, blacksmiths manufactured spears for hunting. Even today, we should not import guns from Westerners but instead, maintain traditional blacksmithing by making use of and developing further the skills of our African blacksmiths. We should all follow their skillful, creative, and productive example and take advantage of the skills that they can offer African society.

My father manufactured farming equipment and gave it to people who needed it in our community. They would pay by choosing a day to come and work on my father's farm. They paid not in cash but with their labor. As a blacksmith's family, we came to understand that to be able to do his job, he had to stay home to blacksmith and allow others to work on his farm. As a child, I was proud to be the son of a blacksmith. I was proud of how he was able to bring people together to work on his farm. I would watch and listen whenever people came to explain to him what they needed him to make for them and observed them meeting with other people who were there to speak with him about their problems. Our house was a center where the people of our community came together to meet each other. My father was famous in his community because of what he could do, for his skills and his profession among the people of the Manjako ethnic group.

Among the Manjakos, when a blacksmith dies, at the celebration of his death, all of the other blacksmiths from the surrounding area and all of the people in his age group come and perform feats of power to determine who among them is the most powerful blacksmith. Sometimes, even blacksmiths from different countries come to perform the rituals that have been passed on to them by the blacksmiths who came before them in their communities. I remember when my father died. Before his burial, all the blacksmiths in our area were informed. All blacksmiths who were in his age group came to the burial. They danced in order to demonstrate how he danced when he was alive. The blacksmiths began making things that people in our community could use and did not stop for twenty-four hours. The final day of the celebration, a Sunday, before the burial, the dead body of my father was placed in a chair. All of his children, including myself, were there. Blacksmiths of his age melted a rod of iron that my father had used when he was alive and brought it to his dead body. I was there so I saw with my own eyes his dead body open its eyes and reach and take hold of the glowing rod of iron before he closed his eyes. All of the people who were there screamed with joy. I was told he had done it to show the other blacksmiths that his profession was going to stay in his family; his action was the traditional way to communicate this fact to the community. Even the black-smith who had handed him the glowing iron rod held it and was not burned. This is the sign of a true blacksmith among the Manjako. This is not fiction. It is something I witnessed with my own two eyes. This has made me feel proud of my father. I see him as someone who believed in what he knew and what he could do. He believed that one day his children would copy his example and maintain his traditional profession.

In April of 1994, a big celebration of my father's death was held in Guinea-Bissau in a village called Tchu-Brik. It was held there because my family believes that our ancestors originated in that village and later migrated to other parts of Africa. It was held in this village because, during this celebration, we believe the soul meets the souls of its ancestors; this is the original area be-longing to the Manjako. Manjako blacksmiths living in other African countries had been informed of the celebration and came to perform this particular ritual. The celebration took three days. It started on Friday morning and ended Sunday evening. People gathered together and slaughtered cows, pigs, sheep, and goats. Food was prepared and traditional music and drumming began. People danced, even people from my father's age group danced. When they rested, they talked about my family, our traditions and his profession.

Saturday evening was the time that the most important part of the cele-bration took place. Even my sister from France attended. My older brother represented our family in the traditional blacksmith performance. A grass-roofed hut was built, and then it was set on fire. When it was completely engulfed in flames, four blacksmiths entered it and remained there until the roof had finished burning. People watched the four fully clothed blacksmiths enter the flaming hut. Musicians sang loudly and the drumming increased, calling our ancestors. This was a wonderful day of traditional blacksmith performance. Videographers were there to record the performances so many people could see the reality of our traditional rituals. My brother, Pierre, was among the four blacksmiths. Some people cried because they thought that the four men would be burned. My brother was the youngest among them. He had been given the courage to use the fire as a means of reaching perfection. This is something that cannot be explained rationally to an outsider, a Westerner. God had given him the power to go through the fire.

The four blacksmiths walked through the fire three times, and the fourth time they had to stay in the blazing hut until the fire had finished burning it. My brother did just that, and it was recorded on videotape. He is still alive and at home in Bakalar Village in The Gambia. This is not a story, it happened in reality. This is the reality of what the Manjako blacksmiths can do. Of all the blacksmiths who went into the fire, none of them was burned, not even the clothes they were wearing. The power of God and our ancestors had been with them in the burning hut. This was not done in secret. It was held in an open place where everyone could see the power of what the blacksmiths' beliefs can do. It was a free performance put on so that anyone to go and see what the Manjako blacksmiths can do.

This is the kind of tradition that our younger generation needs to look into. Blacksmithing is a trade and profession of which Africans can be proud. We Africans have the means to protect our culture if we teach and maintain traditional celebrations and rituals such as this one. We need to support traditional professionals such as blacksmiths so that they can pass on, from one generation to the next, Manjako culture and power. Calling upon traditional resources such as blacksmiths can make life much easier for Africans. We do not have to be dependent on outsiders because the blacksmith provides us with products that we can use that are produced in our own land. If we move away from our traditional rituals, culture, and professions, we become confused, helpless, and beggars in our own land, dependent on the rest of the world. When we ignore our traditional rituals, culture, and professions, we are not only doing something terrible to ourselves but also to the younger and future generations. They may never know about the important role blacksmiths played in African society and, as they become like slaves to Western culture, their own culture will no longer have any importance to them. As we enter the twenty-first century, we should turn back and rediscover every traditional profession in our communities. We should evaluate each of them and find something within them that can benefit us at this time in history, that we can use to build and sustain our African continent. We owe this to ourselves, to our children, and to everyone on our continent.

We must not ignore what traditional professionals such as blacksmiths can offer us. We must be prepared to work with them, empower them, and to appreciate their products. They create products that can be marketed in Africa and bring income to Africans through employment. They can help us manage scarcity within our continent.

We should not depend on importing farming equipment that was not manufactured in Africa. African leaders and agricultural technicians need to turn to blacksmiths and find ways that we can develop our native technology, find ways to make things, using less money, that can last longer in our countries. We need to use more patience and understanding to do this. Our traditional engineers, blacksmiths, are willing to share their skills, which helped our ancestors survive. We need to tell traditional professionals that we will listen to them and learn how to help each other. We need to capitalize on the potential of all of our traditional professions.

Chapter 2

An African Child

Birth

When a child is born in the community, the parents wait seven days, and then on the eighth day, the child is given a name. People come to the naming ceremony, whether they are told about it or not, even passersby, because people feel happy to have a new baby in the community. They believe that one day the child will grow up and will be able to contribute to the community and society. The child does not belong solely to its biological parents but to everyone in the community and it is everyone's responsibility to welcome a new person. The community holds a ceremony for a newborn because it is an important aspect of life to welcome someone new into the society.

This is important to the community because it brings together its members. The ceremony helps the community members understand that they should care for and appreciate people who are different than them, people who are not even part of their family; they may not even be related or belong to the same ethnic group or religion. It is said and believed that this newborn is a saint, a child that knows nothing, that has to be brought up by the whole community. It should therefore be the responsibility of the whole community to name that child.

A naming ceremony in Africa, particularly in The Gambia, is very important. All of the relatives in the community and out attend. There is a feast celebration. People cook and bring food and play music. All kinds of activities occur to welcome the newborn into the community and give the child a name. The family puts a great deal of effort into planning the event. Each group of the relatives makes a contribution to the newborn child. This is a commitment mechanism that builds the community and holds it together and encourages the community to look out for each other. It reaches out to other people who are not in the community to come and rejoice and share the happiness about the newborn, which is considered a blessing from God.

What happens in this celebration? People slaughter sheep, goats, pigs, and cows to roast and eat. They drink alcoholic and nonalcoholic beverages. Also, people share kola nuts. Prayers are offered by the community members in honor of the child so that the child and its parents can have good blessings and health. People call upon the child's ancestors to help guide this child in a positive direction. The naming ceremony helps to eliminate "strangerness" in the community because it encourages people to come out and meet with other people, even though they are busy with their work lives. This naming celebration makes the family proud of themselves, proud of their community, and proud that they are human beings. It makes them feel that they are recognized, valued, and appreciated by their fellow human beings in their community.

The naming ceremony celebration is not limited to the community and family; even passersby usually come and join to rejoice and enjoy with the people who are there. They also give their contribution if they have anything to contribute; otherwise, they can contribute their prayers, words of praise, and words of appreciation. Words of love are very important to Africans. It is necessary and important for everyone to participate because without this involvement, one can become isolated from the community, which then reflects on one at the time of the birth of one's children. The more naming ceremonies one attends, the more people will come when one has the same occasion in their family. Each person's physical presence at the celebration is much more important than the money that one can send if one cannot be there physically. We value the physical presence of another human being. The habit of just sending money and not attending may produce a feeling of being valued less in the community than a poor person who just shows up. A community holding a celebration for a newborn child is a sign of responsibility; it says that this child, the newborn, is in the hands of the community members. The community is entrusted with the task of bringing the newborn by setting a positive example for the child. A celebration for the parents of a newborn child shows the parents that they must reflect upon their attitudes because having the child means they must involve the community. It is not only *their* child; the child belongs to the community. People attend the celebration because they believe that the child will not just benefit this particular family but will benefit the whole community. The child will grow up someday and be someone in the community, the society, and can be someone of whom the community can be proud, who can benefit the community with positive energy and skills to help other human beings. A celebration of a newborn enables people to realize that children are very important and that it is our responsibility to take care of them because we brought them into the world and we should show them that we are proud of them. When someone fails to participate in a naming ceremony for a newborn, that person is said to be a bad example in the community. That person is likely to become a stranger whom people will not trust. This person is said to be violating the norms of the community and will be viewed as someone who hates children. It is important for one to send a message by word of mouth to the parents of the newborn child so that they will know one's heart is with them and that one is thinking about them even though one is not physically present with them. The parents will appreciate it and will be glad of it. They will understand that not everyone can be present and will continue to see one as part of the community.

A child is said to be a fruit of the community as well as its family. Why should we not want to join the celebration of a newborn child? If one doesn't attend, one must not see oneself as a member of the community. Who wants to not be considered a part of a human community? No one! Everyone wants to be seen as part of the community rather than as a threat or disruptive of what the community values. To attend a newborn's celebration is to want to build accreditation for oneself in the society; failure to do so jeopardizes one's reputation. Can one afford to lose one's good reputation? No, because acceptance in the society—the feeling of being valued and appreciated as someone important, and the contribution to the development of the community and the society—are important to all.

The firstborn child is said to be the root of the family and is valued highly by the parents. It is believed that this child opens the way for other children to come into the world in a safe process. The firstborn is a blessing to the family from God, a blessing that the parents and their families embrace in a positive way. The birth of the firstborn helps to ensure that the next children will have good health. It is believed that the firstborn is chosen by God to bless the family and for that reason, this celebration should be the most important celebration the family will ever have.

The firstborn child is seen as a gift from God to the parents. It is a gift that increases the importance of the parents in the community because it gives them more responsibility, and trains the parents to care for the additional children who will be born. It gives them an opportunity to learn from their mistakes and appreciate someone new and different. This newborn child is considered to be the person who will be in charge of the family when the parents are old. This firstborn will serve as an example for all of the other children to follow.

This is why a celebration welcoming this child is of great importance to the family. This firstborn child represents the parents' hope for the future and allows them to plan ahead.

The firstborn child helps to create a bond between the parents and helps them understand their responsibilities because they must communicate to each other about how to care for the newborn child. The birth of the firstborn child increases the status of the parents, which gives them more dignity and greater respect. They enter the class of people who are dedicated and hardworking and who are able to take care of someone. They are trusted and valued more by their community for this reason. They join the other adults, who all serve as consultants in the mutual job of raising all the children of the community. The birth of the firstborn carries them over the threshold into the next stage of their lives. For all these reasons, the celebration of the firstborn child commemorates not just the birth but a change in the parents' lives as well, and the addition to the community of adults who together build and maintain their community and society.

This is why people invest a lot in the celebration of the naming ceremony for their firstborn child. Some go to the extent of slaughtering one cow or even two with sheep as well or pigs. The parents and their families are proud to spread the news of their firstborn. The births of the other children that follow will be celebrated also, but not to such an extent. The firstborn is thought to be guided by the ancestors and is considered a blessing sent from the ancestors to the family. If it is a boy, it is thought to be the father's father or grandfather, or if a girl, the mother's mother or grandmother.

If the newborn is sick, it is said that perhaps the only way it can be cured is by someone who can guess the name of the ancestor who was reborn as that child. A traditional healer is summoned to perform a ritual required to determine this name, and once the ancestor is identified and the name is pronounced to the community, then the child will have a chance to get well. In my tribe, Manjako, even when modern medicine is given to the newborn, it will not get well unless the correct ancestor's name is pronounced. I believe in this because I have seen parents who ignored this tradition and who took their child to the hospital, but the child showed no improvement in health. Later, they were advised by the elders to see a traditional healer who could tell them from which ancestor their child descended. Once they performed the required ritual to determine the correct name, the child became well. This is difficult to understand unless one comes from an ethnic group that believes in it. If one could become a part of such a group, one would see the reality of such a belief, which would become very important to one's life.

When I returned to West Africa, to The Gambia, in the summer of 1994, my cousin had just had a child. My cousin lived in the city so he took his son to the hospital when the baby became sick, but the baby did not improve. Later, my cousin consulted his father. His father went to the child and discovered that his grandson is his brother, my father, who has been dead for many years. Then the child was announced to be my father in the community. The child improved and no longer needed hospital care. The child wanted to be known as the ancestor he was.

Taking care of a child is not difficult in Africa because if one needs a baby-sitter, the parents, extended family, neighbors, or community members will help out. This is a community that cares for each person and understands that people cannot do everything by themselves, and therefore pitches in with support and assistance. Good deeds performed today are recognized and repaid a thousand-fold the next. Payment comes not as money but as respect, value, appreciation, and love. People will know that one believes in God because one cares about the young.

As a child I was told that when we face difficulty today, we will laugh and enjoy tomorrow. This has prepared me to face challenge, to face hardship, and have hope that one day, I'll be happy and enjoy the results of the labors of myself, my family, and my community.

Traditional African naming ceremonies differ from Western-style christenings because the elders of the baby's family make a commitment to be responsible for this child. Also, the child's life is entrusted to the care of people who represent the community and are present at the naming ceremony. The community believes that child does not belong to its biological parents alone. When grown, the person will be able to help the people in their community. If children are not taken care of properly, most likely, they will grow up with no desire to care about the other people in the community. Children must therefore be tended well so that they will later provide benefit for others. Community members make it their responsibility to nurture and care for children so that they will be sure to pass on a similar type of socialization to their children. In this way, the productivity and viability of the community are assured for the future.

This is a lifelong continuous process that involves both the old and the new generations, including babies, children, youth, parents, and elders. Any break in the continuous enactment of this socialization and commitment process is a serious threat to the community and even to the society itself. When people no longer commit themselves as a community to ensuring that each child feels loved and valued by adults in their community, then the children and youth begin to form their own subculture whose values are entirely self-centered and antisocial. The influence of this subculture draws in other young people until it poses a real threat to the safety and peace of the community. The threat can come in the form of gang violence, drug abuse, prostitution, teen pregnancies, and school drop-outs.

When this has occurred, community in a real sense vanishes and all that remains are individuals who are imprisoned in a dangerous and unpredictable world. For this reason, people in any society in which the adults neglect their responsibility to commit themselves publicly as a group to the proper socialization of each and every one of the children who are born in their midst, live with the ever-present threat of being attacked, raped, robbed, or killed. In the mind of such a young person, an insatiable individualistic self-interest reigns supreme so that when a need makes itself known, no feeling of connection to the community inhibits their self-serving behavior. As a result, the humanity of both the victim and the perpetrator is lost. The beings who inhabit the ruins of what was once a community are only predators who hunt and the helpless who must hide from them. The strong desire to avoid this happening created the ancient African wisdom that "it takes a whole village to raise a child."

Age Groups

In Africa, age groups are very important because it is the way the people value and respect children as well as older people. Age groups enable people of all ages to have an important role to play in society, and it is an important aspect of maintaining the self-sustainability of African communities. From a very early age, we take on responsibility for performing certain tasks. Growing up within a system of age groups, we quickly learn how to work with other people in a positive way. The result is that we soon begin to value our own potential as individuals. Young people soon learn that they can join their efforts with those of others to create something to benefit the whole society.

Being in age-group clubs helps individuals to pave the way to a positive future in their lives that will bring them self-respect and dignity.

At the age of six, I went with my older brothers and sisters in our community to my age-group club. Age-group members take new members around and show them their responsibilities to the community such as the things that society expects because the community values "we" more than "I." Age groups foster a time when individuals challenge themselves and re-evaluate their skills. Age-group members have to learn how to work with other people and to understand that one is different, unique, and that one has knowledge and energy that can be channeled in a positive way. As a member of the age-group club, one can contribute to the society and can apply what is learned anywhere that one goes. There is no end to the age-group clubs, as people participate in them until they die. The age-group clubs are a part of our society that builds upon itself. They create a society that wants to move forward, that wants to create a positive community, and that eradicates strangers. In a society where age-group clubs are a right, there one will find freedom.

Discipline of children is a responsibility that belongs to the whole community in Africa, not just to the parents. Any adult has the right to discipline any child. It is the responsibility of the adult, as an elder, to teach children to have a clean heart. Then they will say one day, "We are proud of our elders; we respect our elders because they were there for us." This is the kind of discipline we had in our society and my community when I was a child. One must ask where has discipline with caring and understanding gone? I was taught that to be hardworking is to show pride in one's family, ancestors, community, and society. To apply oneself is a way to say thanks for the ability to do what one can do. To be hardworking brings happiness and joy because one doesn't have to depend on other people to do things for one. One must be proud of oneself.

Age-group clubs are very important to the socialization of Africans, particularly in The Gambia. In my village, age-group clubs start at age six. One physically leaves one's age group only when one dies. When one dies, one joins one's ancestors' age-group club. Age-group clubs connect people in a strong, healthy social network within African society. It is a way to tap into each individual's positive energy to utilize it to benefit the entire community and society. Age groups transform individual self-interest into a valuable resource that can then be used to build and maintain the community and society. Age groups foster an appreciation of each individual's talents and the contribution they can make to their community and society. Age groups promote the philosophy that everyone's role is important and equally necessary, if the society is to be successful and self-sustainable. Age groups help African children realize how they can contribute to their families. African children are socialized to become hard workers in their society. When they mature, Africans believe hard work brings success and joy, in the future.

I remember when I was in first grade, my age group usually took care of animals such as goats, pigs, and cows. We also worked in gardens, driving away the birds that come down to eat the seeds that the parents had planted. We stayed outside playing during the day while we took care of these gardens. We joined our parents and the elders working on the farms. We were proud to do this because our role was considered important and essential by our parents and the elders in our community. We took care of the babies when everyone else who was physically able was busy working in the fields. When someone in the fields was thirsty, we brought water for them to drink or pour on their heads to keep cool so that they could continue working. Everyone saw this role as a unique one that could only be provided by the young children. This was a great feeling because we knew our role was special and that the tasks we did for others in our community could only be done by us. The role we played was valuable. To be a bum and depend upon others to feed one is contrary to African upbringing. The guidance one is given by one's age-group club and the important role one is given to play makes one grow into a whole human being who is proud of what one can contribute at every stage of one's life.

As young children in an age-group club, when we went to work on someone's farm, we were given a payment that we gave to the "mother and father" (that is, the elders who advised us) of our age-group club who kept it for us. When it came time for a feast, they asked us, "What do you, as a group, want to do with your money?" We sometimes decided to organize a party or to use the money to buy new clothes. We sometimes decided to use the money to buy books. We would use it to buy things from which we could benefit. We felt proud of ourselves because this money was the result of our sweat; we worked hard for it.

To help us plan our activities, the next older age-group club members in our community served as our mentors. Each age group had an older age group that served as mentors, all the way up to our parent's parents. This is how the traditional African age-group social structure works. This is how it interconnects all individuals in a community, from six years of age to the oldest person.

This type of social stratification teaches one, at an early age, that each individual's role is essential. From six years of age, children take on their responsibilities and learn how the failure to perform certain tasks will negatively affect the whole community. No one wants to see this happen. Failure to perform one's tasks not only negatively affects one's age-group club, but also the family. Africans believe that those who are socialized by good parents, whose parents set a good example, whose behavior one can emulate, who are leaders in their community, will contribute in a positive way in their community and be able to work successfully with others.

I remember when I was in fifth grade. One day, on the weekend, when I was playing with my friends, a member of our age-group club was asked by his mom to go to the store. This time, he decided that he would continue playing rather than go. His mom told us that he refused to go to the store for her. We called him aside and told him that we did not want our age-group club to be identified as a group of children that refused to do what their parents asked them to do. We did not want to be seen by others in our community as a group of bad children. In fact, we told him that it was rude not to do willingly what his parents or older sisters and brothers asked him to do. We said to him, "Your older sisters and brothers and parents have done a lot for you, up to this stage in your life, so it is your responsibility to give something back to them. Doing this task, this service, is a gift that you can offer your parents in thanks for all they have done for you up to this time."

We knew this was true because we were socialized to believe this by the older age group that was our mentors. They taught us that these things are important. For this reason, we were unified in our conviction that his refusal to go to the store for his mother would be detrimental to the reputation of our age-group club. That is why we would not welcome this sort of behavior and attitude on his part. So we told him that he had a choice. Either he would go or he would, from then on, be excluded from our age-group club. He was at a point of no return; he could not turn back. Because he saw that he had to go forward and do the task, he did it. When he came back, his mother was proud of him. He then felt that he had, on his own, achieved something positive. This is the kind of philosophy that Africans were brought up to believe in. I feel it is great to be able to say thanks by the actions we take in our lives to our ancestors, elders, parents, and older sisters and brothers, for caring for us.

After I completed sixth grade, I attended secondary school in the city of Serrekunda and Banjul. On my arrival to the city, the people with whom I was to stay simply took me to my age group. True, some may say it was difficult to be alone, without my family members, but I remember it as being very helpful because, in my age-group club, I was never treated as a stranger. Immediately, I was treated the same as any other member of the age-group club. This was very important in my life, and it happens to be a unique feature of age-group clubs in The Gambia. The world of the age group was something with which I was familiar because it is a widespread traditional social structure that connects the rural to the urban areas in The Gambia. Being a member of an age-group club made me feel proud to be an African. Though we could not work on people's farms, in the city my age-group club helped people by providing tutoring services to families with children in the lower grades, and we were paid for it. We used that money to buy books for reading and our schoolwork and also school supplies that we needed such as pencils, pens, and erasers. We used our earnings when we went to concerts or wanted to have a picnic at the beach.

Participating in our age-group club activities helped us feel a sense of responsibility to our community, in the city, and the village. Because of the existence of age-group clubs everywhere in The Gambia, a child or youth, such as myself, knew that we would find friends and an important role to play wherever we went. This created a feeling inside of us of being very proud of the role given to us to perform by our society. Though some of the tasks were difficult, we had been socialized to expect that nothing on earth of value that we might encounter would be easy to accomplish.

Our great-grandparents had told this to our parents, our parents had told this to our older brothers and sisters, and our older brothers and sisters told this to us. One must sweat to accomplish something of value. This attitude about life was taught to us in our age-groups clubs, in the city as well as in the village.

As a group, we would attend traditional drumming and dance concerts and organize parties. Each time we held a party, it would be at an elder's home because elders and people older than ourselves provided guidance to our age-group club. They would be there to intervene if there was a conflict. The oversight of our age-group club by elders made us feel safe and secure in our community and during club activities, both in the city and in rural areas. In some cases, we used the money we raised to buy soccer balls and uniforms. Then we could compete with the soccer teams of other age-group clubs. We also used the money we earned to pay for transportation to travel to rural areas to play soccer with village age-group clubs. The participation of elders, as mentors, in our age-group club gave us confidence in ourselves because it was clear to us that they had a vision of us as people who would, one day, become responsible elders of our communities. Supervising an age-group club was important to them.

When one moves out of one's village, one is still a member of the village age-group club. In The Gambia, on the weekends, people usually go from the cities to their villages to work on their family's farm and meet with their fellow village age-group club members. Even those who live for the most part in the city communicate regularly with age-group friends who have remained in the village. Quite often, the village age-group club will schedule important activities on the weekends so that one can come from the city to attend, thus maintaining a vital feedback network that builds love for rural communities in the hearts of city dwellers. For this reason, city residents in The Gambia have love for ourselves because we have love for our roots. The experience of age-group clubs teaches all Gambians that working together makes all tasks easier to accomplish. The concept behind the age group is that of a team that is able to act strategically upon what they believe to solve their own as well as their society's problems.

Age-group clubs help Africans appreciate who we are, the environment in which we live, our unique culture, and the norms and values of our society. Age-group clubs serve as an essential commitment to community mechanism that successfully accomplishes the most important task of all societies, the socialization of the young. They are a strong foundation upon which civilizations are built. Particularly the Manjako ethnic group maintains age-group clubs in both the rural and urban areas because we know that without them we will not be able to socialize our young people in a positive way. When children are not socialized by the use of age groups, they become socially isolated individuals. Not only is this sad, it is also devastating for the entire society because of the resultant costs for treatment of mental illness, domestic and child abuse, drug abuse, and crime. One might ask, "What kind of self-esteem and dignity is possible for children who raise themselves?" Africans have a responsibility to work with our governments to see that age groups are supported and maintained in our countries. If we continue to neglect this important responsibility, we will be responsible for encouraging gangs and violence in our societies, particularly in the urban centers. If age groups disappear, children and youths will no longer have an important and meaningful role to play in their society. They will turn their inexhaustible energy to a negative struggle in which the most violent among them survives and prospers. As adults, they will turn away from the challenge of finding positive answers for the difficult economic questions that face all African countries.

Age groups allow everyone to be well known within their community. This eliminates fear because each person knows who is around him or her at all times. Age groups nurture a strong sense of concern for all people in the community on the part of each member. Because one knows everyone, we all look out for each other. Age-group clubs protect the community from harm from both outsiders and from within the community. If one age-group club is seen doing something harmful, another age-group club will call them to a meeting to discuss a more positive way to solve a particular community problem. When one recognizes the extent of age groups' important role in African culture, one can imagine the kind of destructive societies that we are creating when we do not actively support age-group clubs by our participation in them. We will feel ashamed when we face future generations as they come into our world! When we deviate from maintaining age-group clubs, we create a negative future for our children. We are not allowing them to learn from us, to copy our example. When we do this we are creating and maintaining selfish individualism. We are creating individuals that prey on other individuals to survive or people who have no feelings toward other human beings in their community. When Africans deviate from the tradition of age groups, we abuse the younger generation in our societies; we inflict the most harmful and painful abuse upon our African children.

When I returned for a visit to The Gambia in August of 1994 after having lived in the United States for seven years, I found my age-group club in the city of Serrekunda. Immediately, I was accepted. I was valued and appreciated by the individuals in my age-group club. When I arrived in my birthplace of Bakalar Village, having traveled from Serrekunda, there I found my age-group club again. Because of this, loneliness and the feeling of being a stranger were nonexistent to me. At each age-group club, I found people with whom I had grown up even though I had been outside the country for seven years. They still remembered me and welcomed me as a member of their age-group club. To be given their love was an important and unique experience for me. This illustrates The Gambia and all of Africa was before age groups were threatened with extincttion as a result of neglect by Africans in a hurry to leave behind traditional African culture.

I do not want to imagine what would have happened to me if there had been no age-group clubs for me as I grew up. Can you imagine how different my life would have been? I would not have written this book that you are now reading. In The Gambia, particularly among the Manjako, even though I had been away so long, my age-group clubs provided me with a flood of memories and the sense that my past and my present had met my future face-on. We owe it to our children, our parents, our ancestors, our nations, our communities, our societies, and our African continent to support and maintain age-group clubs. Age-group clubs can help us create prosperity, peace, and understanding among people in our countries. Age-group clubs can empower Africa to become self-sustainable.

We ought to be able to sit down, as Africans and human beings, to evaluate our traditional social structure of age-group clubs so that we can commit ourselves to maintain age-group clubs for their positive benefits to our societies and for their role in providing productive and valuable humans. We must be willing to sit down and contemplate why we should be very proud to be able to give age-group clubs to our younger generation. Why? Because age-group clubs inoculate them against a disease that kills the brain and blinds one to the value of one's culture and upbringing. The pain that we have experienced in our African countries is *enough*! We must not accept it anymore. Each of us, as Africans, is responsible for having, in our lives and careers, a clear destination that positively contributes to the support to age groups.

Age groups teach one to respect, love, and believe in oneself. They help young people to believe in the value of elders in their communities. Age groups help young people to collaborate with all members of their community because their age group provides them with a specified role to play in relation to others in their community.

Age groups assist young people to deal realistically with their weaknesses and teach them how to develop their strengths. Age groups contribute to the self-sustainability of communities by providing opportunities for young people to challenge themselves to face and overcome difficulties in their communities and society, not just in their personal lives. A community's level of self-sustainability depends on the ability of its people to be innovative in solving community problems. In age groups, young people learn how to deal appropriately with issues and to solve problems creatively. Above all, one learns to accept failure as a way to learn how to improve oneself. My age group taught me to not expect that life would always be positive all the time. It also prepared me to both welcome and deal with negative aspects of myself, others, and living in the community. Every human being needs to have a specified positive role to play in the development of a family, community, and society. The socialization that provided by age groups nurtures a view of the world in which the emphasis is on *we* rather than on *I*.

The elders give youth in age groups in The Gambia the responsibility to clean city streets and roads periodically in a partnership with the elder age groups. These youth are encouraged to follow the example of the elders so that they will eventually provide an example, themselves, as elders for the next generation of children and youth. Every society needs age-group clubs for everyone. A six-year-old child is ready to join their peers in an age-group club when they begin school. Children younger than eight often gather in play groups that imitate an age group but an adult supervises them. The purpose of age groups is to build "togetherness" and to discourage individualism and to guard against the growth of "strangerness" in the community and society.

In addition to keeping the streets clean, age group members can maintain community gardens and care for new trees that have been planted. Age groups can take responsibility for maintaining, renovating, and repainting community centers and churches. Age groups are the grass roots where community politics originate. For that reason, if age groups exist, democracy can flourish from the grass roots up. It is the responsibility of age-group representatives to volunteer to serve on all boards that oversee the operations of city or town government departments to ensure that the peoples' interests are protected. Every human being needs to be able to identify with a group. If society fails to provide age groups for youth, gangs will develop, especially in urban areas. Without age groups for adults and children, the family often becomes an arena of conflict between spouses and parents and children (which often leads to domestic and child abuse). Elders without age groups suffer from social isolation, which causes loneliness and a sense of hopelessness and worthlessness.

In societies with no age-group clubs, everyone competes to look "young" because to be old means to be worthless. Children in these societies grow up with little respect for adults and elders precisely because those adults and elders have not provided them with a specific, useful role to play in the community and society. These types of children grow up believing that their goal in life should be the satisfaction of their personal needs and wants. They manipulate and abuse whoever is in their way. These children never think of preparing themselves to be productive members of their communities and society; rather they expect others to wait on and entertain them. When the circumstances of their lives frustrate this aim, they become suicidal because their life is too "boring!"

Each older age group assists the next younger age group to implement their particular community projects and to hold joint celebrations of achievement and holidays. When people are given opportunities to contribute to their community through participation in age-group activities, they no longer rely on government assistance. The need for welfare and many other human services occurs in modern societies in which people are socially, economically, and educationally isolated from each other. Often this happens because groups of people do not mix because of prejudice, discrimination, and oppression. Age groups can provide urban young people in Africa with the positive peer pressure they need to counteract the temptation to drop out of school and participate in drug abuse, prostitution, and crime.

The mentoring of older age groups unifies communities by creating an atmosphere in which everyone cares for one another. In this way, the mentorship process of age groups flushes out individuals' visions of how they can personally benefit their community.

When a community is unified by the influence of age groups, it actively works to create a safe and clean place to live. Every member of the community is actively and positively involved with its children and youth. The task of socialization is accomplished because elders and adults are proud to pass on what they know. A community and society with age groups empowers its young people to become innovative and creative in finding solutions to their community and society's problems.

Schooling

The family's teachings are reflected in the schools in Africa because people believe that a child's upbringing is the responsibility of the entire community, and the school is part of the community. Parents know that they can trust teachers. Teachers respect the parents because they know they have sacrificed a lot to pay for the education of their young children. Teachers must set an example because they know it is one of their roles in the society. Parents believe that, when children are in the hands of the teachers, teachers provide an example that the children can emulate. The way they speak, dress, and relate to other human beings must be up to a high standard.

Teachers know the parents, whether biological or guardian, of their students and visit their homes. This is what community is all about in Africa. We must never forget about this.

After school in Africa, when the children get home, they do not even put their bags down until we have greeted everyone, shaken hands, and said hello to everyone, to make them feel that they are part of them and that they are remembered even at school. Then the parents give the children lunch and take time to enjoy the meal before starting homework. The adults are always around for the children, which helps them to feel powerful. The children feel the adults' love, the energy that every child needs, so everyone does their best to apply positive energy to succeed so that everyone in the community will be proud. This is an Africa where children understand and appreciate the sacrifices that their parents make for them. I hope this kind of love never disappears because we need it.

My elementary school time was great because of the school farm where all students worked from grade one up to grade six. The principal and all the teachers worked on the farm. It was great because we did it to benefit everyone in the school. The money from the sale of its produce was used to buy books, to buy lunches for students in the school, and to sponsor trips to other schools or cultural areas. This was a society built together. Parents often asked how the farm was doing. They would advise the children not to miss when everyone was asked to go and work on the school farm, because its was for the community and it was important to support the ongoing tradition. Parents would tell their children, "If you run away when you are asked to work on the school farm, you will fail me and shame me as a parent."

I remember my parents telling us to be proud of who we are and that no one should try to make us be someone different. No one can help us unless we help ourselves.

We should be proud of what we can do, and that respect and dignity comes when we take responsibility for being accountable for ourselves. With self-respect, self-love, and pride in the family community, one gains respect from the society and the world. In this circumstance, people will move forward and be loved, and will know what it is to be a human and to value other humans. There will be freedom in the community, society, and nation.

Living in Africa is great because we take advice from elders. We listen to them and follow their instructions carefully. We know that they know much more than we do. We know that they are there for us and we must respect that. We must accept what they say because we know it will be of great value to ourselves. We know that they will never put us in danger because then they would feel pain in knowing that they failed their responsibility to bring up the young children in a positive way. If a child is bad, it is a shame to the whole community, not just the parents. Children do not even dream about making their family face that shame in the community. We can never repay our parents for what they have done for us. For nine months, we are inside of our mothers. We cannot repay them for the pain and difficulty they suffered, but we can give them respect and listen to them and follow their instructions.

Parents cannot bring up children alone. It takes a whole African village to raise one African child. In Africa, after dinner, parents take time to gather the children around to tell them stories about their great-grandparents, and about their ancestors and to tell them about their society and about their roles as children. This gives the children a sense of dignity and self-esteem. Storytelling time is the time that every child does not want to miss. The children always want to be the closest one to the person telling stories and want to be sure to show respect to them because their talents are considered very meaningful in the society. These are evenings in Africa that all Africans should remember and be proud of their culture. Storytelling is very important to an African. Children and elders are proud to tell our beloved stories.

Restructuring African Educational Systems

Young Africans need to be reconnected to the community. They need to be part of educational programs that provide them with internships and apprenticeships in their communities. This may include community gardening, adult education tutors teaching literacy, and receiving and disseminating information about family planning and infant and child health. All young Africans must be taught to apply what they learn at school to the real world of their local communities. In The Gambia, there is no high school, even in the capital city of Banjul, where students can participate in an internship program. All of their learning is merely theory. What African countries need is ministries of education, youth, and sports to design and implement summer internship programs as a requirement for all high school students to complete before graduation. In the summer, African high school students should be placed in internships in agricultural, fishing, construction, engineering, health, business, administrative, craft, and preschool apprenticeships. The funding for high school internship programs can originate in a consortium of government, nonprofit, and business organizations and agencies. I believe that adults need to set an example for young people to follow by giving back to our communities by creating learning environments in which our young people experience firsthand the joy of performing a valuable role in their community.

I agree with those who state that they must first tend to their personal needs for educational and economic advancement. Nevertheless, I challenge them to answer this question: "Have you looked back to see how you can apply what you have learned to benefit your home community, to satisfy its social and economic needs, and to solve the urgent social and economic problems of its inhabitants?" I say this because I believe that the purpose of all African institutions and students of higher education should be to transform African society so it can move to higher levels of independently sustainable social, economic, and moral development. Once a society deviates from this path, it becomes weak. Its people are left vulnerable for forces of exploitation to corrupt them from within and oppress them from the outside. The people of these societies find themselves locked between prison walls of censoring dictatorship by leaders on one side and senseless criticism accompanied by lack of innovation by intellectuals on the other side. When this point is reached, the result is governments that believe that they must rule by military force and that the use of weapons is the only way that their country can be rescued from endless cycles of exploitation from within and domination from outside.

Young Africans tend to copy what they see in the media without a thought to the consequences of their behavior and how it will contribute to a culture that younger children will imitate. They do not think about how the values of this culture will affect both themselves and those coming after them in terms of development. These young people do not have the resources and skills required to maintain the culture that they seek to adopt. They are constantly distracted by worries about how to appear "cool" instead of working on figuring out how they can be innovative in helping their community to improve and sustain itself. One possible antidote to this sickness would be to call on the consortium of government, nonprofit, and business organizations that supports high school internships to build television, movie, and radio production facilities in which young people can be engaged in documenting the concerns and activities of people and groups in their local regions. Adult staff members supervising these media internship programs can write proposals to obtain funding from worldwide foundations while they guide the youth to focus on using the media to build on their own and their country's strengths. In this way, our African young people can be transformed from passive, mindless addicts of Western materialistic culture uncontrollably hungry for goods sold by countries outside of Africa.

African governments must make it their priority to provide financial support manufacturing industries that utilize local raw materials to create the type of goods that African youth associate with middle-class status. The national high school curriculum must include practice experiences whereby African high school students observe, analyze, learn-by-doing, research and development, manufacturing, marketing, and management processes. I believe that when African governments lend their wholehearted support to high school internship programs such as those I have described, then Africans will be able to call themselves "self-starters" instead of "followers."

The African educational institutions should be redesigned so that no student should be allowed to graduate after they complete *form 4 or 5* (the American equivalent of eleventh and twelfth grades) but instead after completion of *A-level* coursework (the equivalent of American college-level coursework). Young people would then have time to complete the practicum, apprenticeship, and internship experiences required to graduate. At this level, it is appropriate for teachers to encourage learning to occur in a group context as the result of team projects. At the teacher's college level, high school teachers should learn to welcome personal evaluations of their teaching from students so as to find ways to assist more efficiently and to guide their students toward mastery of subject material. Professors who train teachers and other professionals in Africa should be expected to continue to perform research and publish their findings, as a requirement of maintaining their teaching positions at African colleges and universities. Above all, Africans must be willing to face failure and see it as a path to improvement. The knowledge that flows from both successes and failures is much better than the helplessness of imitation.

At this time, most African students do not interact with their teachers in the classroom because many African teachers have been socialized to define the student-teacher relationship in European-style hierarchical terms. African teachers feel that when students ask questions they are challenging their authority in the classroom. Because students sense that their questions will be responded to negatively, most rarely participate in an active manner in the classroom. When European colonizers and missionaries first opened their schools in Africa, they assumed that Africans had nothing to offer them in terms of knowledge, so they expected their students merely to memorize what was being given to them. For this reason, Africans who were educated by Europeans perpetuated a similar teaching style with their own students. African leaders and intellectuals have yet to sit down to evaluate teaching methods that have been used in Africa. An appropriately African teaching style would involve assigning specific roles and responsibilities to each student in the classroom, making each student equally accountable for the success of the group learning experience of each lesson. At home, African young people participate actively in their age group's activities and in the upkeep of their family's home and garden. I believe that their schooling should provide the same type of expectations for active participation.

This incongruity between school and home incapacitates Africans. Their school experience is alien to their culture. They are expected to behave in a way that is different from how they behave at home in their communities, such that they must be passive and assume the role of an observer. Education involves not merely a body of knowledge but also a certain culture from which that knowledge emerged. The education that Africans have been getting brings with it a definition of the African as a person who knows nothing and who must listen and remember something that they have never heard of before. In this way, African education as it is today teaches Africans to *not* be self-starters. African education denies young people the opportunity to participate actively in the classroom, effectively handicapping them. Thus they are robbed of their potential to become innovators in their adult lives. Regardless of the form of government in Africa, we will never become self-sustainable until African teachers conduct research into our history, culture, and traditional knowledge and skills. They must then transform this knowledge into a curriculum that can teach young Africans how to build an independently sustainable continent.

One important thing that must be done is to encourage African females to take a more active role in the classroom. At the moment, current teaching methods, which reflect some African societies, discourage females from taking an active role in the activities of the classroom. One example of this is the common practice that is used by both male and female teachers of always beginning question sessions by calling on a male student. Another example is teachers allowing boys to make negative noises (booing) whenever a girl asks the teacher a question or responds to a teacher's question. Eventually, girls, who at first show interest in learning, experience a significant loss of self-esteem. As a result, these girls learn that their success in life will always depend on how well they follow the ideas of men instead of on developing their own thinking. This kind of classroom culture encourages female dependency so that half of the African population never is tapped to see whether innovative and valuable solutions to problems can be found.

African teachers need to avoid memorizing text from books so as to lecture directly from textbooks. I believe Africans will not be encouraged to become innovative until their teachers go beyond textbooks to demonstrate to their students how to apply the knowledge contained therein and how to use facts to improve African societies. The example of cramming by teachers tells students that if they do not also memorize what the teacher tells them word for word they will be seen as not intelligent and as having failed to learn. Because Africans are not encouraged to develop analytic thinking (to think for themselves) and their potential ability to synthesize information is not developed, at least half of most African students' mental capabilities remain stunted. For this reason, I am convinced that at least half of our total human potential as a continent remains untapped. It is not being used. Thus I can accurately state that most of our problems as Africans stem from fact that we are being handicapped by our own educational system.

Because teachers respond negatively when students ask questions that challenge their ideology, students withdraw from taking an active role in the classroom. They know that if they continue to challenge their teachers, they will receive failing grades. Having to remain passive in the learning situation creates in Africans a habit of not being innovative. In other words, our educational system trains us to wait for someone to tell us what to do and also to accept what that person says without questioning it. I believe the roots of our educational system can be found in our past. When the colonial masters took control, they brought with them an educational system, which they used to teach Africans what they believed about us: that they are superior to us and that African culture contains nothing of practical value (being made up of rituals and superstitions).

For this reason, African educational systems continue to suppress Africans and hinder our development as a self-sustainable continent.

I challenge my readers to answer this question: "If it is true that Africa is primitive and our culture is inferior and that we have nothing of value to offer the rest of the world, why did Europeans leave their own countries and travel to Africa?" Surely it was not merely for raw materials that were not found to their own countries, for if this was true, how would they have known about all the wonderful and valuable products that Africans manufactured for centuries while Europeans fought over their own meager resources? No. The truth is, Europeans suffered great dangers to reach the sources of our ancient treasures and to snatch control over trade of these valuable goods, which, at that time, was in the hands of Africans. It is time for Africans to wake up and focus on ways in which we can unite to reclaim control of our continent. The colonial masters left, but we are still tied to them because we have maintained the educational system that they established. To justify the exploitation of our people, Europeans had to convince both us, and the rest of the world, that we were lacking. They needed an educational system that would make us dependent on them.

I appeal to Africans to listen carefully. Europeans did not just leave their countries to bring us something wonderful. They are not angels. Although they smiled and offered things to please and distract us with one hand, they stole our continent with their other hand and divided it up among themselves. They accomplished this by destroying our culture from within. What have we done to rebuild and rediscover our cultural wealth, the foundation upon which was built many glorious empires that drew Europeans to our shores? My parents used to tell us that if anyone takes away one's culture, one will become weak and vulnerable to that person and lose the roots of the African skills that enable one to survive in one's own society. I believe that this is what has already happened to Africans.

For this reason, I urge all Africans immediately to establish organizations in which they work together to re-evaluate our current African educational system of primary, secondary, and higher education so as to re-structure these institutions. By doing this ourselves, we will be able to learn from our mistakes. This will enable us to become self-starters once again. When we begin to do this, we will show our children that we are taking up the responsibility of solving our societal problems as Africans. Remember the popular African proverb, "It takes a whole village to raise one child"?

It will take all of us from every nation on the continent of Africa to make our society self-sustainable again. Europeans used our differences to gain control over our continent in the past. If we continue to view European nations instead of other African nations as our best friends, we will remain dependent on outsiders. As long as we continue to depend on outsiders such as those in America, Europe, and Asia to enable us to compete with other African nations, we will never become self-sustainable. We will not be able to control what happens to us as a people. Competing with each other instead of cooperating caused Africans to lose control over their continent in the past. Learning to cooperate with each other, in spite of our differences, is the only road out of the dark time of colonialism. This work remains to be done by all Africans. I believe that before asking for outside help, one should first try to do it oneself and then, when all else fails, go and ask for help from one's nearest neighbors.

We do not go to our African neighbors for help because we would prefer to be able to maintain our status in their eyes so we turn to outsiders instead and perpetuate our dependency. In our communities, Africans depend on their neighbors for survival, yet, on a national level we fail to work together to develop the African continent as a whole. Instead, we depend on our former colonial masters to come and help us develop our separate African countries. Africans need to remember that true (rather than superficial or artificial) prestige and dignity is earned by not only successfully sustaining one's own family and community, but also by offering a helpful hand to those beyond the borders of one's home. True dignity and prestige cannot be bought or traded for. Material possessions alone do not bring true dignity and prestige. One gains true African dignity and prestige by performing self-sacrificial and generous acts without thought for what it will bring to oneself. As long as we are concerned about how to gain or maintain status in one another's eyes, we will never gain true dignity and prestige. It will only be hollow show. To regain our dignity as Africans, we must instead set our minds to discovering how we can better utilize the personal, human, and natural resources that are readily at hand to work with other African nations to build a self-sustainable continent.

The question to consider is, "Are we really satisfied with what is happening to us in our nations and on our continent?" Regardless of how we answer this question, we need to realize that as long as each of us fails to take a positive role in the betterment of our community, nation, and continent, we will remain oppressed. We hesitate to be proactive because we prefer to lean back into the physical comfort of newly acquired material possessions while we criticize and condemn our leaders and never develop ideas that we can implement to solve our countries' problems. I ask those of us who are doing this, "If you are satisfied, why are you complaining? If our problems are entirely the fault of our leaders, what are you doing, in a positive, constructive manner, as an individual, to make African society better?" As Africans, we fail to take a proactive role in working with other Africans who are different from ourselves because we are afraid to fail. Our desire to see ourselves in a positive light hinders us from doing this. Unfortunately, this also limits our ability to learn from our mistakes. When we cannot learn, we cannot be creative and solve problems.

Chapter 3

The Changing African Family

The Traditional African Family: Lifestyles

The African family is an extended family and includes grandparents, uncles, aunts, nephews, and nieces who live in several houses in the compound of the elder parents. As the family grows larger some of the married sons and daughters take their spouses and children and settle in nearby neighborhoods or towns. In most cases, grown members of African families desire to stay near their parents' homestead because they want to maintain their ancestors' link with the land. They do this to keep their extended family together: economically, socially, psychologically, and spiritually. After the parents become elderly, usually the oldest son returns to the family home to take charge of it in the place of his father. If the oldest son cannot do this, the next oldest son does.

Africans choose to live with their parents because they want to set an example for their children so that their children will choose to support *them* financially and emotionally when they become elderly. Africans believe that it is their responsibility to care for the parents who cared for them when they were children. Anyone who fails to do this will not receive blessings from their ancestors and God that are necessary for a good life and will bring disgrace upon themselves in the eyes of the community members.

African family members live together because they believe that whenever there is an emergency of any kind, the appropriate ones to help will be another family member rather than someone who is not familiar with that particular family's dynamics. Living together also encourages members of African families to work together to achieve important goals and not view each other as enemies or competitors. Working and living together nurtures a team spirit in the family rather than feeding into the self-interested aspirations of individualistic tendencies in members. Living together as an extended family helps Africans to understand and know their family's background. This sense of identity, which stretches back in time, provides Africans with a strong foundation of self-esteem because they know and are proud of their roots. In this way, Africans know who they are so they can feel proud of themselves.

Sometimes, in African families, there is a tendency to expect one person to be the only breadwinner. This is especially common in urban areas because often there will only be one person in the family who has the kind of skills required to obtain a job in the urban area to which a rural family has migrated. When this occurs, this person will experience a high level of stress. Either they will die, exhausted, at an early age or simply disappear, later to be found busily working quite a ways away, without the strain of hearing the demanding, hungry voices of family members nearby. I feel that now is the time for Africans to bring issues such as these to the table for discussion to try to figure out solutions to this significant social problem of urban Africans. African governments have a key role to play in decentralizing resources so as to reduce the numbers of unskilled migrants to urban areas.

Several social problems are caused by the lack of an extended family in African urban areas, including teenage pregnancy, prostitution, drug addiction, and theft. The extended family serves as a consultant that is readily available to any member of the family who needs help. Family discussions center on members who seem to be in need of help and focus on ways that other members of the extended family can ensure that members do not lose their way in life. They also confront any member who is about to bring shame on the family name by their behavior in the community. Without the support of an extended family, people are bound to disregard the warnings of a sense of shame and thus they easily succumb to the temptation to give in to their desire for an "easy life" and the passing pleasure provided by it. Eventually, one can be overcome completely by an individualistic and self-interested personality. Every person has within them a tendency toward criminal or nonsocial, purely self-interested behavior, but the strong, close social ties of the extended family maintain and support the socialization of each member. In African as well as Western urban areas where there is a significant lack of extended families, people live in constant fear of criminals who operate with impunity in broad daylight. In urban areas, where most people are strangers to each other, people rely on the law to protect them from crime, but laws cannot create the kind of social ties that are necessary to suppress crime.

As soon as some urban Africans realize that they are still responsible for accommodating extended family members and former neighbors who migrate to the city from the rural areas, they begin to search for methods to avoid supporting people like this who often want to stay with them in the city. Some urban Africans are interested in adopting Western lifestyles so that others can identify them as having advanced toward modern African society. They feel that they are then more "civilized" and have hopes that soon they will gain more respect and prestige in their community. These Africans begin to look upon relatives and former rural neighbors as inferior to them, in this regard, and so for that reason they do not want anyone to associate them with people from the rural areas. In West Africa, when someone adopts Western culture, that person, in the eyes of other West Africans, becomes a *Tubaab,* or Westerner. Once rural elder Africans identify someone as a *Tubaab,* rural people no longer feel safe and comfortable associating with that person. Some urban Africans intentionally adopt Western lifestyles to discourage those who would normally come to join them in the city. Nevertheless, some young people inevitably leave to go to the city, ignoring the warnings of elders, never asking themselves why and never thinking about what effect this will have on the family and community that they have left behind. This creates much conflict in African society.

The trend toward adopting Western lifestyles in African urban areas gives rise to an increase in the number of nuclear families in African cities. Throughout human history, community has always originated with the extended family, which later developed into the larger groups of the clan, tribe, and nation. Disruption of the normal operations of extended families threatens the community, and no amount of artificial community-building activities can bring it back unless extended families are re-established. To do this, nuclear families can be encouraged to become extended families. Leaders of both formal institutions and informal grassroots organizations must encourage open dialog and discussion regarding issues such as housing, employment, schools, and healthcare that affect extended families in African urban areas. By listening to and dialoging with each other, people can develop creative solutions to problems that hinder the establishment of extended families in African cities. This process requires that we address the issue of how to ensure that those who migrate to join family members are adequately prepared to contribute to the support of their family.

The African View of the Self and Symbolic Interaction Theory

I believe that symbolic interaction theory is an appropriate model for viewing traditional African culture because it emphasizes communication and because it emphasizes the essentially social nature of humans. It avoids the trap of isolating individuals so as to view them independently of each other. I feel that the social interaction model is appropriate because it focuses on the system of meanings that guides and motivates African individual, group, and community or organization action. The theory of symbolic interaction poses the important questions that traditional African culture seeks to address for the individual African: How do Africans experience themselves and others? What do Africans have in mind when they say "I" or "me"? How do Africans develop and change? Why do Africans resist change? Symbolic interaction theory states that change involves the development of a new system of meanings and that people change best through methods that address their system of meanings. This theory is congruent with traditional African culture because it views the individual as an active participant in shaping his or her life and social identity, as a learner.[1]

I believe that one can utilize a symbolic interaction model when examining African culture because the idea of person-interacting-with-environment is central to this theory. It focuses on the interaction between the individual and the environment, considers the relationship between the two, and views person-environment influence as reciprocal. Africans typically believe that individuals achieve their identities through social interaction. They believe that individuals in Africa develop their sense of self as a result of their interaction with other Africans and the picture they see of themselves reflected back through other Africans' perceptions of them. In other words, it is not the objective "reality" of their experiences that most influences Africans, but rather their own subjective interpretations of it based upon their previous interpretations of their past experiences. Researchers who study African culture soon become aware that the most important characteristic of the African psyche is the use of symbols and the development of a system of meanings attached to those symbols. Traditional African culture is transmitted via the use of many different symbolic acts and artifacts and is expressed through various symbolic dance, music, and sculptural forms.[2]

Symbolic interactionists believe that an individual's personal meanings are modified as a result of social participation in a variety of social forms. As African children develop fluency in the use of symbols that characteristic of their culture, they simultaneously develop a series of expectations about the behavior of other Africans or what Mead called the "generalized other." For the individual African, the "generalized other" refers to the community's expectations about behaviors that are internalized. The largest portion of an African's self includes internalization of community norms. From the perspective of both traditionally minded Africans and symbolic interaction theorists, the individual and society are simply two sides of the same coin: no individual exists apart from the society in which they grow up. The "primary group" of African children is their extended family, age-group companions, and, in addition, any adult with whom they come in contact in the community, *especially* an elder.[3]

Characteristics of African Families

Like people such as Asians in many other non-Western societies, Africans do not stress independence and autonomy of the individual but rather believe that the family supersedes the individual. The African family adheres to the African tradition of specific hierarchical roles established for all members. Rules of behavior and conduct are formalized in members' roles to a greater extent than in Western (European-based) cultures. In Africa, the extended family network is responsible for maintaining the status of the family name or lineage. Relationships among husband, wife, and in-laws are strictly prescribed, as are relationships between children and parents. Within Western families (e.g., among Americans), the emphasis is on the single nuclear family, which has a time-limited life span. However, within the traditional African framework, the family is *not* time limited. In Africa, the concept of the family extends both backward and forward. The individual is seen as the product of all the generations of that family from the beginning of time. This concept is reinforced by rituals, ceremonies, celebrations, and customs—such as stories told by elders—that express reverence for ancestors and the songs sung by *griots* (traditional musicians). These songs trace family members back over many centuries. Because of this continuity, an African's behavior has a different importance and consequence. Personal actions reflect not only on the individual and the nuclear and extended families, but also on all of the preceding generations of the family since the beginning of time. Individual actions impact upon all future generations as well. Therefore, there is a burden of responsibility that transcends the individual's personal concerns.[4]

In traditional African families, the families on both sides often heavily influence the choice of mate. In Africa, a person rarely marries without the blessing of the family. Marriage does not mark the creation of a new family but rather the continuation of the man's family line. The father is the leader of the African family. After the father has died, and the oldest son takes charge of the family and the wishes of his mother are respectfully granted. Thus, although the oldest son is the ruler of the family, it is frequently the mother who rules the son and, therefore, the rest of the family. The eldest son is expected to be a role model for his siblings and to exert authority over them.[5]

Highly developed feelings of obligation govern much of traditional African life. Shame is frequently used to reinforce adherence to prescribed sets of obligations in Africa. Africans believe that their greatest obligation is to their parents who have brought them into the world and have cared for them when they were helpless. The debt that is owned can never be truly repaid; no matter what parents may do, the child is still obligated to respect them. Shame is the traditional mechanism that helps reinforce societal expectations and proper behavior.

Much of the activity of African life operates on the basis of trust. In Africa, shame produces not only the exposure of one's actions for all to see, but also the withdrawal of the confidence and support of the family, community, and society. In African society, where interdependence is so important, the actual or threatened withdrawal of support can be a powerful motivating force for conforming to family and societal expectations. In Africa, obligation is not just seen as a burden or debt but also as an opportunity to display affection and gratitude. Therefore, in Africa, love is expressed through the fulfillment of obligations.[6]

My Initiation

The important thing is that parents and teachers are not alone in the upbringing of the children. African initiation teaches males and females about their roles and bodies. The initiation of men in Africa is a private and secret thing. The initiation transforms a male youth into a man and brings them understanding of their sexual organs. Young men learn through initiation that the organs belong to the man and to no one else. With this comes the understanding that no one has the right to touch inappropriately. Initiates understand that they are to keep and use at the right time, and that they are something that one can play with but not abuse. The initiation teaches young men about themselves. We are taught to listen, to sacrifice, and to work with other human beings who are different from oneself. I remember when I was in the bush, my parents were not around and my brothers were not around nor anyone who was a member of my family, but I was with other children like me. An outsider who was not in our community came to be with us for fourteen days to train us. This secret society was important to us because it was our rite of passage to adulthood. When we came out of the bush, we were wiser, more responsible, and more dedicated to our community. If one has not been circumcised, that person must not come close to where the group of circumcised males is meeting because that is taboo. Females are not allowed to come near there because that is taboo. If they do, they have to pay a fine. Sometimes initiation is difficult; people cry and they want to leave, but it is a chance to create bravery in oneself and to understand that life is full of good and bad, evil and happiness.

Women are very important to Africans. To have and raise a child engenders respect, value, and prestige. When people have a child, their parents are involved. Parents depend on the extended family and community to bring up the child. Marriage and the birth of a child confer respect. The community respects married parents as an example to the younger generation.

In Africa, women and men have separate initiation traditions and ceremonies. My people, the Manjako ethnic group in The Gambia, do not practice female circumcision. We are against female genital mutilation because we see it as something evil and oppressive to a female's body and mind. Though we are against female circumcision, or female genital mutilation, we maintain the tradition of separate female initiation. At the age of eight, Manjako females undergo their initiation. During their initiation, they are socialized by older females who teach them about their female body parts, give them information about how to develop into a healthy adult female, how to behave as a female, and what their responsibilities are as a female in African society. They are taught to practice self-discipline and to see their bodies as their own. They are taught that they should never allow anyone to abuse their bodies. The Manjako believe that female genital mutilation or circumcision should not accomplish female initiation. They believe that female initiation should be accomplished by socializing females to think and behave in traditionally established ways. Manjakos believe that females should not be subjected to the pain of female circumcision or to its lifelong consequences.

When Manjako females have been taken to a location for initiation, Manjako males do not come near, or they would be in violation of the norms and values of their culture and would fly in the face of powerful taboos. Among the Manjakos, female initiation is a secret society for females only, and we expect that all members of the community will respect the privacy of this secret society. During Manjako female initiation, girls are taught to obey and respect older females. They are taught to understand how they are different than men and that they have certain abilities which men will never have. For this reason, they should not strive to be like men or act in a way that a man might desire. Manjako females are taught how to make decisions that will satisfy their needs in a positive, acceptable manner that is uniquely female.

This type of strong, creative, and autonomous femininity is seen as something very valuable in Manjako society. In this way, Manjako female initiation is a typical example of a traditional African rite of passage. In Manjako society, any woman who has not gone through this initiation is not considered to have been blessed. This person has not been indoctrinated regarding her role in Manjako society. I believe that female initiation of this kind is a way of empowering each female and nurturing the positive energy and talents that God has given her. Among the Manjako ethnic group, when females emerge from this secret society's initiation, their body becomes holy. For this reason, they dress differently than they did before their initiation. Because they see themselves differently, they begin to play a different role in their society. Their behavior and actions change because they have become aware that they have moved on to a more advanced stage in life. This is a stage of apprenticeship to adulthood, a stage of self-responsibility, a stage of self-respect and dignity, a stage of having understood the purpose of ones body and its existence. This understanding creates in all Manjako girls a sense of great pride in being a female. When older women begin the initiation, they teach the girls about Manjako family life. They talk to them about how they will be viewed by men when they reach physical maturity, how men will become interested in them when they have reached puberty and, for this reason, how they must be careful around men from then on. This is the kind of information that is important to a young African female who intends to remain a virgin until she is married. The true purpose of the traditional African rite of passage of both female and male initiation is to create self-esteem in the hearts and minds of African young people.

I consider traditional African initiation, as it is practiced by my ethnic group, to be a way to provide self-empowerment to African men and women and a key to building successful African societies. All of my sisters went through this experience of female initiation. Because it taught them about their positive roles and responsibilities as females in an African society, they are glad to pass this tradition on to their daughters. My sisters participated in this secret society because they have experienced personally its success in shaping a child's behavior and molding that child into an adult who is proud of her gender, ethnic group, and the African society in which she lives.

During the traditional Manjako secret rite of female initiation, girls learn how to become mothers. During male initiation, boys learn how to become fathers, not just in a physical sense but also in a social sense. The learn how to care for children. An important purpose of both female and male initiation is to teach boys and girls how to accept responsibility. I believe that Africans initiated in this manner take seriously their responsibilities as parents and strive to raise their children in a positive way. In the secret rites of male and female initiation, Manjako girls and boys are taught that the joy of sexual intercourse culminates in the successful nurturing of children.

The Negative Effects of Female Circumcision

Historical and Contemporary Roots of the Practice

African female authors Asma El Dareer and Raqiya Haji Dualeh Abdalla reminded us that "to abolish female circumcision, consideration must be given to the deep cultural roots of this ancient custom."[7] Researcher Marie Bassili Assad reported, "It has been found, by the examination of mummified remains, to have originated in ancient Egyptian culture, which believed that humans, like the Gods, were bisexual and that excision of the prepuce created a man and that of the clitoris, a woman."[8] Female circumcisions were even practiced in the United States from 1890 to 1930 with the purpose of controlling female sexuality. In fact, in our modern day and age, circumcision is found worldwide, in Jewish, Arabic, Australian Aboriginal, Indonesian and Malaysian cultures, as well as among Sub-Saharan Africans. At this time, female circumcision is practiced in forty countries, mostly in west and east Africa, but also on the Arabian Peninsula.

Though chastity is highly prized in Islam, female circumcision is not mentioned in the *Holy Qur'an* as a method by which to achieve it. In fact, Islamic law forbids it. Illiterate West African women must take the word of their Islamic religious leaders who falsely claim that the *Holy Qur'an* dictates female circumcision. In Islam, virginity is considered an unmarried woman's most valued possession. Her family will do anything, even endanger her life, to protect her hymen, the symbol of her virginity. I believe that female circumcision will continue as long as religious leaders identify it with Islam.

Traditional African Beliefs Regarding Female Circumcision

Researcher Hanny Lightfoot-Klein discovered that in Sudan, Pharonic circumcision serves to distinguish respectable women from prostitutes:

> In this patriarchal society, a girl cannot marry, and thus perform her primary role in life, that of producing legitimate sons to carry on her husband's line, if she has not had Pharonic circumcision. In fact, the measure of a family's honor is the sexual purity of their women. In (Sudanese) society, women are assumed to be sexually promiscuous, by nature, and morally weak. This operation is believed to dampen their sexual drive. It is thought that if their clitoris is not clipped, it will grow long like a penis. In fact, the smaller a (Sudanese) woman's infibulation opening, the higher the bride price she can bring her family when she marries.[8]

Regardless of the pain of penetration and the disfigurement of circumcision, most Sudanese women whom Lightfoot-Klein interviewed confided that they often perfumed themselves with spices to attract their husbands. They had to pay great attention to hiding their natural sexual response and the pleasure it gave them because many of them knew of women who had been divorced for showing enjoyment during marital relations because considered whores for such expression.

The Gikuyu, the largest ethnic group in Kenya, believe that this operation serves as a rite of passage for girls to prepare them for marriage and that to eliminate it would end Gikuyu morality. As a tradition, it serves to bind together a rural community and provides a source of cultural identity. Young girls of the Shanabla people in Kenya receive parties and gifts at this time, and the rite is a declaration of a woman's eligibility for marriage. It is believed that the clitoris exudes an offensive discharge and must be excised for a woman to be cleansed in preparation for marriage and childbirth. In Nigeria, female circumcision is performed for both traditional and cosmetic reasons and it is believed that the clitoris is capable of injuring a baby at birth.

Dangerous Medical Complications

In conducting her study, Lightfoot-Klein was assisted by two Sudanese nurses who had their own circumcision practice, in addition to being hospital nurses. Circumcised, of course, themselves, they performed Pharonic circumcisions of excision of the clitoris, the labia minora, and the inner layers of the labia majora. They sewed the outer layers of the labia majora together to leave only a pinhole opening, called infibulation. The author of this study noted,

> In urban areas, in Sudan, small girls, four to eight years old, are circumcised in clinics, regardless of social standing; whereas, in rural areas, untrained midwives perform it without anesthesia or antiseptics, often leading to hemorrhage, infection, shock, and urinary retention. Usually marriage follows soon afterward because menstruation is very painful and blockage causes putrid retention of menstrual blood.[9]

Another researcher, Alison Slack, came upon a study that was conducted in the Sudan, which found that Pharonic virgins needed at least fifteen minutes to urinate and that thirty percent of Sudanese women who had had this operation had fertility problems. One girl was rejected by her family because the blockage of and the lack of an outward show of her monthly flow, along with a swollen belly, led her family to think she was pregnant. Slack noted,

> In the Sudan, often each new birth is more dangerous because wives request re-infibulation after each birth to become "virginal" to please their husbands. When the baby and mother die, it is attributed to God's will or fate, NOT to the build-up of scar tissue blocking the birth opening.[10]

The practice of re-infibulation mocks the idea that infibulation guarantees virginity as a girl could be re-infibulated after a secret affair even before her marriage.

During the Sudanese marriage ceremony, a bridegroom must appear happy and confident and must hide his fears that he may fatally injure his wife when he attempts to penetrate her during consummation by causing her to bleed to death; or perhaps he will fail in his attempts, which will cause him to lose face as a man and possibly tempt him to try to commit suicide. Some men fail to enter but still manage to impregnate their wives, who must be cut open to allow the birth of a child. In some cases, the woman's scar tissue is so thick that doctors have broken scalpels and must resort to very strong surgical scissors. Many Sudanese women convince their husbands to pay traditional midwives to re-circumcise them after each birth so they can be as a virgin again and thus please their husband, discouraging him from looking for an additional wife.

Slack found that in Mauritania, female circumcision is done within the first two weeks of life and contributes to the high infant morality rate, which is twenty percent. Her research also revealed that countries with high infant mortality rates also have high percentages of circumcised women. One example of this is Somalia:

> Unsterilized instruments and unhygienic methods during infibulation cause most complications. Doctors report that in areas of Sudan where no antibiotics are available, infibulation results in death for *one-third* of the girls operated on.[11]

Robert Myers, Francisa Omorodion, Anthony Isenalumhe, and Gregory Akenzua researched circumcision among some ethnic groups in Southern Nigeria, in five rural communities in mid-southern Nigeria among the Bini, Esan, Etsako, Ijaw and Ukwuani peoples to determine the extent of circumcision in this region of Africa. Because female circumcision, as it is practiced there, is not as mutilating as the Pharonic type, low complication rates discourage any campaign against it. Nevertheless, the authors of this study found,

> Clinics and hospitals have compiled lists of possible complications including: anemia, labial adhesions, and vaginal infection leading to tetanus, hemorrhage and urine retention."[12]

Current Obstacles to the Elimination

Though a law outlawing female circumcision was passed just after Sudanese independence in 1956, it has never been enforced. Even in educated families in the capital city of Khartoum, circumcision day is even more important than a female's wedding day. Researcher Alison Slack found a study done in Nigeria that stated that even educated women who were opposed to it gave in and had this operation after feeling pressured by their families. Researcher Marie Assad commented,

Modern and traditional Egyptian women both claim that circumcision is good for protection from temptation, suspicion and disgrace, but often, modern African women's views of themselves change as they gain more education and economic opportunities . . . . She begins to see that her status can be derived from other than that of a wife and mother. Daughters of urbanized women, who are not given this operation, know nothing of it. Because of this, and the taboo surrounding discussing it, it is not an issue for urban women's organizations.[13]

El Dareer and Abdalla agreed:

The concept of womanhood must be changed from one similar to a dog that must be muzzled to one of an equal partner with men in upholding the morality of family and society. This operation has not succeeded in quenching a woman's desire to unite with the man she loves and she will be faithful to a loving husband even if she has been robbed of her sexuality.[14]

It is clear that unless men accept the idea of marrying uncircumcised woman, the chance of abolishing this operation is very slim. Women in these societies must find alternative avenues to social status, approval, and respectability.

Journalist William House noted,

There is no correlation between which women have been circumcised and level of education, home area or family occupation. But the opportunity, for women who have migrated from rural to urban areas, to earn money for themselves, *has* affected the numbers of circumcised women. Now, women are setting an example for their daughters of becoming educated and gaining independence from the dictates of a husband. But, it is believed that rural mothers will not stop encouraging their daughters to undergo this operation until there are greater educational opportunities for them. This will only happen when rural parents decide that economic conditions allow all of their children to attend school, both boys and girls.[15]

Present Action Being Taken

The Cairo Family Planning Association is currently conducting an extensive survey to promote understanding of the beliefs that perpetuate female circumcision and thus to discover the type of educational approach that will lead to its abolition. It is thought that modern health practitioners, social leaders, and educated women will be able to confront this custom with the reality that premarital chastity is a moral and social issue for Egyptian society and that an intact clitoris does not endow masculine characteristics. Established in 1984 by UNICEF in Senegal, the Inter-African Committee on Traditional Practices Affecting the Health of Women and Children in Africa has sponsored sections in Benin, Djibouti, Egypt, The Gambia, Liberia, Mali, Senegal, Sierra Leone, and Togo for the purpose of spreading information about the negative health effects of female circumcision.

A Call to All Africans to Abolish Female Circumcision

It is the responsibility of educators, health professionals, government officials, sociologists, psychologists, politicians, enlightened religious leaders, respected and wise elders, and progressive community members and their leaders to renounce this dangerous practice. National policies must be produced to counteract mothers' fears that their daughters will not receive a good bride price and husband unless they are circumcised. Alternative sources of income must be found for traditional surgeons who perform this operation. Community programs need to be designed and implemented to educate all of the people via public lectures held at schools, even in remote rural areas. It is the responsibility of women's organizations to publicize this issue utilizing radio and newspaper campaigns so as to reach everyone. Following public lectures and media coverage, discussions open to the public should be held in which everyone is invited to come to hash out the pros and cons, the superstitions, and medical realities of this traditional custom. Dramatic troupes can be organized to perform on radio and television, in town theaters, and rural clearings to enact the various aspects of this social problem and to encourage people to consider the positive outcomes of giving up this traditional practice.

The Value of Traditional African Initiation

I believe that we should evaluate traditional African initiation practices and maintain those that we conclude can assist Africans to be successful in the future. We should likewise discard negative practices, such as female genital circumcision, that hinder the empowerment of African women. I believe that eliminating the tradition of male and female initiation will only create confusion among our young people. If we neglect our tradition of initiation, we will become lost because we will have left behind our own culture. Our African societies will be seen as valueless in the eyes of African young people, and their energy will waste itself in futile, meaningless excesses of crime and drug abuse. Traditional African initiation teaches young people to respect themselves and other people. It teaches women to respect men and men to respect women. I am sure that our African ancestors want us to continue holding initiation rites because they know that initiation can maintain a positive society because it creates an environment of safety within communities.

Africans value and respect women because they know that without successful women, Africa would be a complete failure. African women are hard working and intelligent. They have an amazing ability to cope with the most difficult circumstances. They set a wonderful example for the younger gen-eration to follow. African women such as my mother have a vision for the future of Africa because they are willing to sacrifice their needs to secure a better tomorrow for their children. I am convinced that Africa will become a better continent when African males start to work hard to understand our female counterparts and follow their example in expending all of their positive energy caring for the needs of the younger generation.

In African urban areas, secret male and female initiation societies should be maintained because they enable young people who go through the initiation process to know who they are in terms of their adult roles in African society. Initiation helps young people to understand the rights and responsibilities of their own gender. They are taught to value and respect the gender to which they belong. When they respect their own gender, they are more likely to respect people of the opposite gender. Initiation builds the self-esteem of a young women and men. This helps them become good parents. Initiation encourages young people to appreciate and value other cultural traditions and be more likely to pass them on to their own children.

The problem occurs when children grow up in the city. They are unwilling to go to the rural areas to undergo initiation ceremonies because they view anything that is related to rural African society as old fashioned and uncivilized. There is a need for rural and urban elders to discuss openly what can be done to maintain female and male initiation in the cities. One solution would be to invite those elders who conduct the secret initiation societies in rural areas to come and lead initiation activities in specified buildings in the city that are appropriately modified just for that purpose.

Existing neighborhood youth centers could be utilized for this during particular months, once a year. For example, males only could occupy the youth center during part of Christmas school vacation for their initiation; females could then use it during part of Easter vacation. Arrangements can be made to suit the individual circumstances.

More and more urban Africans are neglecting to return with their children to rural areas to participate in initiation activities. As those children grow up, their perspective never expands beyond their own family. For that reason, they are often much more self-centered and self-interested than those young people who have undergone initiation, those who have become aware of and ready to take up their appropriate roles in traditional African culture. These urban young people exhibit little respect for elders. They do not want to listen to or take instructions from anyone, even their parents. In their minds, they create a myth about themselves as being superior to those who grew up in rural areas.

There is a need for people living in modern societies around the world, in the West as well as in Africa, to understand the purposes and value of secret male and female initiation societies. When this happens, all people will realize that this initiation is necessary to provide the glue that holds together the various generations within human communities. I am not referring to practices that mutilate women's bodies, such as female genital circumcision. Governments should implement public policies that fund salaries for elders who regularly travel to communities to perform male and female initiation workshops for youth.

When such policies are implemented, modern societies will be free of the prevalent social disease of "strangerness" because important social ties between adults and young people will have been strengthened. This will make all communities safer and thus much better places to live for children, families, and the elderly. Another good thing it will bring to modern societies is that young people will feel a sense of responsibility toward their communities and society as well as pride their places within those communities. In this way, young people will be able to shed their belief in the myth that their government is responsible for supporting them financially and socially. When young people have undergone traditional initiation, they feel a sense of empowerment as new adults, which make them reject the idea of ever relying on government handouts because it would be degrading.

Marriage

Conflict in marriage exists in Africa, but everyone in the community has the right to intervene when couples are fighting. They have the right to tell them who is right and who is wrong. Even a passerby can enter one's house to investigate when they hear someone screaming. That person will listen with patience and sit down to try to solve the conflict. We cannot deny that there is abuse among couples in Africa but because the community looks out for everybody, when couples fight, neighbors have the right to come and seize the wife and take her away. The wife will not be returned until there is an apology to elders of the community. It is a big shame for men to face the elders and do this so they try by any means to avoid abuse and spousal conflict. They leave the house to vent their anger and stay away for a while until both partners are calm.

In African societies, marriage as a social institution is very important. Women are definitely aware of this and for that reason, they work very hard to keep their marriages together. It is time that African men realized the sacrifices their women make to maintain their marriages. At all times, African men should be prepared to work hard with their wives to create a better future for all African children. When one marries, status increases. In The Gambia, all women are expected to get married. When they marry, they take on more responsibility, and for that reason, are given more respect. As married women, they now undertake an important role in community affairs and acquire a strong voice in all family and community decisions. This is one of the reasons that women in Africa value marriage. Once a female becomes a married woman, it is taboo to instigate a fight with them in public. This would be viewed by everyone as being highly disrespectful to not only the woman but also to her husband and children.

Among the Manjako, marriage is for life. When a Manjako male marries, it is his responsibility to work his in-laws' as well as his parents' land several times a year. This is done to show love and to indicate that one values them because they have wholeheartedly given their daughter. These efforts demonstrate the husband's pride in having one of their children as wife, and prevent the in-laws from feeling that they have lost their daughter. The husband works hard to make the in-laws feel that they have not lost a daughter but gained a son. Working their land helps to defray the loss of a person who contributed on a significant social and economic level to their family. In Africa, marriage establishes a relationship between two families; marriage involves an extended family, not just a wife. Newly married couples are socially and economically connected to the community that raised the wife. It is impossible to disassociate from the entire community. People think long and hard before deciding to dishonor everyone who has worked hard to help create a woman who is attractive because of her value as a good wife.

Traditionally, Africans marry more than one wife. In the past, this was done because more wives mean more children and more land that the family can farm. More children thus confer greater economic viability on the family. Quite often, a man will marry a second wife because his first wife is not able to produce children. Among the Manjako, we deal with this difficult situation by discussing this alternative with the first wife, who then chooses a second wife with whom she is willing to share her husband.

In most African ethnic groups, parents usually choose a spouse for their children. Recently, many parents have realized that this is not practical for their children, who most likely will move away to another city or even another country and there find someone with whom they will fall in love. Many parents have come to recognize that forcing their children to marry someone whom they have chosen themselves is a sin. Among the Manjako, most parents have given up the practice of arranging marriages for their children because they prefer not to suffer public embarrassment when their child refuses to marry someone they have not chosen.

I remember my father telling my older sisters that they had the right and the responsibility to decide whom they will marry. My father's older brother wanted to arrange a marriage for one of my sisters, but my father said no. He explained, "We are not the ones getting married. She is the one who is going. If it doesn't work out, we would be the ones responsible because we were the ones who made the choice for them. We should give our children the chance to decide who they want to marry." After thinking about it, my father's older brother agreed. African parents always want a chance to get to know the family of their child's intended spouse because grandparents have an important responsibility to help raise the children of their children. The African extended family is intimately involved in molding each child that is born to it. Perhaps that is the origin of the famous African proverb, "It takes a whole village to raise a child." At this time, many men of the Manjako have realized that it is no longer economical to take more than one wife, especially in the city, because the cost of supporting many children is too high.

Effects of Forced, Arranged Marriages

Marriage should be an agreement between two people, male and female, husband and wife, who strongly believe that they can live peacefully together and build a family with the support of their parents and extended families as well as the community in which they live. Parents and elders within the community should provide young people with guidance by offering suggestions as to how to go about obtaining an appropriate mate. I believe that it is the role of parents and elders to supply opinions but not to force their sons or daughters to marry someone whom they did not choose.

In The Gambia, some parents continue to promote arranged marriages for their children because they feel that they know who is most suitable. They prefer to select a mate for their children who are of families with whom they already have established social ties. For their daughters, they seek to obtain men whose parents are known to be dedicated and hard-working community members. For their sons, they try to obtain a girl whose mother is known to have had many healthy children. These parents believe that they have the right to extend their authority over their child's adult life. They do this to ensure that their community is maintained. Arranged marriages are attempted because parents learned this tradition from their parents; their own marriages were arranged. At that time, there was less rural-urban migration and formal education was limited to only a few people in the society. In our parents' time, there were less available lifestyles from which to choose.

Problems of Forced, Arranged Marriages

Conflicts between young people and parents arose when more people gained access to formal education and could migrate from rural to urban areas to settle. Young people began to meet others for whom successful marriages had not been arranged, which caused them to develop their own views regarding how marriages should come about.

They began to question traditional arranged marriages in Africa and tried to resist them. Because parents felt that they were losing power over their sons and daughters, they reacted by increasing pressure on them to comply with arranged marriages. Greater emphasis is placed on forcing women into arranged marriages than men.

Often parents make arrangements for their daughter's marriage when she is young. When she is old enough to leave home, they tell her that they expect her to comply with these arrangements, and if she resists, they force her to do so. Often they threaten her with physical violence or deny her opportunities to see her friends. Some parents even withhold food. They attempt to regulate her relationships with others in the community so that they can maintain power over their daughter. If she refuses to accept her parents' choice for her husband, she is viewed by members of her community as a woman who is sending a harmful message to other girls who might want to follow her example and as such is no longer deserving of respect as a person. Some are even forced by their parents to drop out of school to get married.

This conflict causes some young women to run away to avoid having to marry someone whom they have not chosen as their lover. Often they are not psychologically ready to settle down as a wife and care for children. They run away because they can no longer tolerate the beatings that they must endure if they continue to resist marrying their parents' choice. After they run away and someone who knows them discovers them, their parents deliver them to the man who has been arranged to be the husband. Some girls who have found out that their parents have arranged a marriage for them deliberately become pregnant with their lover's child. A few young women in this situation even leave the country and do not return.

Forced arranged marriages cause a brain drain in our country that now affects the progress of sustainable development in our society. Forcing girls to marry someone whom they have not chosen promotes poverty in Africa. Usually, these young women have not been properly prepared nor trained to plan their lives as wives and mothers. As a result, they end up becoming helpless members of society. Before they are forced to get married, young people have to be taught how to raise children. They have to be prepared economically to support their children and to be able to provide them with a positive education that will benefit them in the future.

Possible Solutions

The role of parents in their children's marriages should be to allow open discussion with their children regarding the topic of traditional arranged marriages. Parents and children should consider together all of the advantages and disadvantages of traditional arranged marriages. Parents need to explain thoroughly to their children, why the practice of arranged marriage continues. Parents also need to listen to their children's thoughts and feelings about this matter. Parents must also consider the other influences that are faced by their children. The proper role of parents also includes considering the psychological effects of forcing their children into marriages that are not of the children's choices. Parents need to consider the economic burden that they may be placing upon their children's shoulders if they still lack proper preparation for marriage and supporting a family. Parents who insist on forcing their children into arranged marriages must face their responsibility to be accountable for a failed marriage, if that happens.

The proper role of elders in the community is to try bridge the generation gap between children and their parents. Elders should be understanding of both parents' and young people's concerns regarding the institution of traditional arranged marriages. Elders should counsel parents and their children regarding conflict resolution during this time, instead of siding with parents. By doing this, young people will feel more welcome, the democratic process will be encouraged, and elders will have a role that will bring them great respect in their communities. In this kind of social climate, parents and their children will be empowered to work *together* to build better communities.

The role of religious leaders in arranged marriage should be to meet with and counsel parents and young people, especially young couples, to see whether they are adequately emotionally mature and are not being forced to marry by their parents. Religious leaders should provide spiritual guidance and serve as examples of compassion, love, and understanding in their communities. They should be willing to stand up and challenge those who practice forced arranged marriages. They should avoid siding with elders who condone forced arranged marriages.

I believe that the proper role of young people in the social institution of marriage should be to strive to understand their parents' concerns about them finding a suitable mate that will help them to maintain ties to their family and develop economically. Young people should be willing to be responsible for their actions and realize that these actions may negatively or positively affect their future and the future of their family. They should not immediately reject their parents' advice but should be open-minded and discuss this matter with them. Young men and women can voice their feelings and thoughts in a respectful manner to their mothers and fathers. Young people can present the topic of arranged marriage as something that is important to discuss during youth group activities held in their communities. Youth can request couples whose marriages were arranged and not arranged to tell about problems they encountered and solutions they found.

The proper role of social institutions such as schools in marriage is to provide people in their communities with education regarding the advantages and disadvantages of arranged and non-arranged marriages. Schools should have a complete curriculum that teaches about the history of traditional African culture of which arranged marriage is a part. Then students will have knowledge about their culture that they can draw upon to make choices about their lives as adults. This curriculum must explain in depth both the negative and positive aspects of traditional African customs, such as arranged marriage. School debate groups can address the topic of arranged marriage.

The role of the media (television, radio, and newspapers) is to encourage people to discuss the advantages and disadvantages of arranged marriages by providing a forum wherein this topic can be debated and discussed. By all means, the media should discourage people who want only to criticize and condemn traditional African customs, such as arranged marriage, without offering reasonable alternatives that are acceptable to most Africans. The media need to take up their responsibility to be accountable to the people in society and not always be looking out for their own best interests. The media are responsible for assisting in the development of Africa as a modern region of the world.

The role of government in arranged marriage is to support all groups, religious and social, that are striving to deal with the problem of forced arranged marriages and their negative consequences. The government can help by providing these organizations with technical support and training to help them be more effective in their attempts to solve this serious social problem in Africa. Government officials and politicians have a responsibility to address the issue of forced arranged marriages on a national as well as local level when they speak in front of groups of youth, elders, religious leaders, business people, and citizens.

African governments should become more proactive on this issue and develop a public policy that seriously addresses traditional African cultural practices such as arranged marriages. For this to happen, African women will have to be included in the decision-making process of designing public policies regarding arranged marriage in Africa. I recommend that governments establish nationwide secondary school essay competitions, the title of which would be "Arranged Marriage in My Country." The purpose of this essay competition is to awaken and empower Africans to address the problem of forced arranged marriages in our countries and to come up with solutions that can be adopted by African society.

Self-evaluation is necessary because Africans need to examine traditional customs so as to develop strategies to use to create a society that suffers from less conflict.

All Africans should ask themselves what are the reasonable alternatives to forcing young people into arranged marriages against their will. This self-evaluation process should allow all Africans to look at subjects in our culture that have been considered taboo in the past. Subjects that have been taboo should *never* be discarded, but instead, evaluated and their positive contributions to our society welcomed and strengthened while we free ourselves of the negative aspects of our traditional practices that hinder our progress as a nation of strong families.

When elders and religious leaders side with parents a conflict over arranged marriage, it damages the social fabric of African society because young people then stop trusting the elders and religious leaders in their communities. When this happens, young people turn to each other rather than listening to elders and religious leaders to find norms and values. This nurtures the growth of a subculture that is contrary to traditional African culture and does not include a sense of responsibility to the community or society because the social bond between the generations has been broken. When this essential social bond is destroyed, the glue that holds together human society is gravely weakened as each generation looks not to each other for assistance but to itself for survival. Thus each generation competes with the next, tearing the social fabric even more with each new generation as more and more positive, tried-and-true traditions are rejected. When young people create their own subculture, it erects a communication barrier to screen out the words of parents, elders, and religious and community leaders.

I do not propose to abolish traditional African arranged marriages. I am proposing that African elders, educators, and government and religious leaders create a forum in which this issue can be discussed and evaluated. In Africa, we have to eliminate the myth of the need for "total acceptance" or "total rejection" in regard to modern Western social practices and traditional African social practices. I believe that the African attitude of "total rejection" of modern Western social practices will lead to the destruction of African society because the Africa of the past no longer exists. For this reason, Africans cannot afford to reject something merely because they do not understand it. In addition, I believe that the African attitude of "total acceptance" will lead to the enslavement of Africans because we do not know how our African norms and values will be affected by a total acceptance of Western social practices and beliefs.

Chapter 4

Africans on the Move

African Handshake and City Life

There is a philosophy behind the African left handshake that is used when one travels. It plays an important role in West African society. Why do Africans shake left hands when traveling? Why not use the right hand? Why not just hug the one who is going away? Why not just wave goodbye? Why not just smile and nod? Africans shake with the left hand when traveling because they want that person to remain healthy so that they can come back to the community alive. Why do we not just say that to the person who is leaving? That is not the entire philosophy. The whole philosophy includes the fact that human beings hearts are on the left side of their bodies. By shaking with the left hand addresses their left side and therefore the heart and conveys the wish that their heart continue to beat, to continue to be healthy so that they will return alive. In African society, each person's health and happiness is important to the rest of the community whose members believe that the departing person will be able to bring good things back to the community.

Because this is something that I learned before I went to school, I believe in it. I did not learn it in school. I learned it in my community. Through out my life, over and over, I have seen people who have never been in school doing it, especially in The Gambia. It shows love, respect, and appreciation for other human beings. It builds awareness and understanding among Africans. It shows that Africans love peace.

The left handshake is very important and means a lot to Africans because we value human life. We want to see this flesh go and benefit other human beings because we believe that every human being has something that they can offer to benefit their society. Africans feel that all human beings have worth regardless of their color, wealth, education, experience, or skills. We believe that all human beings should be respected, accepted, and supported in our society so that we can have peace, harmony, and freedom. The traditional left-handed handshake conveys a wish for long life. It expresses caring and understanding and the prayer that *Nasibati* (God) will protect all human beings.

Many young Africans are leaving the countryside and the culture in which they were raised to migrate to urban areas. Africans have been told by our great-grandparents that drought would come again. If we had been listening to our elders, we would have prepared for it. We must plan for the future; otherwise, we will remain as slaves. When droughts come, we will turn to the hands of those whom we think are helping us. Then they will come and take our resources. They will suck out our natural resources, and they will leave us with empty land. When this happens, we will say, "Had I known . . .", which is past tense and cannot lead us to a bright future.

When I moved to the city, life was great but at times it was lonely. Sometimes people find it difficult to make friends in the city because they come from different parts of the country. Sometimes they don't even speak the same language. Sometimes a person from the village is viewed as uncivilized. City life would be much better if we took time to learn from rural life because that is what maintains people in the city. In Africa, rural areas support urban areas. We need to re-evaluate city life and maintain and support rural areas. We need to be aware that we cannot exist without rural life.

There is more crime in the cities, but to be a thief in Africa is to allow oneself to be rejected by one's society and community and to incur the denouncement of one's parents. Even close friends will no longer have time because they often perceive the one departed as an evil.

When someone cries, "Thief, thief!" everyone in the community runs out to help and runs after the offender. The pursuers sometimes take the law into their own hands and may impose punishment or pain such as whipping or scratching. One thus has to seek refuge with the police otherwise or risk being killed. The people believe they are protecting everyone in the community. The thief who has come to divide and destroy the community will have to suffer and face punishment alone. This being the case, people usually leave their doors unlocked. People are afraid to invade other people's homes because they know what will happen to them. They know that they will have no excuse. They realize that it is wrong. No explanation such as mental illness or retardation excuses such behavior. The evil must be punished and will be punished. This brings peace and stability. This keeps strangerness away and builds a better community full of people who have understanding and loving care and who feel concern for each other.

Rural-urban Migration in West Africa

It is important to understand the causes of rural-urban migration in West Africa because cities are being overburdened with too many rural migrants and rural areas are being depleted of manpower. The economic system is out of balance. "The rapid growth of cities has not been preceded by (required) changes in food production which create the surplus necessary for urban growth."[1] Once the root causes of this problem have been understood, we stand a better chance of developing a positive policy strategy with which to intervene to rescue our nations. We have known about this problem for several decades but everything that has been tried to solve it has failed. We must ask why the education system disregards agriculture in poor countries where many are hungry and agriculture is the basis for a higher standard of living? There is one answer that can explain all of the questions involving "inequality, government expansion, neglect of agriculture, and the urban bias of education: the drive toward a style of life that we call middle-class."[2]

Historical Changes in West Africa

"What is the primary force in (all) historical changes? Is it culture change or economic progress?"[3] We will be able to answer this question when I have finished my analysis, and it will lead us to solutions to the problem of rural-urban migration.

Consider colonial times in West Africa:

> The colonial period denied the African not only the opportunity of acquiring modern productive skills for processing the produce of his farms, forests, and mines but also the chance of learning organizational skills needed for ensuring the smooth flow and delivery of the produce to foreign markets. Most Africans saw Western education as a means of escape from strenuous manual work to a life of relative luxury. Every African parent prayed that his son might be educated so that he could turn away from farming and go to the city. (Unfortunately), European-style education did not equip them with the skills to create wealth and self-sustained growth.[4]

The result of European education in West Africa has been the creation of conflict among and division of Africans. It teaches us to value individualism and to reject as old-fashioned the traditional community style of doing things in African society. Many people think that "the broad flow of people to the urban centers is an inevitable process that has occurred in every developing society as newer technologies exert their impacts."[5] Are the motivations of Africans much different from those of other peoples? "What about that spirit of adventure which seeks new horizons to explore, new worlds to conquer?"[6] Long before Europeans came to our coasts, West Africans were moving freely to many parts of the continent to create settlements.

Global Cultural Change

I believe that traditional explanations do not cover all of the motivations involved in West African rural-urban migration. Perhaps that is why all previous solutions that have attempted have failed. Consider another possible explanation. "The middle-class consumerist lifestyle consists of heated and cooled homes equipped with telephone, television, refrigerator and car,"[7] all of which one finds in urban areas. "Worldwide media teach a pattern of consumption that is temporarily beyond the capability of developing nations to support."[8] More seriously,

> Being middle-class is not a matter of consumption alone. Certain kinds of work are middle-class, and other kinds (like being a peasant, even a rich one) are not. Office work at a salary that permits owning a car and adequately equipped house is the ideal. Workers seek to avoid the hazards of entrepreneurship. Much desired is the job of senior administrator in government; even better is working for a multi-national corporation. The work people like to do diverges from the kind of work that produces the goods on which they want to spend their salaries.[9]

In all institutions in West Africa, white-collar jobs are more highly valued and supported. For this reason, people place less value on farming as an occupation.

Demographic Changes

At this point, it is necessary to get an idea of the scope of the problem. What has happened since independence?

> Before the present century, almost every sub-Saharan African earned his living by gathering food (including hunting and fishing), cultivating crops or by herding . . . . Within the span of two generations, millions of Africans have made the trek from the bush to the modern city to become participants overnight in an industrial society.[10]

> In Ghana, the 1970 census showed that, of Accra's total population, just half were born in the city. Comparison with 1960 figures suggests that there must have been a net movement into Accra proper of at least 100,000 people during the decade. A survey of Accra factory workers in 1972 found that only 19% had grown up locally; 7% had come from other large towns, 28% from small towns and 46% from rural areas. In the rural areas, 11% of the adult population whose homes were said to be there, were away in town; 14% formerly lived for awhile in town; a further 9% planned to go to town.[11]

> "Within a generation, the majority of Ghanaians will live in towns."[12]

> In the twenty-year period from 1950 to 1970, the population of the larger urban centers in Africa increased at a rate of over 7% a year. This concentration of

population threatens not only the prospects of real economic development but also the possibility of stable political evolution.[13]

Changes in Social Structures

This sudden tremendous increase in urban population creates the "growth of squatter settlements, breakdown of waste disposal arrangements, inadequate water and power supply and generally poor sanitation."[14] In the western urban area of Sierra Leone, "devastating social conditions have been created: prostitution, neglected children and elderly, and infectious diseases."[15]

Nevertheless, there is a growing number of youths surviving "in the forlorn hope that one day they will gain urban employment. Most of these youths are too young and too unskilled for employment in the industrial fields."[16] "Their frustration may be responsible for stealing, prostitution, poor mental and physical health, drug addiction, alcoholism and violence."[17] As they pick up employment helping tourists who come to West Africa from Europe, young Gambian men also learn and emulate aspects of European culture that is often contrary to African morals. As one ray of hope, people continue to try to make the best of their situation and make money however they can. "In some of the cities, almost 90% of the working population may be linked to the informal sector."[18] "The informal sector uses small-scale, even recycled, materials to make small items to sell cheaply to the urban poor themselves. It also includes selling cooked foods, traditional health care and the construction of squatter housing."[19]

The Attraction of Urban Life

Rural migrants are willing to suffer the indignities of urban poverty because "the urban amenities—roads, local transport, schools—are available to them. The rich cannot make the city better for itself without making it better for the poor, and thereby, encouraging more newcomers."[20] "In Sierra Leone, the western area is socially, industrially, academically and economically developed and continues to be modernized." Perhaps this explains why "of the total population in the western area, over 42.5% are migrants."[21] Why are the cities getting most of the scarce funds for development in West African countries? It is probably because of a strong import orientation of the economy. The most economical location for most of the industries has been the port city. This city is usually the capital and headquarters of commercial businesses and religious organizations.[22] Easily accessible health care is the strongest incentive that draws rural people to cities. West African social welfare policy designers must try to design policy that will both improve conditions for city dwellers and discourage additional rural-urban migration to cities to relieve pressure on existing social welfare programs such as housing. This has proven to be impossible. In West Africa, social welfare programs should be decentralized so as to reach rural areas and should not be concentrated in cities.

Here is (another) dilemma of policy makers: they want to increase urban wages both for political and social reasons—to provide the minimum income needed to maintain a family in town: but wage increases are bound to increase the supply of labor, and in turn create more unemployment.[23]

What makes rural people risk almost certain unemployment to come to the city to live? Part of the reason is that they still are emotionally tied to their village or small town. "Urban residents continue to care about the opinion people back home hold of them. The prestige to be gained in the village makes the relationship particularly gratifying." If they return with presents and hard currency, "in the village context their success is overwhelming. They adopt the conspicuous spending pattern expected of the wealthy. They compete with others in their generosity."[24] Another reason that people move to the cities is lack of educational opportunities in the villages.

I can speak from personal experience about this because I left the Gambian village of Njongon and moved to the city of Serrekunda at the age of twelve to go to secondary school; otherwise, I would not have been educated beyond sixth grade.

Conflict Between Western Urban Culture and Traditional Rural Social Structures

If it is true that culture change is the primary reason for the substantial increase in West African rural-urban migration, then it would be useful to first examine what constitutes culture as it is defined in this book. "Culture provides a reality and standards of evaluation: what is good/evil, beautiful/ugly."[25] Can there be any other explanation for the popularity of skin bleach in West African cities?

> Culture is a medium of communication: from language to physical gestures to modes of dress. Culture provides a pecking order in society: status, rank and class. Culture supplies us with our identity: determining who are we in a given situation and who are they.[26]

Culture eliminates feelings of strangeness in a community by enabling people to share commonalties and appreciate each other. The question to ask is why and how has Western culture had such a powerful effect on traditional African culture? Consider when this process first began in Africa.

> Religion is one way of explaining reality; science is another. The missionaries built schools not simply to teach the Bible, but also to teach mathematics, biology and one or more European language.[27]

> As schools, libraries, recreational and other facilities for the expression of (modern Western) urban life multiplied, the West African town began to develop a distinct way of life. Western cultural forces emanating from the town which tended to undermine traditional rural West African life were Western

education and religion . . . (because Western) education created needs which could not be realized in the village community.[28]

Western education turned traditional rural African social structures upside-down. Instead of status based on age, hard work, and dedication, status was based on literacy. "Acquiring aspects of the imperial culture opened doors, first of influence and later of affluence itself."[29]

As the city matured, there began to develop a distinctive pattern of life which contrasted with the traditional culture. Not only has the physical environment improved, i.e., sanitary facilities, roads, street lighting, health services including clinics, hospitals, community centers but (modern Western) urbanism took root as a way of life in contrast to the traditional way of life.[30]

In terms of personal motivation, "the basic needs of the wider clan were beginning to be subordinated to the imperative of personal advancement." Colonialism had these effects on traditional African culture because "Western systems of production and distribution carry with them cultural implications. Capitalism itself erodes aspects of African traditional fellowship and collective life."[31]

The intrusion of (urban) culture into the accepted (traditional rural) culture generates culture conflict. Rural-urban and return migration have this effect on rural society . . . and are responsible for changing the social cultural order of the rural communities. They affect the rural culture through changes in the knowledge, attitudes and value systems of migrants.[32]

European education taught West Africans individualism. Since colonialism, it has become institutionalized and is maintained by urban West Africans who use it to survive.

Rural-urban migration breaks cultural ties to the family and rural social system. It is an open refutation of the existing order and could also change the views held by those that remain. Individuals living outside the rural area and functioning in different cultural settings develop new attitudes, goals, and new ways of doing things in the advanced urban culture. Also, they may begin to assimilate the new culture and simultaneously reject the relevance of the rural culture. The returnee may have ideas about restructuring the rural culture. He may be unwilling to accept his old position in the rural social structure. This may result in resentment by the rural community. The rural political structure probably feels threatened and thus detests and prevents the expertise of the returnee from influencing the rural norms and social structure.[33]

Often, parents of returned rebellious school children are blamed as perpetrators of community conflict for sending their children to the cities for education. The extent of this cultural conflict cannot be over estimated. It amounts to the most immediate cause of rural young people relocating to the urban areas of West Africa. "This conflict situation leads to maladjustment to the local community which may result in a decision to move to the city permanently."[34] Urban culture has also been incorporated in a positive way into traditional rural social structures in that it serves as an opportunity to participate in the initiation into a modern West African adult lifestyle.

> Boys approaching initiation and youths just after initiation go away to work for short periods to show their manliness and earn some money for their personal use. Young men usually need to make money in earnest if they are to achieve the ideal of having their own homestead. Moving to town has become the thing to do; the freedom that the town offers from the control of the older generation constitutes an incentive to migrate for rural young men.[35]

It is wrong to think that traditional social structures and culture no longer affect the motivations modern urban West Africans.

> Even Africans committed to a full working life in town maintain close links with a rural area they consider their home. They live in a dual system. Throughout sub-Saharan Africa urban dwellers regularly visit their rural homes where they make gifts, find wives, maintain land rights, build houses, and intend to retire eventually and want to be buried. They receive gifts in return, offer hospitality to visitors from home, and help new arrivals in town.[36]

Unfortunately, there has been a recent trend in the 1990s for young urban West Africans to refuse to be identified with the village from which they came.

Chapter 5

Rethinking African Social Policy: Policy Changes Needed to Combat the Causes of Rural-urban Migration in West Africa

Urban Social Policy Reform

The terrible problems of the urban poor are so numerous that urban social welfare policy designers hardly know what to focus on first. Unfortunately, "the response to the crisis has been short-term and political rather than one of systematic development planning."[1] "The poor are involved only as a source of cheap labor and take almost no part in the overall planning and decision-making process."[2]

> Social practitioners should: (1) come to the aid of individuals and institutions that have specific problems and are unable to solve such problems; (2) help communities organize community and social welfare programs; (3) combat social issues by both preventative and medical measures; and (4) involve themselves in policy formation, at both higher and lower levels of government.[3]

West African social workers and social policy designers must support programs and polices that emphasize collectivism instead of individualism and encourage self-starters.

Rural Educational Reforms

The urgent need to institute educational reform that will provide all West Africans with an education to enable them to not only earn a good living within the rural and urban areas but also to contribute to the development of Africa is of utmost concern to anyone who has studied this problem. Africanized education must encourage West Africans to value, consume, and produce West African agricultural products.

> A 1976 survey by Byerlee in Sierra Leone, indicates that migrants to urban areas regard the availability of schools to be one of the major reasons for migrating. Likewise, urbanists are almost always reluctant to return to rural areas because of the unavailability of schools.[4]

It is well-known that "without a technical revolution in agriculture, the prospects for the production of the surplus needed to support urbanization and a growing rural market for consumer goods are grim."[5] The main problem is that

> The strong emphasis in education remains on training largely for clerical and other white-collar occupations. In West Africa, in 1965, for every one hundred students receiving a general education, there were only nine receiving some form of vocational training.[6]

Rural Labor Shortages

At this time, "unmarried males in the economically active age group needed to create, organize and staff an agricultural revolution" in West Africa are not available in rural areas because of rural-urban migration. Because the peak ages of migration are twenty-five to twenty-nine years, in rural areas,

> The older population cannot cope with the physical operations confronting them in the agricultural industry, so some rural communities are experiencing stagnating, or even declining, agricultural output and higher production costs. The disruption of agriculture effects the rural economy because the migration of rural individuals perpetuates the transfer of (human) capital from rural to urban areas.[7]

Some young females also migrate to cities to earn money as housemaids to send home. All too often they end up as unwed mothers who are too ashamed to go back without a husband.

Rural Women's Educational Development Projects

Who is growing the food to feed West Africans?

> In rural sub-Saharan Africa, women now constitute eighty percent of the rural labor force and produce seventy percent of the food, (but) technology farmers need to solve problems and boost yields is delivered by men through agri-

cultural extension programs. As a result, it often has emphasized cash crops produced by men with large land holdings and money for machinery while ignoring small farms where women produce much of the food for poor families. Women in Africa have thrown away fertilizer their husbands brought home because it stimulated weeds along with crops. Weeding is one of women's backbreaking chores. No one asked them if they were willing to accept more weeds in exchange for high yields. Now, with husbands and fathers missing from the countryside (because of rural-urban migration), many women get no extension assistance because local extension agents—nearly all men— are uncomfortable training other men's wives.[8]

Rural development policy designers need to work within rural traditions by training rural women to become extension agents in their areas.

Women are a large component of the labor force that goes underdeveloped without education. Education pays big dividends: farmers who have completed four years of school out-produce their less educated neighbors by more than eight percent, according to the World Bank.[9]

Rural development policy designers will help Africa to become self-sustainable only when they begin to invite women to the decision-making table.

Social Amenities

If one plans reverse rural-urban migration, it is not good enough to just bring more schools, better health care, electricity, and roads, telecommunications, clean water, and even sports centers to rural West Africa. "Rural infrastructure and industrial parks, decentralization of administration, social amenities, cultural programs and health services are all vital factors to be considered in reverse-migration programs."[10] It is easy to be misled. Do not imagine that

. . . every nook and corner of the rural sector will be supplied with amenities comparable to those available in the urban centers in the near future. (Most West African) towns do not even have cinemas and night clubs; small towns are still acutely short of water and many small ones have no electricity.[11]

Also, rural as well as urban areas need municipal parks and recreation centers for all residents.

Development of Small-scale Rural Industries

In economic terms, the most promising rural development policy design ideas involve small-scale industries.

Countries (such as Ghana and Ivory Coast) who [*sic*] have combined provision of social infrastructures with rural employment opportunities, have succeeded in retaining a sizeable proportion of potential out-migrants in rural areas.[12]

At this time, it is unrealistic to locate large-scale industries in rural areas because of poor road systems, inadequate water supply and electricity and poor means of communication . . . . [It is essential that all new plans create] agro-based industries which will use local materials to increase agricultural production.[13]

The funding of small

. . . enterprises makes sense because they create jobs cheaply and use local materials, skills and technologies. [New] industrialization, which is the key to the problem of urban mass unemployment, should be planned on a divisional basis using small-scale industries. These industries should be centered in the principal town or administrative headquarters of each division.[14]

Any policy that is serious about population redistribution in West African countries must include a way to "decentralize government administrative institutions. Two-thirds of all government institutions and jobs (in Sierra Leone) are in the urban areas."[15] It is important to design policy that includes the development of regional "cities, which would serve as centers of efficient exchange of goods and services."[16] Rural policy must encourage both men and women of small towns to become self-starters.

Chapter 6

Protecting Africa's Natural Environment: Where Did All the Elephants Go?

Instead of pointing accusing fingers at Africans who poach protected wildlife in African nature preserves, I believe a more constructive activity for all of us would be to consider this pivotal question: Can conflicting demands of African economic development and wildlife conservation be reconciled and to whose benefit should they be reconciled? I am convinced that for the two conflicting demands of African economic development and wildlife conservation, to be reconciled in a win/win manner for both rare African wildlife and local people, everyone has an essential part to play. To discover the nature of this essential role, I recommend that we waste no time in asking ourselves, "What can I do to facilitate the accomplishment of a win/win outcome in Africa and am I willing to commit some of my resources to facilitate this happening?" To facilitate this self-evaluation process as well as the eventual, and, I hope, positive resolution of this crisis, I present historical information on the topic of this problem.

Principle Causes

Before Europeans came to Africa, wildlife was an integral part of an African's life. Local African peoples communally owned and sustainably managed all of the land of Africa, together with all of the continent's natural resources, including wildlife. Local community leaders maintained control over the wildlife in their region. Hunting of wildlife was performed only with their prior authorization. Only they had the power to approve and appoint the hunters for the community. When Europeans colonized Africa, they instituted game laws to usurp power over African wildlife as they had done with regard to all the other valuable natural resources of the African continent. The voracious appetite of Europeans for things African extended to include wildlife, arable land, precious minerals, and human beings. In most African countries, those colonial game laws are still in effect to this day. The colonial game laws discriminate against local people because those laws were established as part of a colonial social and economic system that was designed to disenfranchise and push to the desolate and barren sidelines all Africans with regard to all of the natural beauty and wealth of their native continent. These colonial game laws show an absolute lack of respect for traditional communities and their leaders, who formerly, since man's first upright step eons ago, sustainably managed the fabulously beautiful and diverse life forms that can still be found inhabiting all corners of the African continent up to this moment. Indeed, if African peoples had not successfully managed these wild citizens of humanity's "garden of Eden," they would not have existed there to stimulate European avarice. Even now, they are the centerpieces of a raging global debate in which people express their anguish as they look back in apprehension at our species' recent history and face wildlife footprints that suddenly end, leading only to extinction.

These colonial game laws, which are still being enforced, are the root of the wildlife conservation problem in Africa today because they perniciously suppress the traditional African overriding sense of responsibility to manage local wildlife in a sustainable fashion. The trigger that ignited the inequitable state of affairs inflicted upon Africans by Europeans with the institution of colonial game laws has been a continuing high demand for ivory, rare skins, rhino horn, and gorilla parts outside Africa since the 1800s. A continuing high demand for wildlife products on the part of the rest of the world has had a destabilizing effect throughout Africa. It has destroyed the remaining ancient traditional social and economic systems that had escaped the corrupting influence of colonial practices. Because of these game laws, many rural people now regard all outsiders to their communities and central governments in Africa, whom they regard as the agents of outsiders, as a dangerous force that disregards the reasonable minimum economic and social needs of their families and communities. They look around themselves and see in every direction local African wildlife being financially exploited and reserved for future exploitation for the pleasure of outsiders to their communities, while they receive nothing in return to assist in their survival. They are reduced to homeless, penniless beg-gars on their own land while, as they watch from the rocky, sterile periphery of human society, outsiders, even other Africans, ogle the natural inheritance that their ancestors, with infinite love for unborn generations, prepared for them. Is it any wonder that to survive, some Africans must hunt in national parklands and conduct illegal trade in rare wildlife products? The result of being thrust into such a degrading role is that many young Africans react by confiscating, for themselves and their family, local wildlife that is currently protected by laws made and enforced by these outsiders, but which, in terms of social justice, rightly belongs to them.

Sustainable Recommendations

An obvious remedy for the understandable local hostility to African wildlife conservation entails giving the land and wildlife back to the local people to utilize in their traditional African way of life. All of us who want to see African wildlife sustainably managed should encourage central African governments to cooperate with local community residents and their leaders to utilize traditionally African management methods of "consultation, discussion, and consensus" to negotiate the design of and accomplish the formation of new social and economic structures in these regions of Africa. Present wildlife management practices in these areas can be changed so that local people and community leaders regain their traditional responsibility to screen, hire, and train local wildlife field management professionals who come from the ranks of local youths. We can encourage central African governments to establish ecological stewardship education programs that will reawaken the traditional African cultural reverence for wildlife in local people. We can help find financial support for these programs at the primary and secondary level in local schools. We need to find corporations that will fund scientific higher educational scholarships to train local young people to manage their people's wildlife resources.

Central African governments and all those in the West who seek to protect African wildlife from the present threat of near-future extinction must clearly demonstrate by their attitudes and actions that they desire to make up for their part in inflicting past indignities and injustice on local Africans. They must demonstrate that they are willing to work hard to lay the foundations for a future in which they will have a respectful relationship with local people. This kind of relationship should have but never did exist before. To me, the best way for us to help start this process is to put our heads together with the officials of central African governments and leaders and residents of local communities to consider ways in which the management of African wildlife by local Africans can economically and socially benefit the people who live in these regions.

Specific Proposals

Wildlife Game Farms

Western scientists have discovered that African wildlife is immune to the diseases that are transmitted by tsetse flies. Africans have always known this. How else could wildlife have survived so long? With this scientific fact in mind, African governments can work with local Africans to encourage them to utilize traditional herding practices to facilitate the production of local African wildlife that is genetically related to domesticated cattle. The natural products of wildlife managed in this way can be made readily available for local people to transform into food for themselves and into useful items that can be sold in the global marketplace to generate wealth that can sustain their communities and educate future generations.

African business people have skills that they can donate to central African governments to use in the design, with the input of local community leaders and residents, of cooperative ventures between the commercial farming sector, based on large privately owned farms, and the small-scale, largely subsistence farming sector on communally owned land. African business people could assist central African governments to provide financial support to local people to set up their own communally managed and owned game farms. This option is especially recommended because cattle herds have traditionally represented financial security and social prestige in many African societies. Nevertheless, when thinking about this option, an important consideration is the reality that indigenous species use the rangeland resource more efficiently than cattle that originated in places outside these regions. Research has proven that indigenous African wildlife can produce more meat on the semiarid rangelands of these areas. We can encourage central African governments to dismantle present regulations and subsidies that favor the current livestock industry, which is based on utilizing nonindigenous types of cattle. African corporations can help fund wildlife meat pilot projects so that they can eventually become a commercial wildlife meat industry that produces affordable food and employs local Africans. The most important aspect of a new wildlife meat industry that must never be overlooked is that it must be locally controlled and owned.

Tourism

As an important source of foreign earnings, tourism is a highly valuable economic option for all African countries. To be part of the creation of an economically sustainable Africa, however, tourism must always provide direct social and financial benefit to local people. African governments can halt the negative social effects of tourism by producing educational programs for tourists that are designed and administered by Africans. Only successful cultural orientation graduates of these programs should be allowed as tourists. Only those people who have demonstrated over the course of participating in this educational program that they harbor a genuinely sincere desire to experience a complete picture of Africa should be allowed to invade rural Africa. They must prove by their actions that they are ready to learn about and respect traditional African culture.

African governments provide financial support for the efforts of local people to accommodate worthy tourists and provide these tourists with the kind of educational and spiritual experience that will change their lives and certainly their perspective. They can contribute to the movement to maintain homes in rural areas that will temporarily house tourists from both Africa and elsewhere. African governments can see to it that local people establish appropriate fees for tourists to pay in exchange for this priceless experience as well as tourist gifts that the whole community can utilize. This will ensure that the impact of future tourists will be to enhance instead of to threaten traditional social structures. In traditional African communities, everyone shares. Networks of social obligations require people to benefit each other. It is imperative that tourists perform an important role in maintaining these beneficial traditional social structures.

Creating a Sustainable Environment in Africa

The uncontrolled exploitation of African wildlife and trade in its products, which began in the last century and continues unabated to this day, proves that the ability of African governments to exert ownership over wildlife has never been effectively mobilized. I believe that this can be changed once and for all. I am convinced that it is time to involve local African people in the sustainable management of their own wildlife.

My recommendations involve organizations and businesses in Africa, as well as in other countries around the world, assisting central African governments to help local people to manage their wildlife. Any new method implemented to accomplish the task of conserving African wildlife for future generations must come from people who live in regions inhabited by this wildlife. These methods must be culturally compatible with their traditional social structures and must be adequately labor intensive to provide economical support for their families and communities well into the twenty-first century. It is clear that there are many ways in which African business professionals can join with African governments to empower local people to support themselves economically and socially. What I have mentioned are only a few ways that we can help Africans regain their rightful role as stewards and educators. Perhaps the future role of local people will be to teach people from around the globe to worship the natural beauty that is Africa. Surely, they deserve to be more than adequately compensated for this unique spiritual treasure that only they can share with everyone. They hold the keys to the door behind which lies a truly incredible experience: to learn firsthand the ancient traditional African way of life as it is lived by local African people themselves.

Rethinking Urban and Rural Development Policy Design

Those involved in the design of policy and development schemes for West African countries must be aware of

> the inter-relationships between rural-urban wage differentials, job creation, and migration. Unless these inter-relationships are fully appreciated, policies directed towards only one aspect of the problem are likely to make a minimal lasting impact. Fortunately, there has been a fundamental shift in thinking towards rural development, regional planning, balanced development, land policy, growth centers, organizing the countryside, and so forth—all basically intended to reverse, divert, arrest, or regulate urbanization.[1]

I believe that, one by one, those in power in West Africa will give up the race in which

> . . . centralization is perpetuated by the compression effect. They will give up catching up with the (economic and) social development of Western and European nations in the shortest possible time and will reduce their efforts at modernizing the most highly developed area of their countries.[2]

They will soon turn from programs of mismodernization in rural areas.

> Mismodernization occurs when governments select a single social factor, instead of all social factors, for utilization in revitalizing depressed rural areas in order to encourage reverse migration. The government's choice of education, agriculture, and community development as criteria for rehabilitating the rural economy is a mismodernization practice.[3]

West African governments should work to unite their people by decentralizing industry and by redistributing resources equally to all regions in their countries regardless of ethnicity and political support.

Chapter 7

Becoming A Unified Self-Sustaining Continent: Finding the Solution to Rural-urban Migration

Competition Between Import Goods and Native Products

How can African nations solve their problems while they rely on outside markets to feed them? It is a prerequisite to rural development to encourage internal markets for native West African agricultural products. "Although a high proportion of food consumed in the cities [is] drawn from the rural areas, it is worth bearing in mind that, as of 1972, Nigeria spent N90 million importing food from abroad."[1] We are actively supporting conflict and hindering progress toward democracy in Africa when we refuse to invest in what we, as Africans, produce. When we neglect to value our culture, we become slaves to the West and no longer can call ourselves self-starters. At this time,

> Development focuses on import substitution, which means that instead of importing finished consumer goods, we import the machinery, skilled personnel and often the semi-processed raw materials needed to produce these goods locally.[2]

> While all productive effort is focused on making available a wide range of consumer goods, import-substitution industrialization has meant that industries in our cities do not derive their raw materials from the rural areas [but from outside Africa].[3]

[The] worsening of social and economic conditions in rural areas is not just a measure of the failure of our urban centers to adequately service the rural population. Such servicing goes beyond mere welfare functions of making educational, health, and other social amenities easily accessible to people living in rural areas. In particular, it includes the function of stimulating increased rural production through creating a constantly expanding market for (native) agricultural products.[4]

Disentanglement from Foreign Loan Debt

The leaders of all African countries understand very well the trap into which Africans have fallen by trying to copy the West. Now it is time to heed their warnings and get ready for the sacrifices that will be required to rebuild our self-respect and our continent. We must work together to find ways to create markets for African products if we seek to discourage African demand for imported goods. Many African countries produce unique, highly artistic fabric designs that express the many different cultural backgrounds of the various peoples where the cloth is decorated. African fabric designers utilize both traditional and contemporary uniquely African fabric designs such as Batik and tie dye techniques that originated in West Africa. At this time, these fabrics are not mass-produced, nor have the techniques used been replicated elsewhere.

As soon as clothing designers begin to show Western style clothing made from fabric from, for example, The Gambia, a great demand will begin for African-produced cloth. Yoweri Museveni, president of Uganda, recently introduced African scientific researchers to *muteete*, a traditional grass that he chewed as a child to clean his teeth. Researchers found that it could be made into superior dentifrice, which is now named "Nile Toothpaste." Museveni had stopped chewing *muteete* when he attended a British colonial secondary school. He was told that using Colgate™ toothpaste was far better for his teeth than the grass he chewed. This was not true. The British schoolteachers, who had never chewed *muteete*, were merely teaching Museveni to imitate them.

African governments need to launch marketing campaigns by which to re-educate Africans regarding the superiority of their own products. Also, any imported product that might supplant an African-produced product, which can satisfactorily serve the same consumer need, should have a high tariff placed upon it, such as clothing produced in Africa. When I went home after my university studies to The Gambia, I was able to purchase several hand-tailored Western-style suits for the price of one machine-produced standard-sized suit in America. The fit, seams, cloth and colors of my Gambian-made suits were all superior to anything I could have found in the West, at a fraction of the cost. In addition, when I wear them to work in the U.S., everyone compliments me on how great I look. This is because the colors and the fit enhance my physical appearance. I appear professional, which brings me opportunity and respect. I am able to make a favorable first impression on others before I speak to them. Instead of worrying whether I fit my clothes, I have the confidence that my clothes fit me.

Regardless of the inferiority of mass-produced, machine-made Western goods, Africans have come to value Western goods over African goods because of their long colonial socialization experience. We were taught that anything produced in the West is superior to something similar made in Africa. Western colonial and neocolonial powers, such as Britain, France and the U.S., did this to create a market for their own products. In seeking to imitate Westerners, Africans assist them to penetrate existing African markets. Continued low demand for African-produced goods threatens to bankrupt African economies. Because Western exporters set prices, African governments cannot control their own economies. Unfortunately, high import tariffs are politically impossible at this time. Unless African governments become proactive and educate their citizens regarding the superiority of locally produced African products first, leaders who attempt to institute high import tariffs will soon their political downfall.

Every African leader must see to it that the media in their country promote African products. African governments need to support journalistic talent with the financial backing needed to produce African magazines for the public that display the positive attributes of African-produced consumer goods. In addition to subsidizing local industries that produce consumer goods, African leaders can take a proactive role by encouraging leaders of nearby African nations to join them in forming regional markets where locally produced goods are supported and promoted continent-wide. Although import substitution brings more industries to Africa because goods are actually produced in Africa, it still leaves Africans vulnerable to the West. The raw materials needed for African import-substitution industries must be purchased from the West. They still control the market. We must stop running after the West. We must say to each other, "We are African. We should no longer seek to imitate Westerners. If we have the patience and perseverance to develop uses for our national resources and indigenous African materials, not only will we someday manufacture products far superior to any the world has seen, we will have built an economic foundation that can support the standard of living o which we dream for our children." We can do this if we remember why the West came to Africa in the first place. Past African empires produced superior goods including gold jewelry, leather, spices, cotton, and beautiful dyes for cloth.

Import substitution, as the basis for national economies in Africa, limits self-sustainability because it ensures that Africa will remain dependent on the West because either the raw materials or the products themselves must be imported from the West. As long as Africans import consumer goods from the West, African rural resources will be neglected. By valuing imported Western consumer goods, Africans are actually discouraging traditional African rural industries that satisfied the needs of Africans for centuries before European colonialists came to Africa. By providing imported Western consumer goods to their people, African leaders are sending them a mixed message. With one side of their mouths, African leaders are telling Africans that they should stay in their rural homelands and produce the cash crops that African leaders use to buy these imported consumer goods from the West. At the same time, African leaders boast about their accomplishments in importing increasing levels of Western consumer goods for people in their countries.

Rural Africans are aware of how their leaders are using them. It is simple to see when they look at the amount of money that is brought in from the sale of their crops. It is not enough to buy them the imported Western consumer goods that are so valued by people in their country. They therefore remain poor in their own eyes and in the eyes of their urban friends and relations. Their income remains low because the price paid for African cash crops is *set by the west*. Both coming and going, African nations remain at the mercy of Western countries as long as import substitution forms the basis of their economies. If this is so obviously negative, why do African leaders allow this state of affairs continue to exist? It is because they benefit from it.

African leaders have been taking loans from the West to cover the shortfall between the prices they get for exports and the cost of imports. They want to remain popular with their people, and thus they stay in power long enough to milk their personal advantage for all the money they can afford to embezzle before their corruption is stopped. President Julius Nyerereof Tanzania reminded us that

> The people who benefit directly from the development that is brought about by borrowed money are not the ones who will repay the loans. Thus, those who do not get the benefit of urban hospitals carry the responsibility for paying for them. Tarmac roads, motor cars, electric lights, water pipes, hotels, and other aspects of modern development mostly found in towns have been built with loans and most of them do not benefit the farmer directly, although they will be paid for by the foreign exchange earned by the sale of his produce.[5]

What African leader would ever send any of his children to school in his own country's rural area or send them to rural areas to get medical treatment? The behavior of African leaders proves to their own people that their leaders are shamelessly neglecting the valid needs of rural Africans. I believe that this is the reason that African leaders are not interested in decentralizing government institutions. If government offices were relocated to rural areas, government workers would have to face how their country's economic policies have impoverished these areas. Soon, local people will demand that they do something to challenge these policies. Decentralization would enable African nations to decrease corruption and while building democratic institutions from their grass roots. For this reason, I believe that the decentralization of government institutions is the first step in bringing self-sustainability to Africa.

Nyerere also noted,

> The money we spend in the towns comes from loans. To repay them we have to use foreign currency obtained from the sale of exports. We do not now sell our industrial products in foreign markets because the current aim of our industries is import substitution.[6]

Unlike developing nations in Asia, African industries are not now producing valuable consumer goods for export. Instead, they are using imported materials to produce consumer goods for Africans that are import substitutions. Africa can never become self-sustainable as long as foreign investors from the West own the majority of large African industries and the rights to Africa's most valuable resources. As long as this continues, the West will extract Africa's wealth, produce valuable consumer goods with it, and set the price; and *then we buy it back from them at their price.*

President Julius Nyerere also stated, "We must get foreign currency to pay back loans used to develop urban areas from the villages and from agriculture."[7] Where does this foreign currency come from if the West sets prices for our exports so low? We constantly need to borrow more. The West has successfully fooled us into thinking that accepting their loans will enable us to become self-sustainable. We do not think about how these loans come with conditions and requirements set by the West that are favorable for them and not for us. Does the ordinary African know about these conditions and their effects? No. African leaders who accept these loans do, but they are interested in their own immediate benefit from them, in the short term. By the time their country is further impoverished, their family will be resettled in Europe or America with a good-sized bank account there.

Negative Effects of Western Food and Rural Development Aid

Accepting offers of needed food aid has only compounded problems and made the situation much worse.

[Because] marginal farmers cannot compete with subsidized food aid, they are compelled to survive on food assistance. This not only increases the number of dependent people but also further depletes rural capital. Food aid depresses farm prices and worst of all, shifts food consumption patterns away from local foods to imported foods. Amazingly, it actually reduces the incentive of recipient nations to develop and carry out agricultural policy reforms. Few realize that only a small proportion of economic aid was actually invested in Africa's agriculture. Of $7.5 billion given during the 1970s to eight West African countries, only twenty-four percent was spent on agriculture and less than twelve percent reached rural areas. Even less got to small landholders thought to be Africa's most productive farmers.[8]

Generally, the effect of Western development aid has been proven to have more negative results than positive ones.

The World Bank, in a report issued last September, said donor nations had pressured African governments during the 1970s to take on projects that were expensive, inappropriate in design and selection, and too large, and that contributed little to economic growth or to generating foreign exchange to service their debt. During the 1970s, African governments inaugurated a range of projects aimed at increasing domestic food production. The ones most widely favored—funded by USAID and the World Bank—were large, mechanized, and highly capitalized. Moreover, investment in food production often favored crops consumed by people in the cities: wheat, rice, and sugar.[9]

Donor nations with a genuine desire to help us should support Africans in design development projects that incorporate collectivity.

Dependence on External Markets

Remaining dependent on outside markets to provide the economic foundation of African nations will no longer work.

In 1983, we witnessed the adverse effects of the openness of Africa's economy, with its excessive dependence on industrialized countries, for the region's growth and development. Because the basic industries of the industrialized countries have not recovered enough (from a worldwide recession), the demand for the region's iron ore, copper, cobalt, uranium, and other metals of export importance to Africa has remained weak. Fiscal constraints, mainly from the difficulty in the external sector, remain severe. We saw in 1983 a continuation of the policy of cutting public expenditure. Despite the curtailment of expenditure, deficits have not been eliminated, and since the deficits have been in a large measure financed by bank borrowing, inflation has persisted.[10]

Chapter 8

African Unification

First Steps Toward African Unity: Improving Communications

It is obvious that moving toward a more unified Africa is the only way that African countries will be able to alleviate the dire straits in which they have found themselves. For unification to occur, all African nations must contribute to a social, economic, and technical forum. For example,

> An area [that] cries out for improvement is opening up the continent to itself by strengthening communications east/west, north/south and diagonally. Transportation in Africa is notoriously rudimentary. In many cases it is easier for one part of Africa to communicate with Europe than with another part of Africa. Certainly telecommunications and air transportation still bear the colonial stamp, which makes them serve Africa's interaction with Europe rather than with itself. It is possible to dial the United States directly from one's private phone in Nairobi or Mombassa, but it is not possible to dial Lagos or Abidjan from that same telephone.[1]

The Urgent Need for African Unity

It is obvious that culture controls economics. A change in African economics that will allow the solution to the problems of rural-urban migration involves a significant re-Africanization of African culture and a

. . . new lifestyle. The results of a lifestyle that consumes what Africa does not produce while neglecting its our own products are disastrous. The indigenization of the West African economy, the attainment of self-reliance, the expansion of domestic production capabilities and markets, innovation, etc., cannot come about if we remain psychologically dependent on outsiders. Thus, new cultural values have to become important features of Africa's socioeconomic development by the coming century. The whole African continent must be convinced that effective co-operation among African states is an absolute necessity. All Africans must see that regional co-operation is a critical complement to national self-reliance. Africa must co-operate in all fields—food, energy, industry, transport, trade, finance, and human resource development.[2]

All Africans must co-operate by accepting the leadership of those who encourage responsibility and work to solve conflict without the military intervention of the West. They need to support leaders who work hard to support and maintain gender equality and believe in the vision of a united, non-violent, nonracial, nonethnic, independently self-sustainable continent. Above all, we must believe in ourselves and value our land, native products, and culture.

African Community Theory

If changes in culture influence economic changes within countries, perhaps it would be useful to apply a sociological analysis to various economic theories that have left their mark in Africa. In this way, social policy designers can realize the importance of working with economic planners to create state policy in Africa that will actually have the desired results in the future.

[Capitalist] Adam Smith believed that until the call to city employment came from a productive enterprise, the peasant would remain in his ancestral village, doing what he and his forebears had been doing since time immemorial, in a static society that was no burden to urban industry. Mao Tse-Tung offers an alternative; on an egalitarian pattern, which is indeed the relief of poverty. Everyone would go up at the same time. It would not be a matter of a few joining the middle-class each year, but rather of everyone in the country having a small increase of income each year. But those who obtain some part of it (middle-class lifestyle) want the rest quickly; they are not willing to be held back by the slow pace that raising all of their fellow citizens simultaneously would require. One who obtains a transistor radio wants to up grade to a television set.[3]

Neo-Marxists O'Connor[4], Offe[5], and Poulantzas[6, 7] believed that capitalism requires the support of the state. The state "assists in private capital accumulation" and "increases the productivity of labor and the profits of capital."[8] The state's role in this partnership requires it to assume industry's responsibility for "subsidizing the costs of education, social insurance, research and development, and transportation and communications."[9] The other job of the state is to maintain social harmony by providing "public assistance, food, and housing subsidies" to "nonproductive parts of the population"[10] (i.e., the capitalist's reserve labor pool). This is exactly what governments in Africa have done since independence.

What is the result? "With subsidies from the state, capitalism grows in the short run, but in the long run, it overproduces, contracts, and lays off workers."[11] Because of low taxes on capitalists, "the state receives few of the profits during periods of economic growth and must support surplus workers during periods of economic recession," so that "public costs exceed revenues"[12] and a huge deficits grow. That is the state of affairs at this moment in most African countries. What we need is a way to tax the wealthy elite and raise tariffs on imported goods. This would result in a needed redistribution of wealth that will take the burden of the urban poor off of the state and also would stimulate agriculture and internal markets by making native products attractive to Africans. It is easier said than done, however, because there are forces that block such initiatives within African governments. African nations are being exploited via state-initiated economic and trading ties as well as political and military relations with more developed countries.

Because industry is unwilling to compensate the worker for the fragmentation of the family, the burden of maintaining the social safety net, formerly the function of the extended family, has been thrust upon the state. The state needs to decentralize industry to make it the servant of the family instead of the other way around. Public welfare and private charity, whether in Africa or abroad, is a mechanism of social and economic control. All foreign aid to Africa builds dependency, corruption, and dictators. There is a dichotomy between the needs of the people and the needs of indigenous industrialists and multinational corporations, and the state must decide to whom they should attend. The African people have been brainwashed by industrialist-controlled media to believe in ultimate individual freedom as the highest good. This value divides us and plants self-interest in our minds so that we can be easily exploited for the profit of others.

In Bakalar village in The Gambia, West Africa, where I grew up, children are socialized against unlimited individual freedom and self-interest. Sadly, at this time in The Gambia, unregulated industrial development threatens traditional African culture and its value of group achievement. Highly populated cities and growing urban areas continuously attract rural migration with the hypnotic myth of The American Dream. The centralization of wealth in the cities creates the growth of a small upper and middle class, a well-educated elite, and the mass of the people remain without adequate health care, educational, and economic resources. The influence of Western institutions in the cities creates a fading of traditional African values as a result of the increasing pressure to assimilate into Western customs that insinuate that traditional African values are inferior. Thus, urban Africans are forced to give up traditional African culture because to maintain it would involve a risk to their survival in the city environment.

Urban benefits, such as higher quality and more readily accessible health care and education as well as more job opportunities, continue to draw more people to African cities. Unregulated industrialization creates extremes of rich and poor in countries such as Nigeria. What we need is decentralization of resources: communication services, Africanized education, health care, electricity, and better roads are needed for rural as well as urban dwellers. I believe increased technical and entrepreneurial knowledge and educational opportunities could use traditional and Western crafts to develop both rural and urban areas in Africa whereas Western-style unregulated industrialization will soon completely destroy the traditional African social structure.

The economy of countries such as The Gambia is controlled by the economies of the biggest cities that are controlled by Western institutions. Posters showing the wealth of Western nations on office walls tell new employees that traditional African culture is worthless if one wants to get ahead. The education that Africans such as myself have enjoyed contains within it a bias toward Western culture because traditional African culture has not yet been incorporated into African educational materials and curriculum. Like Western-style education, Western-style industrialization will benefit the few in Africa, not the masses.

In contrast, I contend that industrial development can benefit all Africans *if* it is introduced and maintained in ways that incorporate traditional African values of the *community*. Since the first contact with Europeans, the education brought to Africa by colonialists and missionaries was welfare policy designed for social control that was intended to exploit Africans for profit and rob them of their traditional culture. Today, modern Africans from both rural and urban areas must be involved in all social policy decisions at the grassroots level to incorporate traditional African community values. The traditional *African community theory* of social welfare dictates that the people must be involved at the grassroots level in all decision-making processes that create social policies that may affect their lives and the lives of their descendents.

The Interaction of Rural and Urban Problems

Because young rural Africans will always want to leave their family's farms and travel to the city, one key to reducing one-way rural-urban migration is to ensure that all African schools are adequately equipped with sufficient academic, scientific, and vocational learning facilities and materials. African schools must strive to teach all African young people practical skills that they can take with them into the real world and succeed in business, medicine, and the public sector, for example. African curriculum must swiftly move away from a present over-emphasis on theory. The emphasis must now be on preparing young Africans to make the most of their intelligence and creativity by teaching them how to utilize materials that close at hand and readily available in their home regions to provide economical support their families, communities, and nations. African governments need to decentralize all ministries so that each ministry maintains an office in each division of their country. This will encourage youth to remain in regions with smaller cities because, at this time, many young people are drawn to the capitals of African nations by the lure of possible employment in a government ministry.

Decentralization will provide African governments with direct access to rural citizens of all ages. The hope is that this will encourage government officials to engage them in dialog regarding public policies that would create locally sustainable economic and social projects that can revitalize these areas and eventually eliminate poverty. African governments need to help rural people export the crops they produce, such as fruits like oranges, tomatoes, and mangos, to countries outside of Africa. The same planes, trains, and ships that transport foreign import goods to African countries could be utilized to transport Africans export goods out of Africa. This will happen when African governments realize that it is up to them to create a market for African products overseas while discouraging Africans from purchasing imported goods. To accomplish this, African governments must provide leadership in efforts to unite all African nations into one economic body.

Every African knows that drought will come again and again in their lifetimes. We have been told this over and over by our grandparents and ancestors. Now, African nations need to create the infrastructures that can facilitate future redistribution of urgently needed water and food to a regions experiencing drought. African governments need to invest in irrigation systems that can be used in the event of a drought in their country. National irrigation and infrastructure systems must be evaluated continually to determine whether there exist ways in which they can be periodically improved. African governments must work closely with local rural people to sustain the viability of any system of this kind. African governments will discover that creating self-sustainability in regions where drought is endemic requires involving local rural people, especially youth, in handling the operation and maintenance of all irrigation and infrastructures that are designed to combat the negatives effects of drought. When this happens, rural people, including youth, will feel a sense of empowerment that will motivate them to take responsibility for the economic survival of their communities, even during drought.

I believe that both rural and urban Africans will begin to feel a greater sense of responsibility for the economic and social well being of their communities and nations when African intellectuals and government officials support and maintain sustainable democracy. I believe sustainable democracy in Africa will only occur when all African political leaders are allowed a maximum of ten years in office (no more than two consecutive five-year terms). All Africans, including leaders, must become more accountable for what they say. They should not say that they want to develop their country while investing money outside of it. This is an obvious sign of corruption. They must be able to transform their words into practical actions.

To me, accountability means having the ability and the desire to identify the root causes of problems and propose solutions that develop African societies to those problems. For sustainable democracy to be established in Africa, every African must be willing to accept the challenge to find ideas that, when implemented, can solve Africa's political, social, and economic problems. Unfortunately, this will not happen unless Africans stop pointing the finger of blame for our problems in Africa at each other and at the West. Once Africans begin finding solutions to our own problems, evidence of sustainable democracy, such as freedom of speech, will appear. Africans should not expect that freedom of speech will bring them a sustainable type of democratic political system. I believe that Africans will never bring true sustainable democracy to Africa until they are willing to unite freedom of speech with accountability.

I believe it is the task of rich and middle-class Africans to create new jobs in their countries. They must establish financial institutions that offer loans to Africans to start businesses and to non-profit organizations that contribute to the well-being of African communities. They must encourage entrepreneurial activity in each country in Africa. Their efforts are needed for fundraising to support civic education programs in all African countries. Most important, rich and middle-class Africans are desperately needed to endow foundations that offer higher education scholarships to deserving young African scholars. At this time, most wealthy and well-to-do Africans spend their money investing in property outside of Africa, or they use their money to prop-up puppet dictators who neglect the citizens of their country while they rule for life. Most of them spend vacations shopping in Europe and America. Their attitude toward their own country is that *they* have succeeded, and that is all that matters. They do not care about their fellow Africans, even those from their own country or ethnic group. Their African psyche has been totally transformed into that of a Western individualist who feels no responsibility for the well being of other people in their own community.

The root of political instability in Africa is this attitude. Those who come to power, by either peaceful democratic means or by bloody, violent conflict, somehow always end up hanging onto power long past the time when it is appropriate and in the best interests of their country to share or pass on leadership to capable others around them. I believe that when African leaders are willing to limit themselves to a maximum of two consecutive five-year terms, the political instability that causes wars and economic hardships for Africans will be reduced. In Africa, wealth always facilitates access to political power. Unfortunately, at this time in Africa, wealth is not measured according to its benefit to the community or nation, but instead by the amount of expensive Western-style material goods that Africans can accumulate. For that reason, one can find many African leaders who manage to acquire a monopoly over their country's valuable resources. The Western colonialists in Africa brought with them a foreign definition of wealth: the freedom to pursue personal gain. In Africa, colonialism meant a transformation of the meaning of wealth. It is specifically this peculiarly Western attitude of individualism that perpetrates the destructive social, economic, and political instability one finds in Africa today.

When Africa was colonized, Africans were taught to reject their own cultures and languages. To this day, in school, they are still taught to speak in European languages about European ideas. When a language is torn from a people, they are robbed of their own culture. The context in which learning occurs is culture. When a people have lost their culture, they can no longer learn. For this reason, most Africans have become mere shadows of their ancestors, similar to them in appearance only. Unfortunately, it is clear that the process of colonialism succeeded in socializing Africans to accept Western attitudes and values and to reject traditional African languages and cultures as "uncivilized." This destructive myth that was propagated by Westerners propagated is still being force-fed to Africans. It has reduced their existence to mere imitation of Western culture. Whereas learning is a dynamic, creative process with new experiences being integrated into a flexible core identity, by contrast, imitation is an unbending, repetitive reaction. It is the purpose of this book to show how Africans will not be able to build a socially, economically, and politically self-sustainable continent until they find ways to regain connections to their roots and their African cultures. When this happens, we can move beyond mere imitation of the West to becoming a society in which the wealthy class realizes that it must be accountable. Those with wealth are responsible for providing leadership in all aspects of African life, including leadership that supports and maintains African social, economic, and political stability and self-sustainability.

The Influence of Global Western Culture

Africans have not taken time to sit down with each other to ponder this question: "How has Western capitalism contributed positively and negatively to African society?" We fail to look deeply into the advantages and disadvantages of the influences of Western culture in African society. For capitalism to be viable in Africa, Africans must be able to incorporate traditional African cultural norms and values into the economic systems that we design and utilize in our countries. If we are unable to incorporate our traditional African cultural norms and values into Western capitalism, then capitalism will create social, economic, political, military, and psychological chaos in all African nations. At this time in our history, we need to define capitalism in true African terms. In our rush to adopt Western capitalism, we have lost sight of who we are as a culture. We must take time to look at our own history to appreciate, understand, and learn from it. In this way, we begin to know who we are as Africans. Then we will be able to speak about what we want for our people and our continent.

The cultural value of individualism, an integral aspect of capitalism as it is practiced by Western countries, is antithetical to the traditional African value of community in which *we* is more important than *I*. When Africans adapt Western capitalism, instead of examining the implications and effects of capitalism's cultural values, as a rule, they tend to set aside the traditional values of their upbringing. The difficulty resides in the fact that most people do not realize that economic systems are manifestations of many individual economic transactions within a society. Because people whose behavior is governed by unique cultural values conducted those transactions, all economic systems display specific value systems. When Africans set aside their traditional value of community, or *we*, this begins a cycle of psychological conflict. When an African sets aside traditional African values, an inner emptiness results that cannot be satisfied by the superficial adoption of foreign values. The inner emptiness becomes a significant psychological weakness that makes the person vulnerable to dependence. By doing this, they have lost their self-sustainability.

When Africans lack personal self-sustainability, they exhibit an unhealthy dependence on their leaders who, in turn, depend on the West. The roots of this dependence can be found in the African experience of colonialism and its results in the twentieth century. Colonialism taught Africans to regard Westerners highly as the source of all solutions to their problems. It taught them that their own ways of doing things were unproductive and backward. What Africans fail to discuss is, "If we were actually so backward and unproductive, what did we have of value that made the Westerners leave their own countries to come here?" When Africans begin to look at their own history, they will see that all products and knowledge that fueled advancement in Europe and the Middle East originated from African thinkers and craftsmen working in fields ranging from mathematics to metallurgy. Africans have a great need for a transformed educational system that emphasizes an African—not European—based curriculum. Incorporated within this new knowledge should be a psychological component that will help Africans to appreciate the techniques that were used by Africans, over the centuries, to survive and to build civilizations. Africans can be shown how other people around the world have used the wisdom contained in these techniques.

The African style of capitalism is an economic system that supports and maintains traditional African norms and values. Any form of capitalism that does not assist Africans to become self-sustainable should be evaluated to discover why it is not viable in Africa and then discarded. At this time in Africa, all that is happening is criticism and condemnation. Africans are not holding forums in which dialog occurs so that solutions to problems can be proposed and in which commitment to implementation is offered.

The type of dialog to which I am referring is the kind that encourages people to be accountable and to take up responsibility. At this time, Africans are merely identifying things that are wrong in Africa without asking themselves, "What role can I play in the implementation of solutions to problems in my community, nation, and continent?" African national and community leaders and intellectuals must work together to find ways to bring the issue of personal accountability and group responsibility to the attention of all Africans. By their personal example, they must demonstrate to their people that the era of criticism must now come to an end because it has not achieved anything.

Because they sought to manipulate Africans for their own benefit, Western colonial leaders ruled Africa by gaining the allegiance of different tribal leaders and instigating conflict between them. In contrast, traditional leaders of African civilizations involved all citizens in the activities of government via community group dialog, discussion, and consensus of all important issues for which a decision must be reached. The traditional African form of government is antithetical to the modern Western style of government, which encourages groups to compete for resources and power by following the motto, "Divide and conquer." When Africans adopt Western style capitalism, including its cultural value of individualism and its motto, they inject an element of social and political instability into their societies. This results in groups of Africans whose needs are being neglected and who see other groups benefiting from government projects. These groups then feel a need to organize and overthrow their government.

The Value of Traditional African Social Structures

The family is one of the most important aspects of traditional African social structures and must be immediately strengthened because not quickly working to strengthen it will create conflict between rural and urban areas in Africa and also encourage negative individualism. This negative individualism is mostly found in urban areas, but soon it also will pollute traditional social structures in rural areas. Those who have received their formal education in urban areas have been socialized to adopt the Western cultural value of individualism. Some of these people, who were originally from rural areas, will not even return to their villages for this reason. In these people, their culture has been suppressed and devalued. They view others who continue to value the traditional African social structure of the family as uncivilized and uneducated. They do everything to avoid contact with anyone from their family and village. This creates division in African society and reduces opportunities for innovation and development.

The traditional African social structure of the family dictated that for a male to be a man, he should not just produce children, but also be able to support his family spiritually, socially, and financially. In Africa, if people say a male is not a man they mean that he is not supporting his family. In African urban areas, this traditional social structure of the family is less valued. Men have children before they have means to support them. They have adopted the Western value of individualism and feel that no elder should tell them that they couldn't do this. They feel that they have the individual freedom to live their lives any way they please. This way of thinking is contrary to the traditional African way of thinking, which says that one must follow the community's norms in everything one does, including parenthood. All Africans must begin to re-evaluate their institutions, which are all based upon Western culture, norms, and values. There is a great need to re-establish our institutions so that they incorporate traditional African culture, norms, and values. The traditional African social structure of the extended family is not an aspect of Western culture; for this reason, it is ignored in the curriculum in most African primary and secondary schools.

African teachers, school administrators, and curriculum developers need to consult with local community elders and leaders to find the best way to involve traditional African cultural activities and values in the material that is taught to children. This will teach African children to value and maintain the traditional social structure of the extended family. Community groups in urban and suburban areas must be encouraged to address the need for focusing on helping their members discover how they, as a group, can contribute to strengthening the traditional African social structure of the extended family. Those Africans who have had the opportunity to obtain formal higher education abroad should feel that they have a responsibility to value and maintain the traditional African social structure of the extended family, not just to bring Western culture and values back to Africa. African scholars and intellectuals should evaluate the ways in which modern African societies have been negatively influenced by Western culture and values, especially the value of individualism. Then they can find ways to develop more appropriate public policy by incorporating feedback from men and women who maintain the traditional African social structure of the extended family in rural areas.

I believe that weakening the traditional African social structure of the family has resulted in a preoccupation by African leaders with centralizing resources and national institutions in urban areas, which creates overcrowding. Overcrowding causes unemployment, crime, poverty, and disease and eventually destabilizes African governments.

This causes African countries to fall into a downward spiral of debt crisis in which outsiders dictate the domestic policies of African governments. Africans must first acknowledge that they hold the primary responsibility to address and find solutions for African social, political, and economic problems. I believe the only escape from this trap is for Africans to return to their traditional social structures, such as the extended family, and to re-evaluate them so as to incorporate positive aspects of them that will strengthen and unify African societies.

The Western education that Africans receive contains norms and values appropriate to European-based societies such as Britain, France, and Portugal. Many of these norms and values are anti-ethical to traditional African norms and values, such as individualism and the extended family. Culture consists of shared norms and values based on a group's experience in coping with problems of survival. Africans should build on their unique cultural norms and values first, before they adopt aspects of other cultures, both Western and Eastern, which may facilitate the strengthening of a truly African society. By maintaining the value of individualism that destroys extended families in countries around the globe, societies that consider themselves civilized actually hasten their own demise, for upon the family are built all other formal and informal institutions in human society. For this reason, I believe that establishing modern social structures and policies that strengthen traditional social structures, such as the extended family, can reduce social problems such as crime and violence in all countries, including America.

Chapter 9

Revitalizing Modern African Society: Traditional African Commitment to Community Mechanisms

I believe that traditional African commitment to community mechanisms can be used to revitalize today's African society. To start, we need to look at attitudes and values that discourage commitment to community. In her book of utopian communities titled *Commitment and Community: Communes and Utopias in Sociological Perspective,* Rosabeth Moss Kantor[1] stated that something is lacking in modern communities. Many commitment mechanisms are weak or missing. Renunciation and sacrifice for the sake of the community are very limited. Behavior that evidences these values is discouraged and usually belittled. Investment in the community is mostly on the basis of personal gain.

I assume that the commitment mechanisms that I find in use in the African city where I have lived, Banjul in The Gambia, West Africa, are similar to those anyone could find in other urban communities. They are designed for individual achievement and gain. Membership in community groups such as clubs or churches is entirely voluntary. Even the right to vote, to which most Africans point with pride, is exercised by a decreasing percentage of the population in most African elections, today.

Consider each commitment mechanism individually to examine how it is displayed in Africa these days. *Investment*: People buy land and build homes, but it is not irreversible in that they can sell such property and move away at any time. *Renunciation*: In Africa, everyone is increasingly transitory. Members of extended families are spread out across the country and people are constantly moving out of and into communities for personal reasons such as employment or education. *Communion*: All organizations are now voluntary and offer regular group activities. Churches and Mosques conduct religious rituals. All are voluntary and none involve *everyone* in the community. *Mortification*: In urban Africa, television dictates social norms for most people. Aggression in males and manipulation in females is valued, but neither characteristic lends itself to benefiting the community.

If we are willing to admit that we have weakened commitment to community mechanisms in Africa today, which has been caused by certain attitudes and values that discourage them, and we decide that there is a need to accomplish a commitment to community on the part of all members of our local communities across our continent, then we must start in our own homes with ourselves and our own families. We know about the value of contributing to our community, but most of us refuse to accept personally our responsibility for being an example for our children to emulate of a contributing member of our community. We are seen by our children as pursuing our own individual pleasures and leaving it to "the other guy" to sacrifice time and energy for the needs of our community.

Eventually we end up leaving the community in which we have lived (this is inevitable, as we all face death). At the moment, we should commit ourselves to the community. We should not say, "I don't care because I'm not going to stay here long." If everyone does good things for their communities while they are there, all communities will be cared for regardless of the degree of mobility of its residents. Adults need to sacrifice childish self-centeredness to become members that benefit their community. All adults and children should regularly give up some of their time and energy to perform community improvement projects.

Sacrifice: In so-called "advanced" African urban society, adults must start providing examples for soon-to-be adults of a willingness to sacrifice themselves for the needs of their community and its members. *Transcendence*: It is too bad that our national heroes are no longer used as models for everyday behavior; we have deviated from their example of the value of self-sacrifice for the benefit of the whole society.

To restructure contemporary African society to create a commitment to community on the part of all members, we must replace the current emphasis on individual achievement with the importance of group achievement. If we look closely at our current goals and values, we discover that they are based on short-term comfort for the individual. Right now, urban African society is based on the value of individual gain, which is the opposite of commitment to the group. We *can* accomplish the goal of commitment to the community on the part of all members in this society *if* we substitute the credo, "I am free to do what I want to do provided that it will benefit my community and not myself alone," for the current popular credo, "I am free to do what I want to do as long as it does not harm anyone." We will *not* be able to restructure our communities to create a feeling of commitment to the community, on the part of all members, until we move in out minds from *I* to *we*.

In modern urban Africa, one is tempted to identify oneself as a member of a particular group and to do things with the group that benefit oneself rather than the community as a whole. In urban Africa, the philosophy of ultimate freedom for the individual encourages people to flit from one interest to another searching for peace of mind. As people jealously guard their personal freedoms, the possibility for communities to unite withers and dies. I believe that community organizations are needed by a society as an integral part of a dynamic community to provide continuous education for the younger generation about their social responsibilities and to create solidarity among all members of the community ongoing into the future. Unfortunately, in urban Africa, often community action groups form to solve particular pressing social problems and then disband when those problems are temporarily solved. In contrast, I feel that community groups are needed as the foundation of a society to perform the essential task of socialization of young people.

Ongoing community groups encourage those who participate to feel proud of themselves and to value their community and thus work for its betterment. In urban Africa today we find that separate organizations serve separate sectors of our society and rarely work together for a common goal. In traditional African communities, representatives from each community organization form a body to discuss the activities of each organization so as to avoid replication. Once a month, they make plans to embark together upon an agreed-upon community-wide project. In contrast, in African urban areas each individual believes that they know what is best for them and that they have an inalienable right to pursue it. In Bakalar village where I grew up, people look down upon an individual who chooses not to participate in group projects. In rural areas, that kind of person is rare because all children are socialized to participate in the group. Even if one disagrees with the group, one is encouraged to come to meetings to voice one's thoughts and feelings. No one is ever considered an outsider and even members on opposing sides of issues are considered integral parts of the whole community.

In African urban areas, the elderly are increasingly isolated and denied any important role in modern society. In traditional African communities, the elders' group plans and implements community projects and invites youth groups to participate in these projects with them. To change African society for the better, individuals must be willing to set an example by sacrificing some of their time and energy to organize neighborhood clubs for every age group. These kinds of clubs would meet in a neighborhood home and have no formal affiliation. A parent of one of the members would be available for guidance. As the club rotated its meeting place among members' homes, distrust, ignorance, and prejudice on the part of members' parents would be eliminated. Through neighborhood clubs, ties of trust, respect, and caring between individuals in the community can be built even in modern cities.

Existing organizations in African cities are voluntary and are not sufficiently at the grassroots level. The method used by age-group clubs to develop commitment to community among their members is encouraging them to work on projects that benefit the community. These kinds of clubs create awareness in the mind of child and adult members of the value of commitment to one's community. As children grow up, they develop a love for and a desire to share their time and energy with their community.

My own personal experiences as a member of the West Serrekunda Youth Group in The Gambia from 1980 to 1987 are revealing. Every teenager who lives in West Serrekunda is required to be a member of this group. We met bimonthly to discuss the personal problems of individual members, community social problems, and the self-help projects that we designed to solve these problems. For example, if a club member experienced the loss of a family member, we would take up a collection to pay for the funeral and take time to visit the family. If a member had a sibling who was getting married, we would take up a collection to buy a wedding gift. We would also take up a collection to buy a baby gift if there was a member in our group having a naming (Christening) ceremony in their family.

If someone in our group noticed that the streets in our area needed cleaning or resurfacing, we would approach the elders and enlist their help in obtaining the equipment and supplies needed to do the job. Quite often, elders joined us in the actual labor. As I look back, I now consider this group a community action group because members worked together to address and solve the problems of their own community. Because there were both Muslim and Christian members in our group, we often volunteered to clean both the Catholic church and the mosque and to weed the cemeteries of each. If a school needed new buildings, our group volunteered to mix cement to form the blocks for the walls. If a person building a home needed help, we assisted them.

I believe that the reason that West Serrekunda did not experience the social problems, such as drug addiction, suicide, drunk driving, crime, and teen gangs that are found in the neighborhoods of most large cities is because everyone was expected to act in a responsible way to care for the community. At our meetings, we discussed community norms and values so that every teenager would know how they were expected to act. If an adult saw a teen violating any of these norms and values, they would report it to the elders' group, which would send a representative to our next meeting. They would discuss what they had seen with the teen involved in the presence of a committee drawn from the youth group to find out why the behavior had happened and how to avoid another such incident.

Once a month, an elders' committee would meet with a committee from the youth group to share ideas about both individual and community-wide problems that had come to the attention of either group. The purpose of these joint meetings was to coordinate the efforts of both groups to support the projects initiated by either group. As a result, West Serrekunda was a secure place to live because everyone knew everyone else. Each person who lived there participated in an appropriate age-group club, and all age-group clubs worked together for the good of the entire community. Anyone could knock on any door at any time of the day or night and find a friend to talk to or a person who would gladly provide help. This community has eliminated the word *stranger* from its culture and a scream in the night brings neighbors running to investigate. If they had ignored a cry for help because it did not affect them directly, then a criminal might escape, and fear and mistrust would begin to grow in this community. Any newcomer to West Serrekunda was immediately introduced to the appropriate age-group club, and their new neighbors would take turns hosting them and showing them around the community. In this way the chance of anyone remaining a stranger was eliminated, and everyone was immediately integrated into the neighborhood.

I am personally convinced that the peace and security of our communities and nations around the world depends on the establishment of similar age-group clubs in which everyone is included. The age-group club, a tradition of African village social structure, can make the transition to modern urban African settings and stands as a guide to the solution of social problems in modern societies around the world. African villages have created the successful social structure of age-group clubs over thousands of years of living together in a society. It is time for us to recognize that the answer to the social disintegration of modern society resides in this tradition of African village life. Age-group clubs, such as the West Serrekunda and Bakalar Village Youth Group in which I participated, work to solve problems in their communities, socialize young people to become responsible citizens, and encourage commitment to and develop pride and love for a community in the hearts and minds of all of its inhabitants.

Chapter 10

Building A Sustainable Democratic Africa

Using Cooperation

People in Africa are now blaming other people for the social, economic, and political problems of our society. I believe that this is because many people living in Africa hold a negative view regarding the use of alliances, reciprocity, and exchange to accomplish work and solve problems. They believe, "I've failed if I have to go to my neighbors for help; I will look bad." We tend to seek someone to blame for problems and to view persons we cannot control as our enemies. This tendency limits our perception of the many possibilities of a particular situation, and it distracts us from developing positive ideas that may help to solve various social, economic, and political problems. We try to influence the people who we believe are to blame for problems by criticizing them because they control financial and human resources that are needed to solve our nation's problems, and we have to cooperate if plans to solve those problems are to be implemented. We need to remember that these people cannot be ordered around and will only work with us to solve mutual problems when they so choose. For this reason, I believe it is very important for us to understand how reciprocity works and how to set up mutually beneficial exchanges. To do this, Africans need to understand the principle of exchange.

Reciprocity is the foundation of all social and economic transactions among people. Most people view an employment contract as an exchange: "An honest day's work for an honest day's pay." People who help others may not expect *immediate* payment for their efforts but some *eventual* compensation *is* expected. Whatever the forms are taken by these exchanges, unless they are roughly equivalent over time, negative feelings will develop. For this reason, exchange enables people to help each other and to work together for long periods of time without evoking strong feelings of injustice. Times of rapid and extreme change, such as our modern day and age, confers particular importance on the process of exchange because the need for help to adjust to those changes increases tremendously. I believe that during this current time in our nation's development, we should ask ourselves, "Am I contributing to the improvement of African society to the best of my ability?" I believe that Africans need to realize that each of us will be able to influence others *only* if we can offer something they need because *power* comes from the ability to meet others' needs. We need to ask ourselves, "Are my actions and attitude contributing to the positive development of a peaceful and democratic Africa?"

What happens if one person's idea of fair repayment for help is very different from that of the one who provide the help? The basic problem that faces those of us who wish to establish equitable exchanges in Africa is reconciling the differences in the ways people perceive and interpret the same activity. To solve this problem, it is necessary for us to understand the values of the person whom we want to influence. Usually people know exactly what they want in return for giving help, but often they will settle for a rough equivalent as long as positive feelings continue to exist. For this reason, I feel that it is the responsibility of each of us to share our knowledge, experience, and skills with *all* of the people on our continent. Instead of only thinking how we can enrich and strengthen our own family's and ethnic group's resources, each of us has an important role to play in the social, economic, and political development of our country by reaching out to assist with the solution of problems and to collaborate in the support of positive projects that are being initiated by people from families, ethnic groups, and political beliefs that are different than our own. For Africa to develop successfully, we need to view the people whom we wish to influence in our society not as enemies but as our allies. We need to be willing to explore and work hard to understand our world, especially the pressures they face in this world, from their perspective. We must *thoroughly* understand and respect each other's needs. Knowing all this will help us become aware of each other's key goals. When we no longer view a person who is from an ethnic group that is different from our own as an enemy but instead as potential ally, we can more easily understand their world and thus it will be easier to discover what they value and need.

We need to remember that everyone in an alliance has the freedom to continue to pursue their own interests, as long as it does not threaten established and potential areas of mutual benefit and the development, support, and maintenance of trusting, sustainable relationships. In other words, for Africans, pursuing self-interest cannot take precedence over searching for and building areas of mutual benefit. If each person in an alliance truly understands and respects the needs of the others, all people will discover how self-interest can be transformed into mutual interests. The establishment of alliances is an ancient method that our ancestors have used to ensure the ongoing satisfaction of the social, political, and economic needs of the people of Africa up to this modern age, and we should not let this important tradition die.

Our society is in danger because many of us are so concerned with material gain that we have become blind and deaf to the cries of our elders who constantly warn us that if we continue this way, our country will fall apart. All Africans who desire to avoid this need to turn away from blaming others for our continent's social, economic, and political problems and instead refocus their energies on the task of finding solutions to these problems. I challenge those who love Africa to take responsibility for assisting our leaders and join all Africans who work in a positive way to help Africa.

Like all people, Africans have psychological needs that must be satisfied on five different levels: spiritual, occupational, status, social, and personal. I believe all Africans desire to be involved in an important task that is greatly needed by their society and, as well, they seek the ability to excel at it. I believe that most Africans gain happiness from being able to provide the financial, material, or human resources needed to support existing community projects and to implement new ones. Traditionally, in Africa, assistance has been given to the younger generation by the older generation, in the form of knowledge or wisdom. I believe our people yearn for recognition, that is, the public acknowledgment of their efforts and accomplishments, which they can use to build a reputation of importance that links them in a positive way with others in our society. While doing this, all of us need to remember that building one's positive reputation in a community or society is *not* accomplished by merely glorifying oneself with material possessions and rising in status in a bureaucracy. Rather, true value as a person is obtained when one is able to propose ideas and suggestions that can help one's entire community or society. I am convinced that everyone's positive efforts are required to maintain and support the development of Africa. One can do this by going to work on the farm if one does not have a useful position in a business, company, agency, or government office that actually benefits our people. An African who does this is being accountable for contributing in a positive way to the improvement of our society. I am convinced that, as Africans, if we do not give up the habit of sitting at a *Bantaba* (that is, under a big shade tree) and drinking *Ataya* (a traditional wine or Chinese tea) for almost the whole day and evening, our society will become a destructive influence on the younger generation and as a result, our culture and society will disintegrate. When that happens, we will lose our identity as Africans. Daily, Africans listen to one another's concerns so as to give and receive the emotional closeness and friendship that they crave and for a feeling of security. All this, however, is not enough if we do not provide our young people with opportunities to challenge themselves to grow and change by working to increase their skills and abilities. We can provide them with opportunities by merely showing them, by our example, how to seek out and create opportunities to work cooperatively with Africans from different ethnic groups to attack and solve the urgent social and economic problems of our nation. In this way we will be able to affirm our African values in a very concrete way so that our young people can actually hear and see these values in action. We will thus nurture in them a sense of self-esteem as Africans.

I am convinced that Africans fail to influence each other because we do not bother to try to see the world from the other people's perspectives. This is because most of us are trapped by our own definition of what should be and what is right. Because our desire to influence other people so is strong, we only experience our *need* for other people's cooperation. Usually, the frustration of meeting resistance from a potential ally usually gets in the way of our understanding the world from another African's point of view. When it becomes obvious that they are not being understood, our potential ally usually responds by "digging in," which stimulates us to repeat inappropriate strategies or even to back away from the relationship in frustration. Instead of attempting to see the situation from the other person's point of view, I see us just soothing our anxiety and irritation by building up a negative stereotype about the other person, which changes them into an enemy in our minds. When this happens, we no longer care to investigate what the other person needs or values.

To complicate matters, when we wish to influence others, we are rarely precisely aware of just what we want because we do not take the time to consider which aspects should have the most priority and what could be left for later. Africans find themselves always fighting over the wrong things because we confuse our goals with specific means of accomplishing them. The most successful people, in any society, never lose sight of their ultimate objectives while being *flexible* about the means by which to accomplish them. An awareness of one's own style of interaction also is essential. For example, we will never evoke cooperation from a person who likes to get work done first and then relax by approaching them with small talk. A person who likes to look at solutions first, before defining the problem, will not be influenced by us if we approach them with attempts to involve them in exploratory problem-solving.

I believe that there are three factors that can hinder the successful growth of positive exchange in Africa: (1) failure to treat those with whom we disagree as potential allies instead of enemies, (2) ignoring the need to understand the world from others' unique points of view, and (3) lacking awareness about our own interactional style. Maturity helps us to be aware of the needs of an ally, to seek only mutual benefit, and not to use that knowledge to manipulate others to further one's own aims. Unfortunately, those of us who consider ourselves professionals are not good examples to follow because we usually stubbornly stick to our own ideas because we are so sure we hold a monopoly on "truth." Our failure to accommodate our potential ally's needs and desires often doom collaboration. Precisely because we have been especially successful using a particular approach or method, we find it extremely difficult to see that our overuse of it obscures the need to use different, more appropriate approaches.

I am convinced that joint experiences are the best teacher. As more Africans working together will create more trust between us so that the exchange process will become easier in time. I believe that our greatest problem is that *we just do not have much time left*. That being the case, we must immediately close our quarrelsome lips, as our parents would say, and get to work today on the task at hand or the problem to be solved with our focus on improving our *relationships* with our allies, that is, Africans who are different than ourselves. Successful exchange involves not only achieving task goals or solving problems but also establishing *valuable collaborative relationships* based on the satisfaction of mutual needs so that the next interaction will be even more productive. This kind of relationship can be reached by always keeping mutual benefit as the central outcome of each word we speak to each other and each action we take during each day of our lives as an African whom our great ancestors can have the honor to praise where they dwell with the creator.

The Resolution of Conflict in Africa

Conflict has been defined as a difference or misunderstanding between two or more people, groups, organizations, institutions, or nations. The positive resolution of conflict requires all parties involved to identify problems, search for the roots of the problems, generate possible alternative solutions, and take responsibility for an active role in the creation of consensus by compromise. In any negotiation of conflict, there must first exist in each party a willingness to accept and value modes of operating that are culturally diverse (that is, different than one's one culture). Participants in an ongoing conflict who desire a positive resolution must recognize that culture is

> . . . the pattern of basic assumptions that a group of people, who have shared and successfully solved significant problems together, has invented to socially, economically and politically stabilize their group and as such, this pattern is highly resistant to change."[1]

Principals of Problem-solving

Success in problem-solving requires that effort be directed toward overcoming *surmountable* obstacles. Difficult problems in Africa require unusual approaches. A common tendency that frequently leads to failure is associated with the attempt to solve a problem by locating a person or group that is at fault. Available facts should be used even when they are inadequate. When a good deal of information is available, problem-solvers are more prone to work with the evidence. In the absence of adequate information, such as is the case with many Africans, biases dominate the problem-solving process.

> People fail to get along because they fear each other. They fear each other because they do not know each other. They don't know each other because they have not properly communicated with each other.[2]

Africans need to realize that the starting point of a problem is richest in solution possibilities. Starting over again and again from the beginning in one's analysis of the problem is the only way to increase the variety of solution possibilities. This is because statements of problems often hold within them suggested solutions. By stopping the exploration of the problem, Africans limit consideration of alternative, possibly valuable, solutions. We must ask ourselves why we favor a certain solution. What purpose does this solution serve? I believe problem-mindedness should be increased in Africa and that solution-mindedness is delayed because in any discussion the responses of some Africans interrupt the thinking processes of others. The first thing is to agree on the problem.

Disagreement can lead either to hard feelings or to innovation, depending on the role played by our leaders. Africans must feel free to disagree if they are to contribute the best of their thinking. African leaders can reduce conformity by withholding judgment, entertaining criticism, and trying to understand strange ideas. Africans who get along with others all the time are poor problem-solvers because we cannot learn from one another by always agreeing. The solution is to encourage respect for disagreement and turn it into a stimulant for new ideas. The "idea-getting" process should be separated from the "idea-evaluation" process because the latter inhibits the former. "Idea-getting" requires a willingness to break away from past experience. Creative thinking is a radical way to look at a problem.

Choice-situations should be turned into problem-situations. Creative alternatives can be overlooked when choices are made between obvious alternatives. Considerable searching should be encouraged as a way of delaying choices until additional alternatives have been explored. African problem-situations should be turned into choice-situations. Most Africans' natural reaction is to act on the first solution that they find. Research has shown that a second solution to a problem tends to be superior. Solutions suggested by African leaders are improperly evaluated and tend to be either accepted or rejected. Our leaders are in a position of power, so their ideas are received differently than those coming from the rest of us. A leader's previous study of a problem may cause a group to reach poorer decisions. The role of African leaders should be to conduct the discussion and avoid introducing their own views or passing judgment on ideas expressed by ordinary Africans. "The main obstacle to successful problem solving is interference caused by old habits."[3]

Aspects of Bargaining

Active Versus Reactive Positioning: Africans should allow each other to lead because this helps increase their participation in finding solutions to mutual problems. It is easier to "read" ones neighbors when they have been allowed to "lay out their cards" first.

Extreme Versus Moderate Demands: Extreme demands result in polarization, yet moderate demands leave inadequate room to bargain down.

Soft Versus Hard Styles: Africans should try not to be handicapped by a style based on personal need. The person with the flexibility to react with a range of styles holds the advantage.

Off the Record Versus on the Record: "Using a third neutral party to define a beneficial compromise can be valuable."[4]

Negotiation and Conflict Resolution

The window of opportunity for successful negotiation among Africans exists at the balance point between cooperation and fighting. Nevertheless, a mutual analysis of the diverse cultural aspects of conflict-laden situations with the objective of understanding the underlying interests of all Africans can transform problems into search models that can be used to locate novel solution alternatives in a united effort. All successful negotiations indicate mutual respect and a joint history of free-flowing communications to examine, discuss, debate, and propose. The role of each African in negotiation should be to impress upon others the implications of their common interests or interdependencies as an incentive to motivate them to come to consensus on a satisfactory compromise. For negotiations to conclude successfully, all Africans must welcome change and the tensions of new interdependencies that are created by compromise. Africans must encourage each other to be vigilant in resisting the temptation to reduce the ambiguity that is inherent in compromises by adopting a competitive, combative stance (to make other Africans submit) or by yielding to the impulse to run away from the responsibilities of implementing agreed-upon solutions. "All successful negotiation results in agreements that meet the legitimate needs of each party while taking community interests of all parties involved into account."[5]

An Old Fable

There once was an important problem to be solved and everybody was asked to solve it. Everybody was sure that somebody would solve it. Anybody could solve it, but it looked like nobody would do it. Somebody was sick and tired of the problem going unsolved because it was everybody's responsibility to solve it. Everybody was waiting for anybody to solve it, but nobody realized that everybody would never take the responsibility to solve it. So it ended up that everybody blamed somebody when nobody did what anybody could do to solve the problem.[6]

Who Hears Our True Leaders?

"What advantage is there in the earthly things which men possess? That which shall profit them, they have utterly neglected."[7]

O you who believe! What excuse have you that when it is said to you: "Go forth in Allah's way," you incline heavily to earth; are you contented with this world's life instead of the hereafter? But the provision of this world's life compared with the hereafter is but little.[8]

"Behold, I say unto you, 'Lift up your eyes, and look on the fields; for they are white already to harvest.'"[9]

I believe that the challenge faced today by all Africans is to assist our leaders in their work of designing more flexible public institutions by replacing the ineffective European vertical bureaucratic hierarchies of our past with modern horizontal networks that link together African people in a continental alliance. It is clear, however, that if they are to accomplish this, our leaders will need every African to understand and adhere to a vision of a strategic mission for our continent. I believe our leaders are trying to help us knock down the walls that separate us from each other. At this time, we are hindered by the European-style institutions of the past in which independently functioning departments coordinate people with specialized expertise. In the Africa of our past, it was clear who reported to whom and who was responsible for what because the Europeans believed that this was the best way to harness us to their purposes. The problem for our leaders today is that the world in which Africa once existed no longer survives. The world is now composed of new technologies, fast-changing markets, and global competition. All countries must quickly become more flexible so as to respond successfully to a more fluid world economic environment. Recently, our leaders have been trying to show Africans what kinds of roles they need to play and what kinds of relationships they need to maintain with their fellow Africans to do productive work in our modern day.

In our countries today, creating the right kind of relationships with others at the right time, is the key to *productivity and innovation.* Our leaders want to stimulate Africans to generate the good feelings, team spirit, and hard work needed to facilitate these new types of productive working relationships. Nevertheless, this is easier said than done because Africans still view themselves, each other, their subordinates, and their superiors in terms of the outdated European hierarchical systems of the past. Our leaders ask us to put aside what divides us to unite behind their vision of a modern Gambia. All of us must no longer consider differences of authority, talent, and perspective as significant in the old way. If anyone is listening and watching, they will see our leaders demonstrating to Africans how this kind of diversity is essential for productivity and innovation in our country. In The Gambia we need new relationships that are based upon caring, egalitarianism, and participation.

Our leaders are teaching Africans who are willing to listen to them that at all times, some people lead and others follow, and that some provide direction while others are responsible for executing action. All Africans need to take turns sharing the responsibility for leading, planning, and implementing solutions to our problems. In addition, our leaders are telling all Africans that success comes when people challenge as they follow so that leaders can listen as they lead. Africans must accept that these types of changes must occur in the relationships between us if our countries are to be successful today and in the future. We must foster the growth of relationships in which people feel trusted by their superiors. That feeling of trust will free them to be both innovative and accountable. At the same time, we must nurture the growth of relationships in which our superior's feel simultaneously *supported* and *challenged* by us. This will enable them to lead effectively. When these kinds of relationships have been encouraged to grow in our continent, I believe every African will then understand how team-building, a valuable social tool that our leaders are asking us to use, is a mechanism for bringing together people with different but complementary skills so as to harness them to a single goal of the betterment of our country. Africans will then be able to divide up the work for which they share responsibility, not according to the former European hierarchical rules but in a traditionally African manner that efficiently coordinates everyone's separate efforts.

Recently, our true leaders have been having tremendous problems because Africans continue to view this transformation as a change in political structure when it actually requires fundamental changes in relationships (that is, how people view themselves in relation to others). Throughout human history, changes in political structures always have followed and been the result of transformations in the way people viewed themselves in relation to others. When institutionalized, new political structures can then begin to structure relationships between people within them. This has been confusing Africans recently. The change that is urgently needed at this time must begin with a transformation at the level of one person to another. Those who are listening hear our leaders encouraging all Africans to take an active interest in the challenges and problems facing others who contribute in different ways to our continent. All of us must now commit ourselves to the job of defining the tasks that need to be done, allocating responsibilities, and apportioning our resources in ways appropriate to the accomplishment of those tasks. To do this, our leaders are teaching Africans how to negotiate and bargain in productive ways. The key is for all Africans to find ways to define our personal interests broadly enough to discover mutually beneficial solutions to our national problems.

When our leaders speak to us about these matters, I hear Africans asking, "What's in it for me?" As a result, we get tied up in selfish conflicts. Now is the time to stop thinking that way and immediately begin negotiating and bargaining effectively with each other, forming the coalitions among ourselves that will further our country's interests, and developing strategies and tactics for advancing the interests of our country as a whole not just for ourselves as individuals. Our leaders know that increasing our national performance depends on citizen commitment. They are teaching all Africans that their leaders are no longer responsible for ensuring that all decisions are fair. This responsibility fall on Africans themselves. We can no longer rely like a child on "Big Papa." Each African adult needs to evaluate their own behavior critically because the success of our continent depends upon our ability to represent and embody the interests of the whole continent in the example we show to young people. Young people must be able to identify psychologically with their parents and other adults as the representatives of our whole continent.

I believe that by establishing new a relationship with our leaders, Africans will be able to implement new national designs that are necessary to enable our countries to succeed in the twenty-first century. Amazingly enough, the best economic tools that Africans can use are their own feelings. Africans know that they have productive working relationships with each other when they feel at ease and focused on their work, when they believe that everyone has something valuable to offer. When these kinds of relationships begin to flourish on our continent, our people will experience work as not only productive but also as creative. Africans need to realize that such feelings are not just the inevitable residue of positive human relationships. They are *data*, valuable clues to the dynamics of the sort of relationships that our leaders are attempting to create in our countries. Like farmers in their fields, we cannot expect them to accomplish much without the efforts of all of us, their family members. They call us to help them plant the seeds of national greatness and to help them clear the weeds and pests that inevitably come to steal our common wealth. We must plan and work together in a new way for a future in which we will harvest the priceless fruits of valuable relationships between Africans. We must now commit ourselves to listen to our brothers and sisters as they call us to new relationships with our leaders, with each other, and with our nations to help us build a strong and worthwhile society for our children and their children. I know that God will bless our country and each of us if we are willing to stand up when we are called by our true leaders. We must stand up and say, "I am ready and listening. Show me. I will do whatever is needed."

My Message for African Leadership

African leaders must look deeply into themselves. If we cannot lead our own people, what is the point of having independence? Independence means depending on oneself, one's people, and one's environment. It means not being one hundred percent dependent on the colonizers who maltreated the indigent people. Postcolonial leaders tell the people that they can do a better job taking care of their people, yet they often do a worse job than the colonial masters. This is a shame to all African leaders as well as all African citizens. Why do we continue killing our own people? Good leaders care about their people. Good leaders are accountable and value the lives of the people in their countries. Africa needs democracy to allow the people to express their views, to enable the process of constructive criticism of the government, to be able to point out what needs to be done to solve problems. We do not need weapons. If African leaders are accountable, then we will not need the military to take control. The money we spend on weapons is useless. It is useful to a person who is leading by dictatorship, but it is not useful to the African people.

If people are starving in Africa, should we spend money to buy guns? We should feed those people and give them education and health care. We need to unite to progress in Africa: united we stand; divided we fall. How can we see what is happening in another region of Africa and neglect it? What kind of leaders say, "Yes, sir," to the Western world and say no to their own people? Enough is enough. We have a lot of land in Africa, yet people are starving. It is sad that we keep electing leaders who do not act on the best interests of the people. They should not remain in office if they do not do the job. It is our responsibility that to see that they do the job and to elect people who are capable and who are prepared to work for the development of Africa.

We need leaders who are ready to work with the farmers and are ready to educate to both males and females in Africa. We need leaders who are prepared to share leadership with the people. We need to give high positions to women so that they can become leaders and join Africa's men in positions of leadership. African men have failed, and we need to admit that we have failed our people. We do not need a single-party system in Africa. We need a multiparty system to create balance. In a one-party system, the government will be more loyal to its party than to the African people because there is no one in the government to tell them what they are doing wrong and what they should do. Something is wrong with most African leaders and something is also wrong with most of the African opposition parties. All of them are fighting to lead. They should get together to empower the African people to vote for wise and capable leaders. Why are we so bound up as individuals in trying to become leaders? Yes, we realize that we are all Africans and that we should not exploit one another, but do we realize that we must work for the welfare of *all* African nations?

A capable leader is prepared to listen and allows people to criticize the administration with impunity. Should we continue to use our money in Africa to buy guns and let our own people starve and remain uneducated? We will show our leaders that we can elect people who are for us and not just for them. Our leaders listen too much to the Western world's instructions on how to lead their own people and what kind of education they should give us. I encourage African intellectuals to return to Africa or stay away. Think about how we can make a contribution. Do not say, "I am no longer in Africa so I no longer care what happens there." Even those of us who live abroad are still connected to our homeland. Each and every one of us has a contribution that we can make. It is so sad to see African intellectuals who do not return to Africa. Westerners come to Africa to do research, and we give them information. Then they sell us our information. We give them our knowledge for free! We should write our own books. This is what Africa needs: educated African people who are not individualistic and who share their education with Africans.

When I say democracy in Africa, I mean democracy that will allow all citizens to speak their minds without being jailed. One of the things that causes African intellectuals to stay in foreign countries is when they go back and see what is happening to their people, caused by our leaders. If they speak out, they are put behind bars, never to see the light again. We should have freedom of the press. We have the right to vote, but not the right of free speech. This is not democracy. In Africa, we need an education that will help African people. We do not need Western education. We should not spend money to send people to other countries and to Europe to study, but instead, create institutions where Africans are educated and Westerners come to study and invest in our countries. When I say African education, I mean an education that is provided to all

Africans, even in a village. Every African has a right to a meaningful education. We need educated, capable leaders in Africa.

We need to change the African educational system to encourage research into all fields of study and particularly, how to make good use of our land. African education must provide people with knowledge and skills that they can use to get jobs in Africa. We need to build more secondary schools to give each child the opportunity to continue until twelfth grade. What about good teachers? We do not need someone in tenth or twelfth grade to go to elementary school to teach. They need to go to teachers' training college to become elementary or secondary teachers. We must have enough supplies for a positive classroom environment. In a classroom where a child sits on the floor to write, where dust comes in when the wind blows, the child inhales that dust. I refuse to believe that we do not have enough money in Africa to build better schools and better health centers or to employ better qualified teachers, health professionals, and agriculturalists. If we have money to buy weapons, we have enough money to spend on education, employment, and heath care.

All African governments should invest money in agriculture and land. We should invent equipment to help farmers farm the land. We need proper irrigation. We should not depend on Westerners to send us aid to feed our own people. We do not need so many colleges in Africa if we do not have jobs for people who graduate from those colleges. When we do that, we create more unemployment, riots, drugs, prostitution, child neglect, and divorce. We should not let the Western world sabotage the African plan for unity. When the West African Peacekeeping Force (ECOMOG) tried to maintain peace, the selling of weapons by the French sabotaged their efforts. We do not need anyone outside of Africa telling us what to do, how to become a better people, and how to have a better life. We need to look into how Africa can become one interrelated economic market. We produce peanuts, cotton, rice, and oil. We have gold and valuable minerals. We have fisheries in many countries. Why can African countries not come together and agree on a price for anything that is produced in Africa that we export to the Western world, and tell them the price that we want them to pay us? Why should they tell us what price to charge? If we let them do this, we are being colonized by the Western world even if we have our own African leaders. Yes, we can do it if we come together as one African people. To adopt change, people must realize that it is not easy. Even so, they must be willing to say, "Even though I may not benefit personally from this change, I will try so that my people can benefit from it in the future." This confers honor in this life and each of us must be prepared to do it. All tribes, males and females, must believe in peace, democracy, and freedom of speech. We must work together in unity for Africa.

Chapter 11

My Africa

Peace is everywhere in rural Africa. People can feel it. People can feel safe at home, and that is what I call peace. One can go anywhere to visit, anytime of the day or night.

This is what I call democracy. One can speak and share knowledge and skills; that is what I call democracy and freedom. Africa is great. Poverty is there, but we are able to handle it. We are proud of what we can produce, and that is what democracy and freedom are all about. When I was a child we did not depend on the Western world but on our land and our people. Should we move away from caring about our land and our people? If we do, I believe we will suffer and we will cry and cry, because we will regret that this has happened to us. Who is responsible for Africa? Africans are. We must always be in charge of and in control of our land and our people. The greatest continent in the world, Africa, is ours. We are its people.

> We must work passionately to bridge the gulf between our scientific progress and our moral progress. One of the great problems of mankind is that we suffer from a poverty of the spirit, which stands in glaring contrast to our scientific and technological abundance. The richer we have become materially, the poorer we have become morally and spiritually. We are prone to judge success by the index of our salaries or the size of our cars, rather than by the quality of our service and our relationship to the rest of humanity. When an individual is no longer a true participant, when he no longer feels a sense of responsibility to his society, then the content of democracy is emptied. All too many of those who are affluent ignore those who exist in poverty; in doing so, the affluent will eventually have to face themselves with the question that Eichmann chose

to ignore: How responsible am I for the well-being of my fellows? To ignore evil is to become an accomplice to it. An individual has not started living until he can rise above the narrow confines of his individualistic concerns to the broader concerns of all humanity. Every man must decide whether he will walk in the light of creative altruism or the darkness of destructive selfishness. This is the judgment. Life's most persistent and urgent question is, "What are you doing for others?" Everybody can be great, because anybody can serve. You don't have to have a college degree to serve. You don't have to make your subject and your verb agree to serve. You don't have to know about Plato and Aristotle to serve. You don't have to know Einstein's theory of relativity to serve. You don't have to know the second theory of thermodynamics to serve. You only need a heart full of grace. A soul generated by love.[1]

The Influence of Western Culture on African Nation-States

Increasingly, Western economic, political, and cultural models define and legitimize agendas for local action in all the domains of African life, including business, politics, education, medicine, science, and even the family and religion. Since the end of World War II, organizational development of societies around the world has intensified. Western models are more highly publicized than ever before. International organizations devoted to educating and advising on the importance and utility of Western models are more numerous and active than ever. African nation-states are influenced by worldwide systems of economic or political power, exchange, and competition. Nevertheless, money and force, power and interests are but one of the engines of change in Africa. Some sociologists believe the influence of Western culture on African nation-states is merely a by-product of the West's economic and political dominance of Africa. I protest that this view fails to appreciate the significance of culture and its organizational presence in all societies. Culture is now substantially organized on a worldwide basis, not simply built up from local circumstances and the history of individual African countries.

Marx stated,

> The ideas of the *ruling class* are in every epoch the *ruling ideas* because the class with the strongest resources controls the means of communication. Those who hold the largest resources are able to advance their interests over those of their fellows.[2]

Because of this, I believe that the interests of the Western ruling class underlie the most popular models of economic, political, and social development in Africa today. Thus, Western materialism—the culture of this ruling class—is spreading quickly to even the most remote corners of our African continent. The culture of this ruling class therefore dictates the economic and political systems of African nation-states. This is because this ruling class has the economic power to create incentives for African nation-states to adopt Western models of economic, political, and social development. These Western models are spreading a culture of materialism that psychologically seduces Africans by inducing in them new desires to which they become enslaved.

The current spread of Western culture is a continuation of the Western colonization of Africa and other regions of the world. The present Western economic, political, and social models of African development are merely a highly organized method of neocolonization that is spread by a global media system and controlled by a wealthy Western elite. By promoting these Western models, this elite is able to use the ancient mode of dominance, "divide and conquer." It is successful because the influence of these Western models in African countries suppresses local African culture and stimulates civil conflict between those who support Western models and those who want to maintain African cultural traditions. Civil conflict in African nation-states spreads a state of powerlessness that leaves them dependent on the West. Thus divided by civil conflict, Africa remains as dominated by the West as during colonial times.

Western models are damaging to African nation-states because they insinuate that there is a global consensus on matters such as human rights, the scientific investigation of the natural world, socioeconomic development, and education. These models claim universal world applicability. Western economic models of development and fiscal policy and Western models of the human body and health care delivery are based on the assumption that they are applicable everywhere in the world, in all cultures. Alternative models based on local African traditional social structures have little legitimacy because Western models are articulated with elaborate rationalized justifications. Western models of socialization insist that formal education is necessary for economic growth, technical innovation, citizen loyalty, and democratic institutions. They recommend the implementation of Western socialization methods such as mass schooling systems organized around a standard Eurocentric curriculum in Africa without regard to local circumstances and cultures. The culture of a Western elite dominates mass media, thereby providing an *appearance* of global consensus regarding Western models, which is *artificially* produced.

Weber stated,

> The situation of Western civilization cannot be explained by the operation of general factors that are common to the situation of all people, but by specific combinations of historical circumstance unique to it. The institutional system of the modern Western World is not a "natural order," which has come about merely by the removal of obstacles to it or by a process of "natural" social evolution. It represents only one of several possible lines of social development. Radically different social systems found in non-Western societies around the world are not simply "arrested" in stages of development leading in the same direction.[3]

The rapid spread of Western models of economic, political, and social development in Africa indicates the West's dominance of Africa because they serve as a control mechanism. This is evidenced in rationalized justifications that are used to support the West's claims that these models are universally applicable.

The recent propagation of Western models is the way West dictates its ideology to leaders in developing countries. The seeds of this ideology were sown in Africa during the 1950s and 1960s when many African nation-states were attempting to establish themselves as autonomous countries. This was done to align Africa with the West. During the cold war, the West was afraid of the influence of the Soviet Union. The West socialized African leaders and intellectuals to believe that their local African cultures were inferior and that they must adopt Western value systems and culture to promote the development of their new nation-states. When African leaders adopt world models, they begin to devalue local resources and products and value Western-produced consumer goods. This not only creates a market for externally produced goods but also cedes economic control to the countries where those goods are produced, thus dictating economic policy in African nation-states. The rapid spread of Western models of economic, political, and social development in African since the 1950s and 1960s indicates the hegemony of a wealthy Western elite dominating and exploiting Africa nation-states. This hegemony is the cause of the pervasiveness of Western models in Africa today and explains why they are found even in places where they are obviously incongruent with local circumstances and cultures.

African nation-states must present themselves as adhering to Western models in seeking admission to the United Nations. African nations, whose goals are outside of Western models, for example, in service to God (i.e., Allah) are viewed as suspect because they do not include the standard Western goal of individual rights and progress. The present models of economic, political, and social development being used in Africa today are based on Western culture. Contrary to popular opinion, they cannot be imported wholesale as a fully functioning system. Attempts to do so lead to the adoption of conflicting Western principles that are inconsistent with local African practices. Western models are highly idealized, which makes them impossible to implement. African nations with limited resources find it easier to make it appear that they have adopted the latest Western structural forms than to make them work effectively in actuality. Symbolic reform takes the place of the difficult task of bringing about needed change. African leaders retreat to planning for future progress. African policymakers spend their time finding ways to incorporate the required principles of world models in general statements that their countries cannot adhere, which results in widespread cynicism. African national planning agencies write unrealistic five-year plans. Western sociologists attribute this to the delusions of egotistical African leaders or the interests of dominant ethnic elites.

The need to be admitted to the United Nations forces so-called autonomous African nation-states to conform to Western value systems and Western political systems, thus Western models control African nation-states on all economic and cultural levels, including education. Leaders in African countries know that principles of Western models do not fit their local circumstances and cultures, so they must artificially mold national goals to appear congruent with Western models. Having to do this brings internal conflict in their countries. When conflict inevitably comes, both the West and their own people discredit these leaders. African leaders can see that they are at the point of no return, but the

West as yet cannot see its own role in producing coup d'etat and civil war in Africa. I doubt that they ever will admit their responsibility because it is not in their best interests to do so. It is in their best interests for instability and civil disorder to continue because then African leaders will turn to the West and beg for help to solve the resulting economic problems. When international organizations such as the United Nations and the World Bank come to "rescue" African countries, they establish economic and social structures that mimic Western models and suppress local African traditional economic and social structures, customs, and culture. To appear that they are willing to implement Western-designed economic and social programs; African leaders must first sign documents that declare their allegiance to Western models.

Recognition on a global level is important to African countries. Because African nations are dependent on obtaining formal recognition from dominant Western powers, copying Western models has come to mean filling in forms correctly rather than managing urgent national problems. African national policies begin to look as if they had been created from typically Western scripts. Although African leaders claim to their people that they are resisting dominant Western world models, they develop similar modern bureaucratic institutions such as central banking and educational systems, thereby irreversibly transforming local traditions in the direction of world Western cultural forms. International organizations posture as objective and disinterested helpers who desire to assist African nation-states pursue the goal of achieving national development. If African leaders resist adopting world models as their country's primary goal, Western organizations can rely on local African activists to mobilize citizens to oppose their country's regime based on belief in the legitimacy of Western ideas such as democracy, freedom, and equality. Western world cultural ideology promotes individual rights over group needs. Soon, local groups come forward to claim national resources that they see as their right. Local groups call for national action. At the grassroots level, many groups demand the implementation of Western models with Western cultural principles and values. Antimodern movements are viewed as threats to national development.

Expecting African nation-states to adopt Western models that are not congruent with local African traditional social structures and culture is destructive and oppressive. The propagation of Western models constitutes cultural imperialism in Africa because it assumes that the Western value system, which forms the foundation of Western models of economic, political, and social development, is superior to local African value systems and social structures. It weakens and exploits Africans to be answerable to an external and foreign value system and culture. It creates civil conflict among members of the same society. Traditionally, African nations value the needs, rights, and freedoms of the community more than those of the individual. Africans and many other non-Western peoples are socialized to value the community more than the individual. When Western models are imposed on African societies, conflict immediately arises. The West is responsible for this conflict because just insisting on the use of *I* to define social interaction, instead of using the proper *we*, immediately triggers psychological conflict in an African. African leaders become convinced that they must adopt Western cultural values and social systems that are foreign to local African value systems and social structures. Creation of civil conflict establishes a configuration of power in which the West is strong and African leaders are weak; the dialog between them therefore is conducted on an unequal basis. The dialog is distorted by a power imbalance that makes it ultimately destructive. This dialog is one way because the West is dictating world models from a position of power to African leaders. When Westerners begin to perceive Western models as not universally applicable, then they can begin to work to help decrease the level of destructive civil instability in Africa. This will only happen when they show African leaders that they are willing to value and are interested in learning about African value systems and cultures.

At this time, international professional organizations and non-governmental organizations (NGOs) discuss every aspect of African life: economic production and consumption, political structure, education, science, medicine, sexuality, social relations, and religious doctrine. The United Nations and its related organizations such as the International Monetary Fund and the World Bank establish agendas of concern for African economic development and individual rights. The growth of NGOs since WWII has occurred in the areas of science, medicine, and economics. They have become instruments of modernity that promote Western models of individual rights in Africa. As grassroots movements in Africa, they protest failures in the implementation of Western cultural principles locally and demand action from African leaders. They provide models for policy and training programs in Africa and consultants to conduct evaluation schemes African nations. They collect data to assess population, health care, education, labor force, national production, and political status in African countries. In so doing, they transform the way Africans see themselves by identifying and describing African societies and cultures in Western terms. Weber stated, "People who rise in wealth and power cloak themselves in cultural responsibility because of the need to feel that those on the top merit their good fortune."[4]

Marx noted,

> Western models maintain the myth of upward social mobility because it is a way in which the capitalist class derives economic benefits from having a steady stream of fresh recruits. Capitalism channels individual aspirations on a global scale into desires for mobility within the system rather than revolt against it. All around the world, workers do not even know that they are alienated. Increasingly, more and more people on the earth indulge in passive mass consumption. In capitalism, the desire for consumption tends to take on a compulsive character.[5]

The issue that must be addressed is not whether NGOs are responsible for the way they transform how people around the world see themselves. That is obviously true. The issue to be confronted is the fact that international NGOs are tools of a capitalist Western elite because they are unwilling to allow the agendas of African people at the grassroots level to be brought to the table for dialog. More important, international NGOs are directed and staffed by

Westerners whose perspective originates in a Western culture that defines African cultures as inferior to their own. Most Westerners assume that there is no need to spend time learning from Africans so that they can consider local circumstances in Africa from an African perspective. Most Westerners have been unwilling to confront and re-evaluate inherent assumptions that their culture holds regarding African societies. I believe they avoid doing this so that they can cling to the myth that their culture is superior and that they are the saviors of Africa. This belief allows them to ignore the inherent contradictions of capitalism and the Western value system that supports it: democracy and individual rights. In addition, it encourages them to project blame for failures to implement Western models of capitalism and democracy on African leaders. When Africans experience the imposition of the ideology of Western models in our societies and in our lives, we need to acknowledge that we are being abused because our own cultural way of doing things is being neglected. We are becoming alienated within our own societies.

The socioeconomic development that is required by Western models calls for Western and African economists, scientists, engineers, doctors, lawyers, and psychologists whose knowledge is based on Western principles of moral and natural law. This law is the value system that forms the foundation of Western models. The Western value system is the "religion" of modern life around the globe. Its doctrine is defined and propagated not by Western professors of business and education on rational scientific grounds rather than the arbitrary cultural imposition of past colonial missionaries. Nevertheless, they shun the image of self-interested power brokers. Weber noted,

> Western Man's drive to master the natural world is an integral part of his quest for virtue in the eyes of God. Puritanism enabled Western Europeans to become a world power by transforming the "calculating" spirit of capitalism from a mere means to economy into a principle of general conduct for many nations. Western civilization is dependent on a "rationalized" economy in which decisions are made according to a weighing of usefulness and cost. This has given rise to the modern Rational-legal State regulated by an impartial legal system.[6]

One of the serious mistakes made by Western and Western-educated African intellectuals is that they are fully convinced that Western economic and political principles are universally applicable. They fail to realize that to be applicable, economic principles must be deeply rooted in the culture of the society in which they are implemented. Western models are a way that Western European religious, economic, and political principles penetrate and destroy African societies. Destruction of local African cultures occurs when conflict arises because people are required to adopt belief systems and customs that are foreign to their culture. World models create conflict in Africa by stimulating competition between individuals. This conflict weakens African communities because local belief systems begin are subject to questioning. African societies adopt Western models, which increases the rejection of traditional African norms and values. African nation-states become dependent on the West to guide and sustain them because their people have lost their identity. When they cut off the cultural ties to their roots, Africans become confused, distracted, and obsessed with the materialism of Western culture.

A homogenous global culture that encourages competition among individuals supports materialist consumption patterns and enhances the expansion of Western economic and political systems. Nevertheless, global cultural uniformity does *not* foster the establishment of a powerful global state as some would like to think. A well-organized worldwide authority might view the invention of new consumer goods as costly and the rights of its members to challenge its central authority as disorderly. The expansion of the sciences into everyday life might be seen as wasteful and even destabilizing. A strong centralized world government might even take steps to protect humans from the empty temptations of urban life. Westerners would view this as a violation of individual rights. Perhaps this is why countries such as the United States of America demand that the United Nations implement regional programs for which it refuses to pay, rendering it ineffective as well as bankrupt. Such is the case in a world culture in which competition comprises the meaning and purpose of human interaction and in which capitalism is the dominant economic system.

Economic and political systems cannot be separated from the culture of the society in which they originate and operate. Marx did not foresee the way capitalist world models would penetrate and destroy non-Western cultures to create a world of materialists because he did not realize how economic systems are deeply rooted in the cultural belief systems of societies. Communists attempt to eradicate local religions, but the modern belief system of science, which they substitute instead, encourages rather than discourages the idolatry of the individual that forms the basis of materialism. A strong, centralized world government will never emerge until the culture of materialism and the worship of the individual—the belief system underlying it—disappears. When we speak of Western models reaching every corner of Africa, what we really mean is the Western belief system, norms, values, and culture reaching into every corner of Africa.

As Western models spread their influence into African societies and cultures, both outsiders and members come to view local African traditions as artifacts of a "prerational" culture that should be stored in museums. Soon those who continue to practice ancient, valuable African traditions are seen as the sources of modern social problems. The perspective that local African variations of Western models are anomalies or deviations from an idealized norm also generates ideological conflict that fuels civil war in Africa. Even the strong activation of principles of self-determination and cultural autonomy by African intellectuals is not enough to interrupt this downward spiral into social chaos. The inevitable result is civil conflict that originates in the contradictions inherent in Western models. Either there is too much state regulation, which inhibits development, or too little state regulation, which permits inequality. Too much individual freedom encourages moral decadence whereas too little inflicts stifling censorship. Too much nationalism incites ethnic genocide whereas too little spreads indifference and apathy. Western experts who propose competing Western models fight over African nation-states. Economists view the efforts of sociologists to reduce inequality as threats to economic development. Sociologists view economists' efforts at stimulating economic growth as threats to community. Ecologists view the efforts of scientists and economists to support economic and technical development as threats to the natural base of the ecological system of the region. From all of this conflict comes the potential for the destruction of Africa with the resulting opportunity to divide its natural and human wealth among outsiders.

Marx stated,

> Conflict between racial and ethnic groups in capitalist societies is stimulated because it enables capitalists to "divide and conquer" workers. It provides someone below them to despise so they are distracted from the main enemy above them.[7]

Western models promoted by international organizations create conflict in Africa by imposing foreign ideology on African cultures. The type of conflict goes far deeper than civil war. This psychological conflict traumatizes African nations that attempt to adopt Western models. The materialism that Western models bring to Africa increases social problems rather than decreasing them wherever it is introduced because it does not address the psychological needs of Africans. Rather, the individualism that fostered by materialism brings Western social problems such as increased crime, violence, and drug abuse to Africa and compound existing economic problems. The individualism and materialism engendered by Western models initiate a destructive process of increasing disassociation among Africans and the weakening of traditional African community social structures. African leaders that adopt world models encourage the growth of a subculture of an elite that is different than the prevailing culture there. This nurtures a false myth that the dialog that is required to search for solutions to national problems can only take place between this elite and Western countries.

As recently as a century ago, Western European countries politically and economically dominated African colonies. They believed that Africans did not have souls or were a different species, so they could be enslaved and their lands exploited. African cultures were considered inferior and uncivilized. The justification of those who seek to spread Western models and Western values, culture, and economic and political systems is not just that Africans are primitive; it goes beyond this. The roots of Western models contain an impulse to paralyze and dismantle all cultures, belief systems, and economic systems that are *not* Western. Once another culture is identified and defined as different, there is no movement on the part of the West to learn from it or understand it. Westerners sustain their societies economically by reaping the wealth of regions far from their political borders. Their economic dominance encourages them to imagine that they are the leaders of the modern world. They think that they do not need to understand or learn from African cultures. Psychologically secure as the heroic figures in their myth of superiority, Westerners ignore African cultures and impose their own cultural perspective on African circumstances. Allowing themselves to be open to learning from African cultures would not only deflate their myth of superiority but also would require them to face the reality of their *responsibility* for current African problems. Without an identity as religious heroes, economic leaders and political "policemen" of the rest of the world, Westerners need to redefine themselves.

When the West is able to learn from African cultures, it will begin to be able to assist African nation-states to strengthen their own cultural foundations. Then genuine dialog regarding national, regional, and global problems will occur because real equality will have been established. When this has been accomplished, African and Western nation-states will no longer compete for Africa's natural and human resources. Instead, they will each take up positive roles as equal members of a diverse global community. A world community cannot come into being unless all of its members, including the West, are able to transform their own perspective into one that encompasses the principles of commitment to community mechanisms such as self-sacrifice. A willingness to engage in self-sacrifice prepares societies to undergo the self-evaluation that is required to become constructive members of a cooperative community. It facilitates the necessary psychological transformation from *I* to *we*. Weber stated,

> Capitalism involves the continual accumulation of wealth for its own sake rather than the material rewards it can bring. As a result, Man is now reduced to a creature that is dominated by acquisition as the ultimate purpose of his life.[8]

The transformation to which Marx referred ultimately depends on a

> . . . transformation of individual psychology so as to include feelings of solidarity, altruism and fairness. In the future, members of a global society will cease to regard participation in collective action as costly: it will become a benefit in itself, over and above the public good it is intended to produce.[9]

Education for a Sustainable African Society

> Be not dismayed, O peoples of the world, when the daystar of my beauty is set, and the heaven of my tabernacle is concealed from your eyes. Arise to further My Cause, and to exalt My Word amongst men. We are with you at all times. Whoso hath recognized Me will arise and serve Me with such determination that the powers of earth and heaven shall be unable to defeat his purpose.[10]

> Therefore, whosoever heareth these sayings of mine, and doeth them, I will liken him unto a wise man, who built his house upon a rock; and the rain descended, and the floods came, and the winds blew, and beat upon the house; and it fell not: for it was founded upon a rock. And every one that heareth these sayings of mine, and doeth them not, shall be likened unto a foolish man, who built his house upon the sand: and the rain descended, and the floods came, and the winds blew, and beat upon that house; and it fell: and great was the fall of it.[11]

Who is there that will offer to Allah a good gift so He will double it for him, and he shall have an excellent reward. On that day you will see the faithful man and the faithful women—their light running before them—good news for you today: gardens beneath which rivers flow, to abide therein, that is the grand achievement.[12]

Education for a sustainable African society is something that Africans need to think about deeply to develop with ideas so that we all can be part of its implementation. It is easy for one to say, "I'm going to import all the textbooks that are published and used in Western institutions, such as those in the United States, Great Britain, France, Germany or any other European country," but it is harder to think about whether those type of textbooks, teaching aids, and teachers' guides can be used in Africa. We should first ask, "What purpose will this serve? Will the information contained in those materials be applicable to the current situations in African nations?" I believe that if Africans truly desire to create and maintain education for a sustainable African society, we should look beyond our short-term role as consumer and become citizens of Africa and people who can utilize the things they have at hand in our own nations. By doing this, we will be able to maintain ourselves by utilizing more effectively what we produce in our own society. Then our children will feel more proud of us and be prepared to pass on the skills that we have taught them, from which they have gladly benefited, to future generations. To me, education for a sustainable African society means for us, as groups of African citizens of diverse communities, to brainstorm and then prioritize issues and to develop implementation plans in regard to those issues. In this way, each and every one of us will recognize that we are individually responsible for the results and effects of those ideas that all of us developed via a consensus process. In doing this, we will be proud when we realize that utilizing consensus is a method by which we can develop positive ideas that will enhance and enrich the institutions that we have in our own African society.

How long will Africans be willing to remain beggars? I believe that this will change if we take up our responsibility to become more accountable, to become more concerned, and to realize that we are human beings. As long as we are willing to remain beggars, we devalue our selves, our society, our nation, and our own people. This, I believe. I am completely convinced that this is a shame to all African nations. It is a shame to African intellectuals. It is a shame to have Africans who leave Africa and go to other countries because the only thing they dream about is importing things that they have seen in Western societies instead of developing ideas for how they can create those things in their own land. I believe that we have a long way to go to become self-sustainable individuals in our own society. We have a long way to go to become humans who can be accountable for what goes on in their own society. So often, we spend most of our time blaming, pointing fingers, gossiping, sitting around saying that someone has to do it. The question I ask myself and fellow Africans is, "Who is that somebody we are talking about all the time?" I believe that if we take a minute to think about how we always point our fingers at somebody, we will see that it is our own fingers that we use to do this. If we point our fingers, chances are that someone will likewise be pointing at us. What does it mean when we point our fingers at each other? It means we are each saying, "I am not responsible." If we are not responsible, who else will be responsible for the problems of our society?

Yes, we often say that we have conflict, bad government, that our teachers are not well educated, and we appear to have no resources and materials at this time. No one will ever create those things for us. We have to do it ourselves. I have begun to ask this question: "How long will Africans be willing remain to be like this?" I am deeply concerned. I am concerned that we tend to forget all the things that our ancestors have done for us. They were neither depending on anyone to serve nor help him or her. They were depending on their own skills, their land, their resources and the intelligence that God gave them. Why are we no longer making good use of these gifts, as they have? I ask myself this question. I ask every African I meet this question. We must all ask ourselves this question because it is only when we begin to challenge ourselves that we can realize that we actually do have skills, intelligence, and knowledge. As Africans we can use all of these things we have to work together because no one else will do it for us.

Let us not fool ourselves. Let us not become helpless people. Let us utilize that which God has created in us and that which our ancestors left us. Let us utilize that which our land provides us, which Nature has given us. These are our current available resources. These are what I refer to when I say, "We should use what we have to create education for a sustainable African society." We can do this only if Africans and Africans who are outside of Africa come together and put our agendas on one common table. Both men and women have much to give to each other and much to learn from each other. We cannot succeed without accepting that we can learn from both females and males in our society. Each gender has skills, knowledge, and experience that they can share with the other in order to help sustain Africa and develop African nations.

If we fail to do this, we will face problems that we will not be able to handle. What will be left except for us to run away from our own society? When we do that, we lose our sense of responsibility and our sense of self-esteem. When we do that, we become empty human beings, regardless of society in which we live. As we become empty, our society becomes weak and vulnerable so that it might be blown by any wind that comes from any direction. This will happen if we no longer have any connection to our roots to keep us strong. We will have no roots to help germinate a strong, healthy new generation. Our society is sinking down into chaos, and eventually it may disappear completely. How could our society possibly disappear? This will happen because we do not allow room for improvement. We have created only a small niche for our society that is as tiny as the eye of a needle. We are in the darkness and can no longer see light. Because we are fighting each other in this darkness, we feel that we have no way to move forward or backward, left or right, so we stay where we are and become paralyzed.

This impenetrable and paralyzing darkness is caused by the emptiness inside us, which reflects the emptiness at the center of our society. This emptiness within our society is shameful; it is an insult to ourselves and to every human being in Africa.

Yes, everyone wants to go to America, England, France, Germany, Denmark, Sweden, and the other Western countries, but why? Do we think that all the things that Europeans have in their society just appeared there one day? No, that is not true. Do we think that only one person came up with ideas and created all those material things for which we all cry in Africa? No, it was not one person. Different people with different, conflicting ideas struggled through disagreements because they believed in the hope of a more positive day for their own nations. Their attitude was, "Regardless of our disagreements, there is much of a positive nature that we can give to each other. We all can learn from each other. We can all contribute so that our nation can become one of the best." This was their dream for their society. What is our dream for our society, as Africans? Is it non-existence? Do we not dream? Yes, we dream, but what we lack is accountability. Most important, we lack the willingness to be proactive in our own communities. This is what we are missing. Being proactive means we do not just say, "I'd love to have this" or "I will do this," but you have to motivating oneself to work on creating, with the resources at hand, that which one dreams about and cries for and that one believes will benefit society. We need to do this. We do not get it by sitting down and saying, "I have to have all these things right now." They do not come in one day. They will not drop from the sky. God will not grant them you overnight. We have brains to think of ideas. God has given us all that we need. We must be willing to use what we in a more positive way to benefit society.

Yes, we can do it. I am afraid, however, that we are more interested in talking about them than in performing the actions that are actually needed. When will we be willing to perform the necessary action? Why do we have to wait for our neighbors to take action? The longer we wait, the longer we will be oppressed. As long as we are oppressed, what do we have to show for it beside more oppression? We have to turn around and look at ourselves and stop killing each other. We think that by killing each other we can get rid of what is oppressing us. Why do we continue to think that when it is clear that the more we kill each other, the more oppressed we become? Those who encourage us to believe that some of us are oppressing the rest of us are those outside of Africa. It is time to ask ourselves what purpose it serves outsiders for Africans to see each one another as oppressors. Viewing one another as oppressors creates conflict that wastes Africans' time, energy, and valuable resources. The longer that we believe that it is other Africans that are oppressing us, the more wars and civil unrest weaken us. As we continue to weaken, we become more dependent on outsiders. As long as we are dependent on them, as long as we do not have education for a sustainable African society, outsiders can do with us as they like, and we will not even be able to see our culture and valuable human and natural resources draining away.

My question is, "If Africans who are outside Africa actually have better ideas than those who are in power in Africa, why don't we bring those ideas back to the discussion table in Africa?" We must put everything, all of our ideas, on the table and see what will benefit our whole society. We need to view these ideas as not just our own or those of one political party or as ideas that originate with those who have higher education. We need to look at all of these ideas to see how they can be applied in a way that will be beneficial to Africa from one generation to the next. We need to find ways to implement ideas so that the next generation will easily be able to modify and modernize what we establish and build today. This is what I call education for a sustainable African society. To me, this means transforming Africa so that our society is more accountable for itself. If educational systems fail to do this, they fail to accomplish their purpose in *any* society. This is what Africans must realize. Yes, indeed, we can look at each other and say, "Who is going to do this?" I say, "You and I have to do it." I declare that twenty-first century as the time for self-reflection and proactive behavior by Africans in thinking about education for a sustainable African society. United we stand, divided we fall.

Leadership and Organizational Culture for Twenty-first Century Africa

African leaders who want to use the principles of organizational culture to improve the productivity of their countries must first know how to recognize visual, oral, and behavioral cultural forms and their functions. This chapter identifies these cultural forms and explains them with an emphasis on African leadership's intimate relationship with cultural forms within organizations. I include an exploration of how different thinkers define the task of leadership will be included and an exploration of ten dimensions of organizational culture that African leaders can influence. This is followed by an investigation into different types of rites. Next, I discuss the interactional style of an effective African leader and directly tie its effect on organizational culture in Africa to each aspect of leadership behavior. I further describe African leadership's role in creating the kind of organizational culture change that is needed to produce change in Africa. We will take an in-depth look at several transformative African leaders. I provide as examples for modern African leaders to follow the methods they used to draw out the best in their people. An African leader's consistent behavior, based upon unfailing vision, can mold organizational culture in that country and thus nurture a high level of creativity and productivity in the people.

Defining Organizational Culture

Beyer defined organizational culture as a concept that is both created and maintained by human social interaction, through which people develop shared understandings about how to cope with, manage, and avoid life's dangers."[13]

Human beings are social animals. The advent of human culture was an evolutionary leap that initiated the use of culture as a social tool by humans and ensured the survival of their species over time. Culture creates a secure social environment in which human interaction can occur. People understand the meaning of the behavior of others because they share understandings about the nature of their purpose in the universe. The safe environment that is provided by human culture enables civilizations to develop. Cultural artifacts are the outward manifestations of the strong emotions humans feel in response to events that happen to them. People create images, songs, stories, and rituals to express their inner climate during significant times in their lives. These artifacts serve to evoke in others and reinforce those emotions, creating an emotional climate that people can share as a group. Culture allows for the sharing of emotions and meanings and creates a way of life in which human beings can live together in peace. Culture provides all people with reasons that they can understand for why things happen and their roles to play. Culture is a tool that people can use to understand how their society, community, or organization operates and to know how they should behave within it. It guides them in the implementation of their activities in the social groups, such as organizations, of which they are members. Culture enables humans to develop civilizations and technology by supporting and maintaining shared meanings and thus empowering collective action on a scale unheard of in any other species of living being. Culture creates an ordered, stable social space in which learning and the pursuit of knowledge flourishes, and thus creates opportunities for humans to expand their creativity. Once people are socialized into a culture, they inevitably take steps to participate in its rites as a full member and thus express their "ownership" of a particular culture.

> Over time, these understandings become invested with strong emotions. Culture provides rationales that connect behavior to outcomes. People need a secure sense that they understand how the world works in order to behave confidently and consistently. Cultures motivate people to behave in socially accepted ways and exert effort toward collectively defined ends. People seek out and create opportunities to communicate and affirm their shared understandings with each other through cultural forms such as myths, symbols, and rites.[14]

Organizational culture can provide African leaders the means by which their national vision can be known by their people so that they will be willing to buy into it. To be effective, African leaders must play a key role in the creation and maintenance of organizational culture in their countries by creating and influencing legends, rituals, and celebrations as well as visual images that represent their vision for their nation. Leaders can institutionalize their vision by facilitating the growth of traditions based on legends, rituals, and celebrations. As their people are socialized to this organizational culture, a sense of belonging stimulates them to pass on these traditions to their children, thus providing them with an identity within this organizational culture.

Cultural forms are the visible expressions and chief means of communicating the vision of a leader. Through stories, myths, rites, reward systems, language, and symbols, cultural meanings are communicated, celebrated and affirmed. Closely related to the use of cultural forms are traditions. Cultural continuity requires that members remember and pass on to new members the ideologies to which they subscribe.[15]

Schein believed,

Organizational cultures spring from three sources: beliefs, values and assumptions; learning experiences as the organization evolves; and new beliefs, values, and assumptions brought in by new members and leaders.[16]

When people are initially brought into a founding group, a common history begins develop. A common history provides a shared perspective regarding the purpose of the group and its role in its environment. As this larger group shares learning experiences, it gradually develops assumptions about itself. African organizational culture can provide the social coherence that will allow Africans to learn from their mistakes as a group and that will stimulate the innovation they need to discover adaptive strategies for dealing with change.

Organizations create culture; to be renewed and re-structured, they alter it. The resulting organizational culture is a set of coping skills, adaptive strategies used by members. Organizational culture represents understandings and practices regarding the nature of reality. Organizational culture is manifested in values, attitudes, beliefs, myths, rituals, performance, and artifacts.[17]

Kolb, Rubin, and Osland stated,

The signs of an organization's culture can be found in its visible artifacts—the constructed environment of the organization, its architecture, technology, manner of dress, visible and audible behavior patterns, and public documents such as charters.[18]

African leaders send a clear message to their people and to those outside Africa by choosing to play a significant role in decision-making involving the visual artifacts of their country's organizational culture. African leaders can use these visual artifacts to send a message that creates an emotional climate that reinforces the norms and values to which they want their people to conform. In this way, by actively molding their country's organizational culture, African leaders can choose that values that they wish to be encoded in the behavioral norms of their people. It is important for African leaders to go beyond the tangible cultural artifacts of their country's current organizational culture to seek the underlying assumptions that actually determine how their people perceive, think, and feel. The interrelated, underlying assumptions held by the people form a coherent cognitive pattern that can be understood as a cultural paradigm. By involving African people in cultural forms such as rituals and celebrations, African leaders can socialize Africans to their values. Thus, their people's underlying assumptions about themselves, their nation, and its role in African society become a cultural paradigm that can motivate Africans to act collectively to bring their leader's vision into reality.

> The unique and essential function of leadership is the manipulation of culture. Leaders must become aware that their actions both do and say things. The essential role of leaders is to influence the understandings and networks of meaning that members hold and express through their actions.[19]

African leaders who desire the self-actualization of their people, can shape their country's organizational culture so that it incarnates values that nurture personal growth. African leaders can play a significant role in promoting innovation by encouraging, supporting, and maintaining cultural paradigms. Senge stated, "Leadership is intertwined with culture formation. Building an organization's culture and shaping its evolution is the unique and essential function of leadership."[20]

> Innovation occurs when new sets of shared beliefs, values, and norms emerge within a social group. New ideologies can arise through the influence of leaders who communicate new ideas or more indirectly when leaders use cultural forms (rituals/traditions) or their behaviors (modeling/rewarding) to carry new cultural messages to members of a group.[21]

African Leadership's Role in Organizational Culture

Weber stated,

> It is the task of leaders to bring forth rationales that reduce people's uncertainties, make them understandable and convincing, and to communicate them widely and repeatedly so that people come to share the same understandings.[22]

African leaders can help Africans understand their rationale by promoting a belief system of justification so that their people will feel comfortable taking action and performing behaviors that African leaders believe will improve their countries. African leaders must first show by their example how Africans can put this rationale into positive action, and then they use a reward system to reinforce continuously people who respond appropriately. Weber believed that leadership involves not only leaders who originate new cultures or change existing ones, but also leaders who maintain culture, that is, carry forward previous leaders' cultural innovations. Weber believed the task of leadership is to influence the rationales and understandings that are embedded in a culture. African leaders can embed rationales in their country's organizational culture by communicating them widely and by continuously presenting the rationale to their people via visual and auditory cultural artifacts. An African leader's personal example and the incentives that they give to Africans who follow them can be strong motivators. Weber believed that "Leaders inculcate people with emotionally charged ideas."[23] African leaders must observe their people and actively solicit uncensored feedback from them to gain a clear picture of their value system. African leaders will not be able to obtain their people's commitment to the tasks that are required to attain their vision unless they can shape and then present their rationales in emotionally meaningful forms that sufficiently incorporate the personal value system of individuals in their country. If African leaders want their rationales to become thoroughly embedded in the organizational cultures of their countries, they must make sure that they are reflected in new or modified rituals that are performed by their people. In Beyer's view, the three most important tasks of leadership are

> . . . the creation of organizational structures and procedures needed to carry forward a vision of the future, the transference of this vision to people by means of rites and symbols and the incorporation of this vision into the written and oral tradition of the organization by means of myth.[24]

According to Jay Conger, our recent day and age has brought leaders forward that can be considered "strategic visionaries."[25] I believe that African leaders of today need to be strategic visionaries but also, to be successful, they must involve themselves in an ongoing self-assessment process. The right type of self-assessment process should help African leaders separate their vision into short-term and long-term goals for their country that then can be used to compare with their personal goals for their own lives and with the feedback that they receive regarding the needs of their people. The biggest problem facing African leaders may not be getting Africans to believe in and work for their visions but in motivating themselves to build and maintain a feedback mechanism that can provide them with accurate, up-to-date information about their people. Unsuccessful African leaders are African leaders who became blinded by their own visions. African leaders must not allow their visions to become rigid. A useful vision is one that can respond to the changing needs of Africans. Conger stated, "Leaders, like everyone else, try to avoid cognitive dissonance."[26] African leaders must commit themselves to incorporating into their vision feedback from ordinary African people. Successful African leaders view unbiased feedback sources as essential tools that provide valuable opportunities for innovation. African leaders should consider feedback that causes "cognitive dissonance" to be a challenge that can help them develop the new skills that they will need to lead successful adaptation to change.

> Unsuccessful visions can often be traced to the inclusion of the leader's personal aims that did not match their people's needs. The success of a leader's vision depends on a realistic assessment of the opportunities and the constraints in the environment and a sensitivity to people's needs. Failure occurs when the vision becomes so much a part of the leader's personality that he or she is unwilling or unable to consider information to the contrary. All individuals act to keep the commitments they have made because failing to do so would damage their favorable perceptions of themselves. The leader's vision becomes a vehicle for his or her own needs for attention. When this has occurred,

decision-making becomes distorted, and an objective review of possible alternatives to a problem are precluded.[27]

When African leaders are successful at influencing their country's organizational culture, a very cohesive and highly committed nation will be created. African leaders must work with their people to show them how to give and receive positive and negative feedback. Africans can be taught to utilize negative feedback to create opportunities to improve their performance and thereby improve the productivity of their nation as a whole. By establishing the feedback process as a tradition, African leaders can transform a national evaluation process into a common ritual, thereby ensuring its continued practice even when they are not present. This will encourage Africans to focus on becoming innovative and adapting to change. Once this tradition becomes part of the organizational culture of African countries, Africans will feel comfortable enough to share their ideas and feelings that they previously might have kept hidden. African leaders who desire to building a strong team culture in their countries must work to build and maintain a strong, extensive network of informal and formal communication channels between members of different organizations in their countries. This type of network will nurture innovation through cross-collaboration and coalition-building. African leaders who use self-evaluation to keep their personal needs from biasing their decision-making process show their people how to utilize positive and negative feedback to create opportunities to develop innovations. They stimulate the growth of cross-cultural networks with people and other African nations. In doing this, they nurture leadership skills in all Africans.

> Some leaders create an "us versus them" attitude. Although this heightens the motivation of a group, it further alienates other groups that may be important for resources or political support. This kind of leader finds it difficult to develop others to be leaders of equal power. They enjoy the limelight too much to share it, so when they depart, a leadership vacuum is created.[28]

Drucker (1988) stated,

> True leadership has little to do with "leadership qualities" and even less to do with "charisma." Charisma becomes the undoing of leaders. It makes them inflexible, convinced of their own infallibility, unable to change.[29]

I believe that it is good for African leaders to be charismatic provided that they are able to empower Africans to develop skills that will enable them to adapt easily to change.

African leadership is about coping with change. Leading constructive change in Africa requires setting a direction and developing a vision for Africa and strategies for producing the changes needed to achieve that vision. African leaders need to communicate a new direction for Africa to Africans so that they can create coalitions and so that they will understand the vision and be committed to its achievement. Achieving this vision requires African leadership, which motivates and inspires—keeps Africans moving in the right direction, despite major obstacles to change—by appealing to basic human needs, values, and emotions. African leaders can design and use artifacts and rituals of their country's organizational culture to evoke Africans' emotional responses and echo Africans' values and to communicate their vision, motivating Africans to commit their efforts to its accomplishment.

Kotter stated, "What's crucial about a vision is not its originality but how well it serves the interests of important constituencies."[30] An African leader's ability to design a vision that serves the needs, interests, and values of Africans depends on how thoroughly they investigate and react to feedback. Whether African leaders utilize this feedback depends on how well they focus on the needs, interests, and values of their people, in relation to their vision, and how well they permanently set aside their personal need for fame and attention. Kotter stated, "Good leaders motivate people in a variety of ways."[31] Before African leaders can expect anyone to follow them, they must prove to Africans that they actually believe in their vision by their example and by consistently living up to it in all of their decision-making processes. The positive example of African leaders will motivate and empower Africans to implement their vision by providing Africans with a model to follow. In the process of collecting feedback from Africans, African leaders show their people that their input is needed and important. Representatives from each organization in African countries will then be willing to participate in focus groups whose main activity will be problem-finding. A representative from each focus group can be recruited to meet with African leadership to design the organizational structures that are needed to accomplish change. In this way, Africans will be effectively included in decision-making processes in Africa.

By doing this, African leaders can help Africans feel a sense of ownership for their continent. Africans will feel that their skills and contributions are valued and seriously considered. By encouraging all Africans to feel this way, African leaders can stimulate them to be more innovative and productive. African leaders should take time to celebrate their people's contributions and accomplishments both individually and as a nation. As these celebrations become traditions embedded in the organizational culture of African countries, a continuous process of reward will prompt Africans' commitment to the tasks required to implement a vision of a new Africa. By making sure that Africans participate in important decision-making processes and by establishing a reward system that continuously responds to Africans' positive efforts, African leaders will help all Africans feel that they are part of one African family.

First, they always articulate the organization's vision in a manner that stresses the values of the audience they are addressing. Leaders regularly involve people in deciding how to achieve the organization's vision (or the part most relevant to a particular individual). This gives people a sense of control. Another important motivational technique is to support people's efforts to realize the vision by providing coaching, feedback, and role modeling, thereby helping people to grow professionally and enhancing their self-esteem. Finally, good leaders recognize and reward success, which not only gives people a sense of accomplishment but also makes them feel like they belong to an organization that cares about them. When all this is done, the work itself becomes intrinsically motivating.[32]

Leaders induce their followers to act in numerous ways, such as modeling, goal-setting, rewarding, team-building and communicating a vision. A leader motivates people by convincing them that the organizational vision is important and attainable; challenging people with goals, tasks, and responsibilities that allow them to feel a sense of personal success, achievement, and accomplishment; and rewarding people who perform well.[33]

African Leadership's Use of Organizational Culture

African leadership practices, norms and standards, rules and regulations, attitudes and principles, ethics and values, policies and practices, structures and technologies, artifacts and services, roles and relationships influence organizational culture. To influence these cultural factors, African leaders can establish cultural mandates or traditions concerning dress codes, work hours, work facilities, communications procedures and rewards. Drucker stated, "Leadership strategies are not mechanical; they are above all cultural."[34] There are ten dimensions in which African leaders can influence the organizational culture of their countries.

(1) Rationale—clarification of goals,
(2) Environment—modification of physical and psychological environments,
(3) Philosophy—attitudes, beliefs and myths,
(4) Priorities—values and norms,
(5) Media—communications,
(6) Operational Mode—organizational processes,
(7) Rewards—behavior reinforcement,
(8) Traditions—rites and rituals,
(9) Roles—organizational relationships,
(10) Appearance—style.[35]

African leaders must set an example for Africans by not only designating a dress code that visually communicates national values and vision, but also by consistently following this dress code themselves. Also, African leaders must adhere to the same work hours and afford themselves the same kind of workspace as ordinary people in their countries. African leaders can design work schedules and work-spaces to reflect the needs, interests, and values of Africans. African leaders must be sure that interorganizational communication systems in their country are congruent with the values that they want to embed in the organizational culture of their nation. African leaders can help Africans clarify organizational roles and relationships to facilitate collaborative work and to reduce conflict in their countries. In this way, African leaders can ensure that the quality of ongoing relationships between people in their country reflects the values and vision that they wish to communicate to their people. By doing this, African leaders can encourage Africans—in actions, behavior and relationships—to practice what they preach.

African leaders can use different cultural rites to maintain their country's organizational culture. African leaders can ensure that African young people are socialized to their country's organizational culture by maintaining traditional African rites of integration, such as initiation, which include rituals that teach the significance and meaning of cultural forms such as myths, songs, and visual symbols of their country's organizational values and vision. African leaders can use rites of renewal, such as feasts and ceremonies, to help Africans to evaluate the existing organizational culture of their countries and shape it to more closely match their values and vision for their country. African leaders can conduct rites of enhancement, such as personal endorsement, to engender their people's support for new ideas and behavior that are required for change. African leaders can support rites of passage, such as marriage, to help Africans see that they are responsible for contributing fully to the accomplishment of national goals. African leadership's task is to use cultural rites to maintain social equilibrium while stimulating Africans to be innovative and adaptive to change.

> Rites of integration are used to bind new members to the organization. Rites of renewal refurbish social structures and improve their functioning. Rites of renewal and rites of conflict reduction maintain cultures. Rites of conflict reduction dissipate discontents simply by airing them. Rites of conflict reduction reconcile diverse interests. Rites of enhancement assist innovation by enhancing changed behaviors. Rites of passage facilitate transitions to new roles, ensuring social equilibrium. In this way, people feel part of the decision-making apparatus.[36]

Drucker stated, "A leader's actions and a leader's professed beliefs must be congruent. Effective leadership is primarily based on being consistent."[37] Being systematic in paying attention to certain things is a powerful way for African leaders to communicate a message to Africans to create a certain "climate" in their countries. Consistency in the questions that African leaders ask their people can send them clear signals about their leader's priorities, values, and beliefs. Schein stated, "In questioning people systematically on certain issues, leaders can transmit their own view of how to look at problems."[38] By asking Africans pointed questions, African leaders can challenge unspoken taboos and ineffective traditions in their country's organizational culture. As a result, Africans will begin thinking about how their behavior affects national outcomes and will take time to focus on their leader's vision. African leaders can send an even more powerful signal with their emotional reactions. Another signal African leaders can use to express their values to their people is the things to which they *do not* react. Schein noted, "When an organization faces a crisis, the manner in which leaders deal with it creates new norms, values and operating procedures and reveals important underlying assumptions."[39] When Africans leaders do not react either negatively or positively to certain national issues, their lack of reaction sends a clear message to Africans that these issues are not priorities for the accomplishment of their vision. African leaders need not fear crisis because crisis can be an opportunity for them to bring Africans together, not just to make them feel more secure but also to examine critical issues and obtain commitment for needed changes in Africa. Crisis in Africa is a time when African leaders can help Africans see how interdependent they actually are and to overcome the crisis they must work together by respecting and valuing the contributions each African can make. African leaders should view crisis in Africa as a window of opportunity in which, because of the heightened emotions and anxiety created by crisis, Africans will be especially receptive and sensitive to their leader's use of cultural forms such as rituals. During times of crisis *and* during periods of relative stability, the primary task of leadership in Africa is to focus creative energy on finding ways to "ritualize" behaviors that are consistent with positive values.

> Crises are significant in culture creation and transmission because heightened emotional involvement increases the intensity of learning. Crises heighten anxiety, and anxiety reduction is a powerful motivator. Leaders can quickly get across their own priorities, values and assumptions by consistently linking rewards and punishments to behavior. People seek stability and anxiety reduction so leaders can reinforce their assumptions by building systems and routines around them. Procedures can formalize the process of "paying attention" and reinforce a leader's message. Ritualizing behaviors is a powerful reinforcer. [40]

Schein noted, "Leaders can manipulate what they pay attention to and reward; their role modeling; how they allocate resources and promote people; and the organizational structures and procedures they create."[41] As an African nation develops and accumulates a history, some of this history becomes embodied in the form of a legend. Its purpose is to reinforce cultural assumptions and teach them to young people. Changing embedded assumptions requires using cultural forms such as rites. African leaders should view a crisis as a time when they can provide their people with three things that stimulate motivation for change.

> (1) Data (antithesis) that nationals' goals are not being met,
> (2) Anxiety and/or guilt regarding this data and important goals and ideals,
> (3) A sense that their nation can solve problems indicated by this data. [42]

African leaders must be willing not only to face problems, but also to model for their people positive ways to use information that goals are not being met and a positive response to crisis. African leaders can show their people that problems must be addressed by their expression of emotion during this time. African leaders must communicate to Africans that they *personally* feel responsible and accountable. Schein stated, "Change typically begin with a perceived crisis strong enough to 'unfreeze' people's traditional views of reality."[43]

Bartunek stated,

> Change is interpreted dialectically by people, with original rationale and assumptions as *thesis*, new ways of understanding reality as *antithesis*, and what emerges from the interaction of these two perspectives as *synthesis*. This pro-

cess is analogous to the development of cognitively complex understanding in individuals: learning.[44]

Because this process is dialectical, African leaders need to recognize that it involves conflict between Africans. The important thing for African leaders to remember is that reaching synthesis depends on providing a forum in which all Africans can be heard. To facilitate fundamental organizational culture change, African leaders need to help their nation's organizational structure become more decentralized so as to allow more participation in decision-making because synthesis is more likely to be shared by Africans who have participated in its development. African leaders can modify organizational structures in their countries to allow their people to participate in national decision-making by creating focus groups and task forces. By creating a forum in which Africans can share ideas, skills, and feelings, African leaders can facilitate the birth of synthesis or learning. African leaders need to remember that their country's organizational structure should legitimize action by individual Africans, not just constrain it. African leaders can use organizational structures in their countries to enable the expression of particular rationales. By providing a forum in which different perspectives can be heard (thesis and antithesis), African leaders legitimize these perspectives and action by individual Africans based on them. When they provide a forum in which all perspectives receive equal consideration, Africans leaders legitimize the cooperation upon which synthesis is built in their countries.

Bartunek stated, "Change has a strong affective component."[45] When change occurs, an old rationale has to be "unlearned" so a new one can come into existence.

Schein noted, "Change is often experienced as a series of deaths and rebirths."[46] African leaders need to realize that change is painful and threatening to Africans. Africans need to grieve when they have lost something that was part of their life with which they identified. It is the responsibility of African leaders to help Africans fill the emptiness they feel. Mintzberg stated, "Direct, informal communication and relatively easy contact between members and authority figures can serve this purpose."[47] African leaders can involve Africans in informal discussions that give them an opportunity to vent their feelings about the past and what has recently happened. Once Africans have had an opportunity to do this, and then African leaders will be able to begin to work with Africans to bring about the birth of a new paradigm for Africa. Having a chance to express their feelings will enable Africans to release positive energy that African leaders can direct toward the design of a new vision of Africa.

Bartunek stated, "Leaders shape the course of change by legitimizing the expression of particular perspectives because they have primary influence over which rationales are expressed."[48]

Schein noted, "A leader's vision provides the psychological safety that allows the group to move forward."[49] African leaders must realize that merely talking about needed changes is not enough to motivate Africans to cooperate. African leaders can prepare Africans for change by helping to create situations in which they cannot escape from the anxiety that comes from facing significantly negative information. African leaders can conduct rites in which Africans are encouraged to evaluate their recent performance, individually and as group, and compare it with the current needs of their nations. African leaders can conduct rituals in which Africans accept responsibility for making changes that will be required to transform their countries into one that is congruent with a new set of values and vision.

> New visions are most important when people are ready to pay attention when they are hurting because of disconfirming data. Since organizational culture is a learned defense mechanism that helps people to avoid anxiety, leaders can role model how people can assess their organizational culture and assist in the modification of assumptions. Leaders can model the type of self-insight needed for cognitive redefinition to occur.[50]

African leaders can encourage Africans to redefine their country's organizational culture collectively. Schein stated, "Redefinition involves either changing some of the priorities within the core set of assumptions or abandoning an assumption that is a barrier to needed change."[51] African leaders will find that facilitating cultural insight allows Africans to decide the direction of Africa's future. Once a decision is made to initiate a change, African leaders will need to create new learning systems in which new assumptions are learned and tested. African leaders can help Africans redefine their country's organizational culture and values by setting up new learning systems that provide Africans an opportunity to develop and practice skills that they will need to implement proposed changes. African leaders can utilize Africans who have successfully been socialized to a new paradigm to teach other Africans the new vision.

> It is too painful to give up a shared assumption in favor of an unknown substitute. If some part of the group can learn an alternative way to think and if that alternative can be shown to work, then there is less anxiety as the alternative is gradually introduced.[52]

Transformative African Leadership

African leaders need to create organizational cultures that encourage individual initiative and self-governance. They need to give Africans the freedom to shape their own future and to organize as a team. Africa needs transformative leaders who empower Africans by their commitment to their people's self-actualization. All Africans should be able to choose their own fields of work and find something that no one had ever considered before. African leaders need to encourage Africans to be responsible for the decisions and actions they take. If Africans are told what to do, they will not feel accountable. They will not feel emotionally connected with the consequences of their actions and thus will not learn from them. African leaders should not try to prevent mistakes. "It is not leadership's responsibility to prevent errors but to encourage experimentation and coach people later in analyzing how they could improve."[53]

African leaders can model for their people how they should evaluate the consequences of their actions and learn from them. They can encourage an awareness of the need to develop new solutions to problems that Africans see around them. By doing this, African leaders can challenge their people to become innovative. By being consistent in their actions, as well as their professed values, African leaders can create an organizational culture in their countries that allows Africans to learn and adapt to change.

Kenneth Kaunda, Great Leader

Kenneth Kaunda started life with several strikes against him. Because his father was a Christian missionary, he was in the religious minority. There was almost nothing from his father's income that his family could live on. His family depended on food from their garden and their flock of chickens. His father maintained strong ties with European Christian Missionaries in the area. Kaunda's background prepared him for his future. His faith gave him an optimistic outlook that carried him through exile and imprisonment; he sang hymns to motivate him. As an organizer, his own family lived as simply as he had as a boy with a garden and poultry. He had to struggle to see others as adversaries who might want to crush him only because of the color of his skin because he had grown up in a family that had friends of different colors. To compound his disadvantage, Kaunda lived in a British Colony, Northern Rhodesia, where a Black African such as himself had no freedom, whose lifestyle and economic and political aspirations were stunted by widespread discrimination and oppression that were condoned by a government that offered him no representation.

Moved by a desire to help his neighbors, he developed self-help groups that evolved into a political organization. On a daily basis, he willingly faced the threat of imprisonment, slander, and assassination. He traveled long distances by bicycle, alone, constantly in danger of being attacked by wild animals. After frightening off a lion by shaking his bicycle over his head, he sped on. Authorities reacted by exiling Kaunda and his family far from their home in a tiny house with their friends. When that did not succeed in silencing him, Kaunda was imprisoned. During this time, he cleaned the prison, waited for a chance to see a tree, and communed with the birds that brought hope to him. He struggled to maintain ties of communication with his supporters and endured long absences from his family. As his political organization grew, he found it hard to control the reactions of his followers and even himself to malicious efforts on the part of the colonial government to destroy their attempts to acquire dignity, equality, and the right to vote. Once he found himself on the verge of attacking an official who had insulted him.

> I remember saying: if, because of our policy, you are lifted in the air and thrown to the ground, say "Kill me, but I shall be free." I was determined to combine Gandhi's policy of nonviolence with Nkrumah's positive action. Vil-

lagers had been told that these Zambian men were cannibals. They especially liked children since these provided tender meat. Anyone who would go to this extent to telling lies in order to maintain his position I think calls for mental treatment, but this is imperialism at work.[54]

When Kaunda's friend, who had worked side by side with him during many struggles, strayed from the principles upon which their organization had been founded, Kaunda chose to leave, which meant trying to regain his people's trust and loyalty. Denied official permission to publish a newspaper, he created one using his tiny home as an office. After traveling miles to meet with the British government, his willingness to negotiate was met by treachery and a lack of respect for his ideas solely because he was a Black man.

Kaunda's Leadership Qualities and Skills

Kaunda exhibited the qualities and skills of a great leader in that he set a good example without meaning to. His faith gave him dedication; he was willing to take up responsibility to solve problems, no matter how complex or seemingly hopeless because he was possessed by a vision of Zambia with freedom for both Africans and immigrants. Kaunda was able to mobilize people by getting them to focus on the positive rather than by putting blame on anyone. He encouraged the skills of others to lead and chose to communicate in a simple, truthful manner with both humble countrymen and supporters from the most educated circles. He challenged both his followers and the status quo in a positive rather than hostile manner.

> One critical role of effective leaders is to be skillful craftsmen of their organization's mission . . . of equal importance is the ability to communicate their missions in ways that generate great intrinsic appeal.[55]

Kaunda had a vision of a positive future for his country and a concrete plan of how to reach it. He set a good example by always being absolutely honest and gladly sacrificing personal comfort and risking his life. Kaunda has been consistent in what he says and does; regardless of the situation or the stakes, he never hesitated to follow his principles. "To be persuasive we must be believable; to be believable we must be credible; to be credible, we must be truthful."[56]

"Leaders hold in their minds visions and ideals of what can be. They have a sense of what is uniquely possible if all work together."

By appreciating others' skills, Kaunda encouraged them to take the initiative. His ability to simplify complex problems allowed him to educate by using a communication style that could be understood by all. "Effective framing of an organizational mission will ensure emotional impact particularly in terms of building a sense of confidence and excitement about the future."[57]

Kaunda used negative experiences to build strength by reflecting on them. A good listener, he respected each of his followers, opponents, and enemies. He viewed all humans as inherently good, including those who were involved in evil. Kaunda maintained deep faith in his religion and lived by his African cultural values. It is necessary for African leaders to have a vision of their organization in the future. They must successfully communicate the mission, goals, and objectives of their nation in simple, consistent terms to all of their people. Setting a good example of sacrifice inspires Africans to believe that their leaders live up to the standards to which they are held. This builds trust and creates the organizational strength needed for a foundation to build upon. "Our own self-leadership behaviors serve as a model from which others can learn."

As Max DePree, chairman of Herman Miller, the office furniture maker, stated, "It's not what you preach, but how you behave."[58]

In contrast, the lack of a good example causes Africans to be reluctant to buy into a leader's ideas with the result that their nation will be less productive. By working at the grassroots level and personally taking responsibility for problems, African leaders can empower their people. Encouraging and appreciating their problem-solving skills can help bolster Africans' self-esteem. They will feel confident about taking action. Feeling a sense of ownership of their country and a desire to contribute to its well-being, they will see themselves as members of a family. This builds a strong team that is able to work toward a common goal. Accepting responsibility for crisis is useful to African leaders in finding ways to improve their countries.

Drucker suggested that the most effective leaders are those not afraid of developing strength in their subordinates.

> The most appropriate leader is one who can lead others to lead themselves . . . .
> A leader serves as a source of information and experience, as a sounding board, and as the transmitter of overall organizational goals. For a leader, the essence of the challenge is to lead followers to discover the potentialities that lie within themselves.[59]

By learning about Kenneth Kaunda, African leaders can develop a clear idea about the skills and qualities of a great leader. As a leader, one must possess a vision and be prepared to sacrifice to accomplish it. True leadership requires patience and a willingness to start from the place of one's followers to empower them to use their skills in a positive way. An African leader must be willing to face obstacles and take risks. It is essential that leaders be consistent and careful to practice what they preach. I believe that as their nations develop they may find it difficult to control their people, and for that reason they must always have in mind a strategy. Negative experiences should not be seen as losses but rather as opportunities for change, growth, and learning. Incorporating them can expand an African leader's scope and bring flexibility and strength. If one desires to be a truly great leader, one must strive to trust in the abilities of one's followers and see each of them as equal in importance to oneself within the organization. I believe it is possible to challenge the status quo in one's country using nonviolent direct action; Kenneth Kaunda has proven it. Most important of all leadership characteristics is the willingness to listen to what people want and the ability to simplify complex problems and educate people by communicating so as to be easily and readily understood.

Kwame Nkrumah's Leadership Style

Style can be defined as a manner or method of performing that is characteristic of a person, group, or era. Leadership style is a leader's manner and method of acting to influence individuals and groups. People project onto their leader virtues they value. They perceive in their leaders the capacity to achieve results. This capacity must first be seen with the follower's eye of faith before a leader can demonstrate it. Nkrumah made use of the power of information dissemination to influence his people's individual and collective power of action. His greatest asset was his ability to communicate not just ideas but also sentiment. He gave his people brief phrases that facilitated the spread of his message and created in them a new awareness of themselves as important. In a culture in which communication was basically face-to-face, he made his body and voice his medium of communication. He attempted to speak in every corner of his country at all different types of gatherings. Reporters noticed that he could speak with infectious enthusiasm for hours without any notes. He explained this ability by stating, "My mind is clear and my policy decided."[60] Because he shook hands and spoke personally with everyone he met, he was able to obtain their friendship and support.

Nkrumah started several newspapers in his country and showed his people that he feared no one by being unafraid to speak out, though he was taken to court many times for libel. He also utilized the uncensored mouth-to-mouth method of rumor to disseminate information throughout his country. Often a whole page of his newspaper was filled with an illustration that showed him in a positive light and caricatured his opponents. In this way, he attracted youth and others who did not read much. Nkrumah successfully used many external symbols of individual and collective identification, including a flag and a totem. The colors of his flag held traditional meanings for his people: red for sacrifice, white for purity, and green for youth. These colors could be seen on people's shirts and hats and painted on vehicles and houses. Nkrumah selected the red cockerel (rooster) as his totem (animal symbol) because of its many cultural associations in his country. The cockerel played an important symbolic role in the rituals of every ethnic group in Ghana. The cockerel was on the lips of Nkrumah's people every day as they repeated ancient West African proverbs in which the cock and the hen demonstrate important truths about living. In his mode of dress and grooming, Nkrumah strove to be an example. He used a traditional fly swish, carried a walking cane and refused to part his hair, all things that enabled people to associate him with a traditional African leader. Instead of a traditional gong-beater who announced the laws of ancient rulers, his organization's vans drove through the streets bringing music and his words to the elderly and those with small children. He not only fulfilled his people's expectations for a leader by utilizing traditional African leadership symbols and invented modern methods for communicating with them, he also expanded their image of an African leader by inviting women to take leadership roles in his organization and government. Legends grew as he became popular. Because of his studies with Catholic priests and the Christian, Muslim, and traditional prayers that he offered before each speech, he acquired a saintly aura.

Nkrumah was successful because he concentrated his personal energy on the task of identifying and utilizing the unique talents of the people around him. For that reason, each person who met him *immediately* was filled with the conviction that they were *personally* recognized and *needed* by this great man. His charisma stemmed from a leadership style that transformed groups of people of different backgrounds and abilities into effective teams. His organization included the professional and the student, the religious and the atheist, the rich man and the poor man. He relied on the process of consensus to both inform him of what his people were thinking and feeling and also to inform them of his vision, ideas, and plans. A traditional African method of decision-making, consensus depends on listening to each person's point of view before taking action. In this way, his meetings were not hindered by the kinds of struggles that plague most organizations. At his outdoor rallies, people sang and danced as well as listened. The excitement of the audience was high because they knew that anyone might be called on to join Nkrumah on the platform to speak. Although he worked to assure that every person in his country could identify with him, Nkrumah was careful not identify himself with any ethnic group or religious organization.

Nkrumah's leadership success drew him away from his grassroots supporters. His foresight told him that the exploitative world economy under which African and other third-world nations suffer today was coming. He saw Africa's dependence on the world commodity markets of today. He knew that international financial management would soon rob African countries of their autonomy. His desire to save his people from this fate led him away from them. He recognized that his people could not be free unless *all* Africans were free. African unity could not come until each African had an awareness of Africa's unique identity as a society and accepted their role in that society. All human societies hold at their center a myth or an ideology regarding the purpose and meaning of their existence. The accomplishment of the independence of his country naturally led Nkrumah to this task. While his attention was diverted in this direction, struggles among the different factions of his government began to emerge. His organization was not able to find a new effective role for each institution to play in his government. Each had its own organizational culture. His attention was not given to the leadership tasks that were required to merge them with his organization's culture.

How can one sum up Nkrumah's leadership style? What was his source of charisma? He was a leader whose conduct communicated equality between leader and follower. His leadership was built on tremendous personal humility. His leadership style was essentially intimate and informal. He focused on the individual while addressing the masses. He drew out valuable contributions from within people and rewarded them. He demonstrated massive trust in people by thrusting daunting challenges upon them. He taught people how to turn their individual weaknesses into group strengths via teamwork. In doing these things, he was transformed from a leader to a ruler by his people. For this reason, like all great leaders who are beloved by their people, his leadership style became more formal as he took upon himself the responsibility to fulfill his people's expectations of a ruler of their country. He rode in official government vehicles. To speak to him, his people had to gain permission from government officials close to him who valued his safety and the importance it gave them. When his organization failed, rifts between its founders and the younger generation, the new intellectuals whom he had nurtured by expanding educational opportunities and who then formed its base, had grown too wide for a different, more formal Nkrumah to heal. Nkrumah was changed by his success. He no longer carefully utilized symbols of his people's culture to motivate and inspire them. Televised speeches replaced his rallies in rural villages and urban street corners. As they eased into lives of comfortable stability, which Nkrumah's success had brought to them, the members of his organization failed to recognize their essential task as it slipped away into the shadows that they left behind them. While Nkrumah attempted to step into a leadership vacuum for the continent of Africa, the members of his organization turned away from confronting the self-discipline necessary for creating a system that maintained their accountability to the people of their country. The effectiveness of Nkrumah's leadership style depended on the resolve of his people. When they believed that they had accomplished their goal, they ceased to listen to their leader. The quarrelsome words of their neighbors filled their ears. Nkrumah's words echoed from the mountaintop that he had climbed so tirelessly, but no one listened anymore.

A Philosophy of African Leadership

True African leaders such as Kaunda and Nkrumah always have a vision; they know where they want to go and how to get there. They value others' skills and experiences and build teams that make use of them. They courageously accept responsibility for problems and are able to communicate clearly the mission, goals, and objectives of their organization. Great African leaders are willing to challenge the status quo while trusting and empowering people. They use obstacles to create a positive future. They are consistent and willing to set an example of sacrifice for the good of the next generation. The primary task of African leadership is to establish and maintain "intimacy" (caring) because disciplined unselfishness comes about only through close social relationships. Traditional sources of intimacy such as the family, the club, the neighborhood, lifelong friendships, and the church are all presently threatened by modern African lifestyles. Intimacy is essential for healthy individuals and thus for a healthy society. Once African society devalues intimacy, its young people will not develop a sense of community responsibility. These young Africans will go on to produce the next generation that will have a permanently diminished sense of community. This will soon result in an African society that is solely composed of individuals with no or only tenuous social ties to each other.

All great African leaders know that change must start at the top. For that reason, they take time first to establish understanding and true commitment at the highest levels of their organizations. The most important attribute an African leader must have is integrity. A leader with integrity provides consistent responses that show a sense of equal respect for everyone. This fosters family-type relationships between people. A leader who behaves consistently exhibits the integrity that is necessary to nurture the growth of trust. The first task of African leadership is to establish and maintain *trust* because the success of a nation is determined by the willingness of its people to make personal sacrifices. Before the objective of commitment to the development of a less selfish, more cooperative approach to working together can be achieved, there must be understanding that comes from the open expression of opinions, feelings, and ideas in a process of public debate and group analysis. African leaders can set an example during these discussions by critically examining their country's current, actual operating philosophy, strategy, and goals and the value they place in their people. A way to do this is to examine the five most recent key decisions to discover what principles were consistently applied. A sufficient level of trust must be established first to facilitate honest questioning of assumptions on the part of everyone. The first task for an African leader is to set an example by openly disagreeing with others and actively working to create an environment in which different opinions are welcomed. African leaders can establish a discussion process that reflects the egalitarianism, openness, and participation that are the objectives of the change to take place.

African leaders can set an example when they facilitate the growth of trust that is needed to implement this type of discussion process by positively accepting criticism.

Though it will be painful, any group of people who trust one another to expose their deepest weaknesses is a group that can successfully implement change. It is only by examining all national practices that African leaders can uncover the roots of current organizational culture. To deal with change, everyone must be open; that means being willing to investigate and question each other's work as well as to appreciate the feedback that others give in response when they look into their own work. Change in Africa will require African leaders who demonstrate a willingness to expose their weaknesses to their people; in other words, they must have a willingness to reveal themselves so completely that people may find human weakness there. This teaches people that their leaders are ready to acknowledge that everyone has weaknesses, and it proves that all will be accepted in spite of their weaknesses. When nothing needs to be hidden, a tremendous positive energy will be released.

Skillful African leaders do more listening than talking; they observe the pattern of interaction in the group and know when to intervene. Skillful African leaders utilize frequent periods of silence to give everyone time to process what was said, which in turn allows the true issue or conflict to arise. Good African leaders teach group dynamics to people so that they can recognize group interaction patterns. Everyone must learn to see when a group is moving too quickly, how some behaviors interfere with group process, and how to stay on course. The best African leaders teach leadership.

People should be taught how to provide leadership that facilitates identifying issues, finding the roots of conflicts, and creating solutions to problems that everyone can support. Good African leaders communicate with their behavior more than with their words and then make sure that they immediately recognize and reward positive results of people's efforts. They solicit suggestions from people as a group and move quickly to implement helpful ones. Good African leaders set an example by being prepared to address tough questions during regular question-and-answer sessions about how the country is doing, its successes and problems, and other important issues.

Creating Positive Organizational Cultures in Africa

Organizations are the product of individuals cooperating in some integrated activity. Any group of people that works together for some time will develop an unspoken philosophy, a series of traditions, and a set of morals. For that reason, organizational philosophy must state the means by which such cooperation is to be achieved. An organization's philosophy of values and beliefs implicitly rather than explicitly controls how members respond to problems and facilitates coordination between those members. The philosophy is contained in a broad statement. Each unit should agree upon its own interpretation of the organization's philosophy in terms of how it applies to that setting as well. African leaders can use an organizational philosophy to build a uniform organizational culture that will increase individual autonomy, accountability, and innovation. An example of this is an organizational philosophy that states, "If it needs to be done, you have the responsibility to make sure it gets done" and "Group objectives take precedence over individual objectives."

Organizational culture develops when people have a range of common experiences. This philosophy is communicated via a common culture that is shared by all people in a group. Organizational culture can be expressed in the values that African leaders communicate to Africans by their example in a behavior pattern that is composed of consistent activities, opinions, and actions. Africans follow the example of strong, committed leaders and become an example for all Africans to follow. For example, an African leader can ensure that decisions are made by consensus by stating, "If we still disagree, the other person must know something we need to understand more thoroughly." A common culture consists of a set of symbols, ceremonies, and myths that communicate underlying values and beliefs to members. Rituals incarnate abstract ideas, bringing meaning and impact to each individual. A value embodied by a series of specific stories is more believable and remembered better than an abstract idea.

Nurturing Consensus in Africa

An important task of African leadership is to establish and maintain auto-nomy, empowerment, and accountability. Africans should govern their own workmanship because a group doing the work will take into account all the var-iables required to achieve gains in productivity. In participatory decision-making, all Africans in a group reach consensus on what decision to adopt. Con-sensus yields more creative decisions and more effective implementation. When an important decision needs to be made, everyone who will feel its impact should be consulted. Then, once consensus is reached, everyone affected will be likely to support it. The decision itself is not important, but rather the impor-tance lies in the level to which the participants are committed and informed. Not only is consensual decision-making an effective information dissemination ve-hicle, but also it supplies an opportunity for value sharing while openly sig-naling the commitment of the organization to those values. It is a highly visible sign of a commitment to the value of working together. By participating in con-sensual decision-making, individuals demonstrate their willingness to place their faith in the hands of others.

Rebuilding Community in Africa

Like rebuilding a society, building a nation is not like building a house; it is like building a marriage in that one must coordinate people, not technology, to achieve productivity. The role of African leadership is to ensure increased pro-ductivity by effectively coordinating the efforts of many individuals. This is ac-complished by giving them incentives to adopt a cooperative, long-range view. Productivity is a problem of social organization. African leaders must learn how to manage people so that they can work together more effectively. In a consent culture, members of a community of equals cooperate with each other to reach common goals. Rather than relying on hierarchy to direct and control behavior, this system relies on commitment and trust fostered by commitment to com-munity mechanisms. Group membership has much more influence on the indi-vidual than money. More than external evaluations and rewards, human pro-ductivity ultimately depends on one's devotion to others and the evaluation of one's peers.

Because individual freedom exists only when people willingly subordinate their self-interests to the social interest, many Africans now live in countries in which no one has real freedom. There is no freedom there because people are now at war with one another. This is because African society is increasingly composed of self-interested individuals. African leaders can encourage the growth of informal social networks by using cultural forms to create com-mitment to community in Africans. This commitment will prompt Africans to take on leadership roles in their countries. Leaders in countries with developing organizational cultures must be willing and prepared to share leadership tasks with their people. I believe that sharing leadership tasks with Africans is the best way African leaders can create productive and self-sustaining nations.

Leading Learning Organizations

I believe that it is important for African leaders to ask themselves, "How can I build an organizational culture in my country in which continuous learning occurs?"

Senge stated,

> The primary institutions of human society are oriented predominately toward controlling rather than learning, rewarding individuals for performing for others rather than for cultivating their natural curiosity and impulse to learn. [61]

The young African child entering school for the first time soon discovers that what is important is getting the right answer and avoiding mistakes. All Africans are born with intrinsic motivation, self-esteem, dignity, and curiosity to learn. By focusing on performing for someone else's approval, African countries have created the conditions that foster mediocre productivity. I believe that today's African leaders must make changes in their country's organizational culture so that their nations will be prepared to face the internal and external challenges that the future is sure to bring to Africa. I believe that the best way that African leaders can do this is to create a learning organizational culture in their countries that satisfies Africans' need for intrinsic motivation and builds the social networks, collaboration, and information exchange that is needed to deal successfully with future external forces such as the globalization of the marketplace.

I believe the answer to Africa's problems is a different kind of leadership. Most African leaders have no real comprehension of the type of leadership that is required to build a new Africa. The Western view of leaders is that they are *heroes*, special people who rise to the fore in times of crisis to set the direction, make the key decisions, and energize the troops. This is an individualistic and non-systemic view. In Africa, this myth reinforces a focus on short-term events rather than on systemic forces and collective learning. The Western concept of leadership is concerned with individual achievement. This type of leadership is appropriate only for the short-term. For African leaders to deal successfully with the challenges of the future, they need to re-socialize Africans to a rationale that supports community values. Senge stated, "In a 'learning' organizational culture, leaders' roles differ dramatically from that of the charismatic decision-maker. These roles require new skills."[62]

Kotter stated, "In successful learning organizational cultures, each individual contributes uniquely from his or her own experience and talents."[63] Leaders of African countries with a learning organizational culture will help their people to listen to each other. In this way, African leaders can facilitate the learning process in their countries. African leaders can use cultural forms such as national celebrations to encourage Africans to share their unique backgrounds as well as their special skills. African leaders need to remember, however, that a charismatic leader will discourage honest communication and necessary constructive confrontation of problems. African leaders who put the needs of their people before their personal need for fame can use cultural forms to create a strong organizational culture that provides the sense of community that Africans need to face problems and learn from them both individually and as a group.

> Differences of perception that arise from varied backgrounds, work exper-
> iences, and ethnic origins can enrich a group's basis for creative problem-
> solving and achievement. The group's culture can be the means for capitalizing
> on diverse human resources, assisting all people to accomplish goals together
> as a team. A strong organizational culture enhances group communications and
> permits confrontation, so as to stimulate group growth and cohesion. Strong
> networks of informal relationships—the kind found in groups with healthy cul-
> tures—help coordinate leadership activities. Informal networks can deal with
> the greater demands of coordination associated with nonroutine activities and
> change. The multitude of communication channels and the trust among the
> individuals connected by those channels allow for an ongoing process of
> accommodation and adaptation. Extensive informal networks are so important
> that if they do not exist, creating them has to be the focus of activity early in a
> major leadership initiative. Institutionalizing a leadership-centered culture is
> the ultimate act of leadership.[64]

In our search for the leadership skills that are necessary to create and main-tain effective organizational cultures in African countries, I suggest that those who would be successful African leaders use as their guide a proverb by the an-cient Chinese elder, Lao Tsu, "The wicked leader is he who the people despise. The good leader is he who the people revere. The *great* leader is he who the people say, 'We did it *ourselves*'."[65] I believe that African leaders must begin now to build nations in which Africans feel proud of the community of which they are a part. I believe that African leaders have a key role to play in shaping the organizational cultures of their countries. I am convinced that to be suc-cessful, African leaders must utilize cultural forms, such as focus (feedback) groups, celebrations, and rites of accomplishment, to ensure that their country's organizational culture is congruent with their vision. African leaders must recog-nize the need to establish traditions that relate to the values that they want Africans to call upon to guide their actions and decision-making. I believe that African leaders need to acknowledge the importance of organizational culture because all human interactions are conducted in the context of a particular culture. The role played by African leaders in their country's organizational cul-tures will determine, in a significant way, whether their nation is able to adapt to changes in its internal and external environment.

My purpose is to help African leaders understand how vital the ability to utilize cultural forms is in creating nations that are flexible and innovative enough to face the multiple challenges of the future. I believe that African lead-ers influence their country's organizational cultures whether or not they intend to. In the past, African leaders did not consider the organizational culture of their country to be an important factor in determining national success. I believe that in our modern day, the globalization of the marketplace requires nations to operate more efficiently. For this reason, I am convinced that the role of African leadership in creating and maintaining positive organizational cultures in African countries is paramount. With increasing global competition, I think that *now* leadership's primary task in Africa should be to use cultural forms to empower Africans to share decision-making, take up leadership roles, and accept responsibility for learning from their experiences.

Organizational Change and Leadership in Africa Today

In the past, the old definition of leadership for Africans was that it was the utilization of power; now it is more and more the *giving away* of power to enable individuals to respond creatively to changes. Several skills are new to African organizational management: the ability to inspire people's commitment to a shared vision, to attract and hold the most creative people, to develop cooperative and caring systems, and to foster appreciative relationships based on shared meaningful activity. To gain these new management skills, workers, students, managers, and leaders in Africa have begun to examine the assumptions underlying the traditional Western form of management. These assumptions are centered on Western attitudes about human development and the values, which guide organizations.

If the only modality in which an organization operates is competition, its effectiveness is limited. Would it not be more effective if it could shift to other modalities, such as collaboration or individual initiative when circumstances warrant? [66] Many modern Africans are caught in a "prisoner's dilemma" at work these days. They are afraid of being vulnerable when they attempt to collaborate with other Africans who are still competitive. Because they know things about each other that could be used in harmful ways, their trust is based on an uneasy mutual agreement not to use this information to hurt each other.

Africans have to experience *affectively* as well as conceptually how other Africans feel, think, and move in the world if they are to create relationships that energize and empower each other. Organizational transformation cannot be mandated even though changes in policy and structures help to cause it. I believe that it is time for African leaders to expand the domain of appreciation and caring from strictly personal relationships to institutional contexts. This will be difficult because property rights are quickly becoming more central to Africans than community. In Western societies, individuals and society are believed to have separate, distinct, and often conflicting interests. In Western countries such as the U.S., reconciliation is achieved by organizational, political, and legal conflict.[67] When Africans recognize that their future interest is equal to their consideration of the current interests of other Africans and that their caring for other Africans is a means to affirm their own future interest, they will be able to build a more sustainable Africa. The choices that Africans will face tomorrow are a consequence of their actions today. The individual and the group or an organization and society are not separable and distinct from each other. The future needs to be accounted for in the present. There are three mechanisms that can stimulate participation toward desired public goods in Africa: (1) Creating selective incentives, (2) Organizing large groups into many small teams, and (3) Nurturing associations, such as institutions of religion, art, and education that span many different groups, to reconcile differences and to advocate for policy in the development of a common interest. African leaders are now expected to recognize the value of building commitment through inclusive decision-making in a process in which representatives of differing interests are asked to accept their individual responsibility for the welfare of the whole. African leaders hold the key to organizational cooperation because they determine the frequency and durability of interaction in their organization as well as the degree of inclusivity of its decision-making.

Strategies for Leading Organizations in Africa

Because they are aware that they have the responsibility for improving the efficiency of African organizations, most African leaders opt for a Western-style, closed-system strategy and rational model that they believe will maximize efficiency by planning procedures, setting standards, and exercising controls to ensure conformity. This strategy and model focus on structural relationships among units of the organization. They believe that specializing tasks and grouping them into departments will maximize efficiency. Rules categorize activities and clients. Unfortunately, African organizations are *not* autonomous entities. Actually the organization as a unit is constantly in interaction with its environment. For that reason, African leaders need to begin to focus on variables that are not subject to complete control by the organization and to begin to regard the interdependence of the organization and its environment as inevitable or natural. Although neither model *alone* provides an adequate understanding of complex organizations, what African leaders need is a *synthesis* of the two models because their two strategies indicate something fundamental about the actual culture surrounding complex organizations.[68] African leaders need to view complex organizations as open systems that are constantly faced with uncertainty, but, because they are subject to criteria of rationality, they need to manufacture certainty.

Parsons suggested that organizations exhibit three distinct levels of responsibility and control—technical, managerial and institutional.[69] Because an organization is subject to criteria of rationality, it is makes sense to remove as much uncertainty as possible from its technical core by reducing the number of variables operating on it. At this level, the organization is open to influence by elements of the environment over which it has no formal authority or control. To satisfy rationality criteria, complex organizations in Africa must approach certainty at the technical level while remaining flexible enough at the institutional level to be able to adapt to rapid changes in the economic, social, and physical environment.

In Africa, an increasing desire to find ways to create more and more profit has encouraged the association of instrumentality with the accumulation of capital. For that reason, *long-linked technology*, which involves serial interdependence that produces a single product at a constant rate and permits the use of clear-cut criteria for the selection of machines and their human operators, has become prevalent in the most technologically developed African countries. An example of this is the mass production assembly line. *Mediating technology* involves operating in standardized ways to link clients who are widely distributed in time and space and who wish to be interdependent. Examples of this are African insurance companies and utilities. The selection of the standards to be utilized varies according to how particular clients are categorized but belief in the efficacy of *standardization* to service clients is never questioned. Belief, in Africa, in the efficacy of standardization comes from the desire to apply scientific methods to the needs of Africans. Africans have been taught Western style business and manufacturing techniques. *Intensive technology*, which is the utilization of a variety of techniques and technologies to achieve change, determined by feedback from the object of such change is very rare in Africa. In intensive technology, the combination and the order of application of techniques and technologies depend on the nature of the desired change. For this reason, intensive technology is appropriate for changing circumstances. Right now, Africa is undergoing tremendous social, economic, and environmental changes. Increasing rural-urban migration, lack of economic self-sustainability, and overuse of land seriously threaten many African nations today. African leaders need to learn how to utilize mediating and intensive technology effectively to address the changes happening in Africa at this moment. The main challenge faced by African leaders is how to avoid increasing the spread of rigidity outward from the core of African organizations as they grow and develop, and instead extend flexibility and responsiveness to the environment in toward the core. I believe that African leaders will be able to do this if they remember that the main question facing African organizations is, "What activities are *appropriate* for the anticipation of social, economic, political and environmental fluctuations in the organizations in my country?"[70]

African organizational leaders have previously relied too heavily on the support of government-subsidized aid from countries outside of Africa. Increasingly, the relationship between an African organization and its task environment is one of exchange. Unless Africans or those outside of Africa, view the relationship as something valuable, it will not be able to survive. African leaders need to regard dependence as the obverse of power.[71] Then they will realize that African organizations have power relative to elements of their task environments to the extent that they can monopolize the capacity to satisfy those elements. To manage interdependence, African organizations must employ cooperative strategies by arranging negotiated environments within each African country or within the continent. African unity is an essential goal for African leaders to achieve because uncertainty is reduced for organizations by reduction of uncertainty for others. I believe that it is time for African leaders to acknowledge that creating coalitions not only provides a basis for exchange in Africa but also requires their mutual commitment to *future joint* decision-making and accountability within the continent of Africa.

As complex African organizations extend their boundaries to other African nations, to incorporate sources of contingencies outside of own country, they will find the problem of balance is critical. The root of the problem of balance is the question of size. Therefore, to progress toward finding a beneficial balance, African leaders must address the problem of balance as one of economy of scale.[72] Africans have learned from Asians, Americans, and Europeans that the advantages of "bigness" include easier, less expensive financing; more numerous, highly trained experts to attack trouble spots; sustained research; and more accurately tailored and adaptable marketing systems. This may be true in those areas of the world, but bigness has not been shown to operate in the same way in Africa. This is something that all African leaders must admit to themselves and to their people. Nevertheless, most African leaders believe that achieving the organizational flexibility that is needed to deal with crisis and change in Africa is too difficult because the costs of acquiring resources from outside of Africa are often so high that African organizations must make commitments to future use of those resources.

What Thompson labeled "the synthetic organization" exists, ongoing, in all African communities, and mobilizes their communities in response to an emergency.[73] In a short time, human and material resources being used for other purposes are adapted to disaster-recovery activities. I have personally been involved with many of this type of informal African organization because I participated in the traditional African age-group social system, an ancient informal African socialization system (see Chapter 2), as well as formal Western-style national organizations, such as the National Gambian Scout Association. People bring uncommitted needed resources to an individual, usually a respected elder or group whose *power rests not on authority but on capacity to coordinate.* Unlike in the West where ad hoc organizations dissolve rapidly on their own as the need disappears, African traditional informal organizations continue to work with formal institutions in their country even after the crisis is past. Ancient traditional African informal "synthetic" organizations such as age groups rely on consensus regarding goals for action because their mandate is to operate in the interest and for the benefit of the community. Thus they have the authority to acquire freely and deploy needed human and material resources. When called by their age group, Africans feel free to leave their workplaces and request equipment and materials that belong to anyone in the community. Unfortunately, because they have been taught to value Western culture over traditional African culture, most African leaders consider these "synthetic" grassroots organizations to be inefficient. Sadly, modern African leaders' lack of ideological and financial support for such groups and activities encourages young people to neglect their responsibility to maintain this essential foundation of African society.

African leaders who recognize that African unity is necessary to achieve self-sustainability realize that organizations are especially useful to Africans because the whole is greater than the sum of the parts. The failure of any one part can threaten the whole and thus all the other parts. Thompson termed this *pooled interdependence.* Each part renders a discrete contribution and each is supported by the whole. Interdependence may also take a serial form. Thompson termed this *sequential interdependence* because it is not symmetrical. If the outputs of each part are the inputs for the other parts, he terms this *reciprocal interdependence*. Reciprocal independence is unique in that each part is the significant contingency for other parts.[74] African leaders are needed to strengthen all types of interdependence. Currently, most African leaders attempt to produce organizational *coordination by standardization*. This involves the establishment of rules that require that the situations to which they apply remain constant over time. Much of the crisis in Africa has been caused by African leaders relying on a traditional Western-style form of coordination originally established by European colonialists. The situation in Africa has *not* remained constant over time. Globalization caused by advances in communication technology has reached even the quietest African village, like the one where I was born. Modern African leaders also rely on organizational *coordination by strategic planning,* which involves the establishment of schedules. This approach is more flexible than standardization yet strategic plans designed when conditions were one way are frequently maintained in Africa even after conditions change. I feel that it is imperative that African leaders in every African nation learn how to achieve organizational *coordination by mutual adjustment* because it involves the transmission of new information during the process of action. Thompson calls this "coordination by feedback" because it often involves communication *across* hierarchical lines.[75]

It is clear to me that the crucial problem for African organizational leadership today is not coordination but *adjustment* to environmental contingencies (exogenous variables). Adaptation by rule is the least costly form, in the short-term; therefore, African leaders who are under pressure to be economically efficient prefer it. Because the African social, economic, and political environment is so dynamic, however, rules are inadequate. Cues must therefore be taken from the environment such that regional divisions of the African organizations should be decentralized. In this way, each boundary-spanning unit in an African organization is differentiated functionally to correspond to segments of the African task environment. In addition, each unit should operate on a decentralized basis to monitor and use consensus to design responses to fluctuations to its sector of the task environment.[76] So long as an organization employs simple technologies and faces a simple task environment, it can be large and still employ a simple structure. Those African organizations that seek to address significant social, political, economic, and environmental problems in Africa face a mind-boggling, complex task environment in which ancient traditional African cultural practices and modern Western lifestyles compete for the respect and attention of all Africans.

Some African leaders have attempted to transform their organizations into vertically integrated organizations so that they can become responsive to changing environmental conditions by dividing into units, but they subordinate each unit to central planning. What is more urgently needed in Africa is the diversified organization that consists of several conditionally autonomous organizations with each corresponding to one of the domains of the total organization. Unfortunately, the ever-present conflict in African organizations that are under pressure to operate economically revolves around the temptation to rely on standardization regardless of the need for flexibility. The one type of organization in Africa that is designed especially for flexibility has been labeled *task force* or *project management*, which is surprisingly very similar to the synthetic organization.

There exists disagreement among African leaders as to whether African organizations should be evaluated in terms of their maximum attainment of purposes (*maximization*) or their acceptable attainment of desired states (*satisfaction*). This is because some Africans focus on the *results* that they believe African organizations should actually accomplish while others focus on *motivation*, which is what they believe African organizations should try to accomplish. Organizational assessment always involves creating or choosing a standard of desirability against which actual effects of actions are evaluated in a continuous process. Standards of organizational desirability in Africa originate in modern African cultural values, which contain ancient traditional African values, such as communalism, as well as adopted Western values, such as individualism. Modern Western-influenced African cultural values support the belief that utility is profit and therefore profit should be maximized. Thus increasingly Africans must choose between health and wealth because they are expected to compare all possible effects of their actions in terms of one common denominator: money. According to Thompson, the most important question an organization can ask itself is not what it has accomplished in the past but whether it is fit for future action.[77]

I believe that African organizational change will be accomplished by small committees (in this way, similar to age groups) that meet informally and individually with each member of the organization until the necessary series of compromises and appreciation appear to mesh and consensus has been achieved. In Africa, a vote is not a decision but rather a formal acknowledgment or ratification of this consensus. Organizational survival in Africa depends on the co-alignment of technology and task environment with a viable domain and on organizational design and structure that are appropriate to that domain. Timing is a crucial administrative matter because as environments change, the African organizational leaders must deal with not just domain but also, how and how fast to redesign the structure and technology of the organization. The organizational configuration that is necessary for African self-sufficiency does not come from yielding to environmental pressures but rather from finding strategic variables available to be manipulated in such a way that interaction with elements in the environment will result in a viable co-alignment.[78] African leaders must realize that to achieve the necessary organizational flexibility for self-sustainability, the leadership process is not something done at *one* level in the African organization, but spans and links *all* levels. The leadership process should not simply flow down from one level to the next but should inform the interaction of all levels and units of the organization.

When African leaders attempt to solve organizational problems, they use simple concepts of causality that direct them to (1) search for solutions to symptoms, (2) search for solutions based on currently available alternatives, and *always* (3) search for solutions in organizationally vulnerable areas (i.e., finger pointing). I feel that it is very important for African leaders to teach Africans monitoring behavior that scans the environment for opportunities, which does not wait to be activated by a problem and which does not therefore stop when a solution has been found.[79] I blame the widespread bias toward certainty in African institutions that shows up as a preference for short-term rather than long-term considerations and precedent rather than innovation especially in government bureaucracies maintained essentially unchanged since colonial times, for the crisis of self-sustainability in Africa today.

African Unity and Sustainable Development in Africa

I call for all African sisters and brothers to listen to my concern. This is for all human beings who care and who are willing and prepared to sacrifice. It is easy to say, "I am an African." It is easy and simple to say, "I believe in Africa." It is easy to put on African clothes and say, "I belong to the Motherland." It is not easy, however, for one to sacrifice for the Motherland. It is not easy for one to be accountable and responsible for the Motherland. It is not easy to think about creative things that can benefit our Motherland, Africa. I hope that each and everyone of us, whether living in the Motherland or outside of Africa, either in the West, Asia, or any part of the world, will start asking ourselves about our role as individuals who belong to the continent of Africa. "What role can I play? What knowledge and skills do I have to share with our Motherland? How should I go about sharing my knowledge, skills, and experience? What action should I take to make Africa become more successful? What positive stance do I have for Africa?" These are important questions that we, as Africans, should be asking ourselves every day of our lives. It is so easy to criticize our leaders. It is easy to blame other people. It is not easy, however, to blame oneself because blaming oneself challenges one to become more accountable. Blaming other people does not challenge us to think about creative ways to make things that better serve the African people.

How long will Africans continue to blame one another and to pretend that we who blame are not part of the problem? Some of us do it unconsciously. For some, it is deliberate. Others think that blaming is a way to achieve prestige. For some, it is their way of showing people that they are intelligent and educated. I say that an educated person is one who is creative and innovative, who thinks about positive things to implement in their own society.

Educated people are able to transform their society so that it will become more self-sustainable. Educated people must make this the focus of their life's service for the sake of all humanity and all nations. Failure to do so indicates an incomplete education that serves only oneself. That fact is, itself, an insult: one becomes a person who will constantly run away from responsibility to serve one's own people. When we do that, we no longer value and respect the culture of our own society. When that happens, we begin to lose more and more of what exists in our own society. When this starts happening, we cannot control this loss because outsiders are controlling us. When we allow this to happen, we become as light as a kite that can be blown in any direction by the wind because we have lost our roots and our self-sustainability.

Some people may say, "Who is this Michael Ba Banutu-Gomez, who thinks he can address all Africans?" Others may say, "What he says has a truth and is real." Some people may say, "All these things he is saying do not concern me because I will go on with my life the way I want it to be." Others may say, "I have a job so what do I care!" Still others will say, "I'm not in Africa so this doesn't concern me!" To all who have ready answers to what I say, I must say that I truly believe that we all have a key role to play in making ourselves, our nations, our society, and our people better for the sake of the next generation, our children, and future generations to come, our children's children. This is a vision that every African should have. The question I ask myself, as well as my fellow Africans, is, "Why are we so concerned with leaving Africa to emigrate to America, Great Britain, France, Germany, Denmark, Sweden, Holland, Finland, Norway, or any other country besides any African country?" We do that because we want the kinds of things that people have in these countries. My next question is, "How did those people, in these nations which Africans are so eager to go, create and develop these things that make us want to leave our own nations?" They did not make all these things in a day. No one came to their countries and gave these things to them or made these things for them. All of it was not done entirely by one ethnic group or one religious group or one gender. Despite the fact that they have many disagreements, all humans in that society have brought their knowledge to work together. The difference is that they were able to look to a context that was larger than even their own nation.

What is stopping us from working with what we have among our own people? It is not going to be easy. It is going to be difficult. We will not be able to accomplish this in one day. It involves patience, concentration, creativity, love, respect, and understanding. It involves our acceptance of others who are different from ourselves. It also involves our cooperation with them to build and sustain our own society. Above all, each and every one of us must sacrifice to achieve those things of which we dream and the vision that we have for our own children, our own people, and our own society. When I hear Africans talk about our African leadership, I question myself and I question them: What is *your* role in working with those leaders, as you say our leaders lack leadership skills? I am convinced that we will have positive leadership in Africa when Africans show our leaders that we accept and appreciate each other by performing complementary roles in service to our society.

We are the very people who have put our leaders in the positions they hold in our governments. We are the very people who support the type of government they practice in our nations. We, who talk about the lack of leadership in Africa, are the very people who would do the same or even worse things if we were in leadership positions than the leaders in our own nations whom we criticize. Have we not learned anything from colonial days up to now? If we have not, when are we going to learn? If we are not willing to learn, then we should not talk about bad things done by leaders in our own nations. To be able to learn requires us to accept that we are going to fail. We cannot deny nor can we suppress failure in our own nations if we want to succeed at becoming self-sustainable. At some point, every nation has failed. At one point, every human being has failed. Those who are able to build on their own failures and the failures of their nation are people who are willing and prepared to sacrifice, to accept responsibility, and to become more accountable for what goes on in their own nation. They are people who are focused on what *they* can do, as Africans, and as citizens of their nations because they love and care about their own people.

Are we, as Africans, prepared to serve the African people? Yes, one can say, "I am; we are," but what is lacking is the action. When I speak of action, I am not referring to military or physical violence. I am speaking about proactive, positive action that enables us to choose and change our own leaders without any weapon being pointed at any human being. By proactive, positive action, I mean action that is deeply rooted in the consensus process, which is the foundation of traditional African society. Freedom stems from consensus, *not* from elections. Elections accomplish what the consensus process previously laid down. Elections can never be the foundation of African society. Africans often make this mistake when they are in the process of choosing their leaders. We think that by merely holding elections, we have accomplished democracy. *An election without consensus is not democracy.* Consensus enables people of any society to express their concerns and points of view about issues that affect their nation and local community.

> Democratic reforms are naturally well suited to African conditions. For me the characteristics of democracy are: the freedom of the individual, including freedom to criticize the government, and the opportunity to change it without worrying about being murdered.[80]

We should be able to find ways in which we, as Africans, can have a positive open discussion about issues with which we must deal to build a united, nonviolent, nonethnic, independently sustainable Africa. As I said previously, accomplishing this is not easy and maintaining it will never be easy. Achieving this has not been easy for any other society, so be prepared to accept that it will not be easy for us, either. Yes, we should not ignore the reality that African leaders have done much good, despite their errors and mistakes. We need to appreciate the good things that they have done. We also need to understand that our leaders have made mistakes because they are human like us. This does not mean that they are evil: they are not. They are not perfect. Nevertheless, I am convinced that this vision can be achieved if we are prepared, as citizens of Africa, to work *with* our leaders. I am sure that if we show them that we are prepared to do this, they will be willing to listen to us. Be aware that the beginning of anything in life is not easy. We need to be persistent with ourselves to make our vision of a new African society become a reality for our children.

Look at the type of educational system that we have in Africa. We all know that it is not the type of educational system that can develop an independently sustainable Africa. This is because it is a system that is deeply rooted in a culture from outside of Africa. Our educational system does not incorporate our own African culture. We ought to be able to sit down, as Africans, to re-evaluate the type of educational system we have and to develop one that incorporates our own African culture, serves and benefits our own people, and can help our countries develop into self-sustainable nations. How many of us, as Africans, really know about the history of our own nations and regions? How many of us, as Africans, really understand the true value of our rich oral history? How many of us know, as Africans, about the natural and cultural history of our regions and about the traditional African way of socializing young people? Africans and African intellectuals, both inside and outside of Africa, view this as something that is not important in the development of a self-sustainable African society. Why is it not considered important? Because one can say, "It is not written." Nor is it from European society. Those who think in this way have been socialized to believe that anything from the West is the best.

This belief has psychological power over us. Westerners succeed in socializing African intellectuals to reject their African culture, adopt European culture, and value European-type institutions. We ought to be able to look far beyond any written history that exists in books about African society. One might ask, "How can we bring back our own history? It is not written in a textbook that one can find in a library." No, but as long as we have Africans who are still alive and remember our oral history, we can write it down. We should thank God that in this century, we have complex technology. We must use the technology we have and go sit at the feet of our elders to videotape them so that we can transcribe our own history and publish it. Of course, it is difficult to do that, since it is a big sacrifice. We will be willing to accept the difficulty and sacrifice only when we are able to see far beyond our own personal needs to the larger context of the needs of the African people and our children's future. We need to begin to measure our personal success by our individual efforts to build a self-sustainable African society from which all of our children can benefit. When we do that, we will be able to face these challenges and be prepared, as Africans, to sacrifice our time and energy in service to our own people.

Look at the health systems in Africa. What is happening in our hospitals? Not only do we need to watch out for expired medicine, but also we are experiencing a great amount of medical malpractice in Africa. Why? Because the masses of the people have not been provided with an adequate understanding of the health system that is supposed to be helping them. This is because we are still using the type of health system the Europeans left us. It socializes us to believe that the doctor knows everything and we, as the patient, know nothing about medical matters. No one dares to challenge or even question a doctor in Africa. Because of this, doctors in Africa feel so powerful that they refuse to listen to the patient describe what is wrong at any hospital or any clinic in Africa. Their word regarding medical conditions is final because supposedly they know what is wrong. It is our own bodies; we know how we feel inside. The doctor cannot feel how you feel. The doctor cannot understand the body more than the one who is in it. The doctor cannot feel the pain. The doctor is not experiencing the illness and must take time to listen to the patient describe the symptoms.

I challenge every African and African government to stop accepting things that are not useful to Africans from the West, especially in the field of education. Instead, consider a larger context to determine which things will better serve the current and future needs of the African people in general. So often our governments get off the right path when they start to prioritize what would be in the best interests of the African people. This has harmed us in the past and will continue to hinder our progress unless we begin *now*, not tomorrow, to re-evaluate our beliefs and practices as well as our actions in service to our own people. We should be able to prioritize correctly. We should be able to empower our own people. We should encourage formally trained doctors to enter into productive dialog with practitioners of traditional African medicine in all African nations. The West is now using the holistic method of treating patients. For us to be able to become self-sustainable, each skill in Africa, including each traditional skill, must be welcomed. Once a skill is welcomed into modern African society, it can be evaluated and modernized so that it can be effectively utilized to serve the best interests of the African people.

We cannot continue to condemn all the things that have been produced in Africa if we want Africa to become an independently sustainable continent. As I said previously, it is not easy to accomplish this goal. It will involve much sacrifice and patience to reach our vision of a great Africa. I often say to myself, "Even though I may not be alive to see Africa become united and independently sustainable, I still have a vision that one day this will happen and our children and their children will benefit from it." They will be happy that we, as Africans, created a positive future for them. Africa is a continent that has many valuable resources and talented human beings.

> Our country produces food to feed itself. We can even surpass our current production. But unfortunately, because of our own lack of organization, we are still forced to hold out our hands for food aid. This food aid is an obstacle to us, instilling in us and planting in our minds the habits and welfare reflexes of the beggar. We must do away with this aid through increased production.[81]

Why do African nations welcome wasteful and harmful materials from other countries so they become the world's dumping ground? It is our responsibility, as Africans, to say to the rest of the world, "Enough! We are not prepared today, nor will we be tomorrow, to allow you to make Africa your dumping ground. Nor will we continue to be a place where conflict can be sustained so that you will have a market for your weapons. We are tired of it, we are sick of it, and we are not prepared to take it anymore." I am convinced that we believe that our ancestors are not happy with the way Africans operate in our nations. They are not happy to see us divided with African descendants around the globe. They are not happy to see us remain in poverty. They are not happy to see us have poor educational systems. They are not happy to see us have a lack of adequate clinics and hospitals that can cure our own people. They are not happy to see us suffering from a lack of agricultural and industrial materials and equipment to produce the things we need in our own countries. I believe that they are surprised because they accomplished many difficult tasks for us so that we would be able to appreciate that and build on it to move Africa forward toward a more positive future for the twenty-first century world economy.

United we stand; divided we fall. Which way, Africa? Are we going to continue falling down or are we going to stand in unity for Africa's sake? We must awaken and create a clear vision of Africa's future and then remain focused on it. Believe in God and God will give us the power we need to accomplish our vision of a better land for our own people because Africa can do it.

I believe in Africa. A society that has no vision for its people is doomed to fail. A vision without accountability cannot be implemented. A vision that cannot be implemented is useless. Are Africans useless people? The choice is ours and no one else's. How long will we continue fooling ourselves thinking that somebody, somewhere, somehow will come and build Africa? Have we seen that happen? No. We must build Africa ourselves. *We* have to do it. *We* have to sacrifice, to work together, to become more creative and accept our responsibility to take up our own individual and group tasks to build a better Africa. We should not expect Europeans, Americans, Asians, or any other people to build Africa. Africans, not by outsiders, must build Africa. Once outsiders have seen the type of positive work that we do in Africa, they can come to Africa, but only if they are prepared and willing to follow and work *with* us. We will begin to build Africa when we stop following behind them. We think this is the way to build an independently sustainable Africa. Not only is this a false belief, it is also a shame to all Africans. It is a shame to every human being who loves and cares about Africa.

Sometimes Africans fool themselves by thinking that a particular nation in Africa belongs to a certain ethnic group. We must not fool ourselves. We must become mature and capable Africans and look at the larger context. When we do that, we will see that no single ethnic group can alone build and sustain Africa without the help of the other ethnic groups in their country. No ethnic group in any nation in Africa can run any national government, alone, without working with other ethnic groups in their nation. No ethnic group in any nation in Africa can alone build better educational systems, clinics and hospitals, and industrial and agricultural projects without working with other ethnic groups, so why are we fooling ourselves thinking it is possible? Have we not learned anything? When *are* we going to learn? When are we going to grow up, as Africans, and realize that we owe it to our children to work with each other, regardless of which our ethnic or religious group, to build better educational institutions, health centers, hospitals, industrial and agricultural projects in our nations?

Muslims, Christians, Bahais, and traditional believers are all Africans. Islam alone cannot build Africa, nor can Christianity, Bahai, nor traditional African religion cannot alone build Africa. All of us need to work together to build a better Africa. I want us all to understand that we must be prepared to work, not just for the benefit of our own religion or our own ethnic group, because that is not healthy for any African, nor is it healthy for our continent, Africa, Beloved Land.

We must act for African unity. We must together strengthen our individual and group dedication, accountability, consensus, and democracy because from these, true freedom will come to African people. Then, at last, we will be able to shout with joy, "Unity! We have freedom because we did it ourselves." That is what Africa should be like. Are *you* prepared to dedicate your life to African unity for the sake of our children and our children's children? If so, we must join hands, hearts, and minds with other Africans and proclaim that we love Africa, and that even though we die, we believe in African unity and nobody can change our minds. We are convinced that one day we will achieve unity and become a self-sustainable continent.

Queen Mother Africa Model

Queen Mother Africa

We received so much from Queen Mother Africa
We owe it to Queen Mother Africa
We owe it to our Ancestors, our Children and Ourselves
We must give back to Queen Mother Africa
Queen Mother Africa is here for us all.

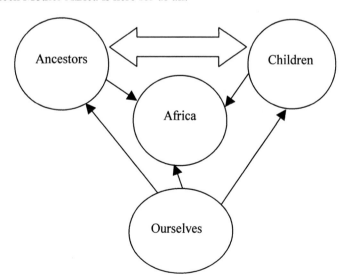

Chapter 12

Conclusion: I Have a Vision of a New Africa

I have a vision of a positive future for Africa. This vision is deeply rooted in the hearts and minds of all true Africans. It is the vision of a day when Africa will be a united, independently sustainable continent in which divisions of language and conflicts of ethnicity, gender, religion, and class have been overcome. It is a day when Africa will be a united, non-violent society in which oppression and conflicts of gender, religion, class, and race have been overcome. I have a vision of a day when Africans will practice true equality in which women take leadership roles and men work to support them to develop our continent. I have a vision of an Africa where violence and abuse toward women, children, and the poor have been abandoned and all humans are treated with respect and dignity. I have a vision of a day when traditional African religion believers, Muslims, Christians, and Baha'i all work together to develop and create a more peaceful continent.

It is a vision of a day when our African leaders foster African unification and the development of our continent by democratically distributing high quality services to all Africans, regardless of ethnic group, gender, or religion. I have a vision of an Africa where corruption and monopoly have been eliminated and heads of state are no longer dictators but instead support and maintain true democracies. I envision a day when the abuse of military power and violence in Africa has been eradicated. This will be a day when African presidents serve no more than two five-year terms and when African heads of state are restricted from investing money outside of Africa. It will be a day when no African is above the law and those who commit crimes against Africa will be dealt with severely by our legal system. I have a vision of a day when our chief justice and our criminal justice system become more effective, making Africa no longer a dumping ground of prostitution and drug trafficking. I have a vision of a day when the use of knives and guns to enact violence and commit crimes in Africa has been eradicated, when our homes, neighborhoods, schools and communities will be safe and clean. I see a healthy environment in which people of all races are proud of where they live and go to school and will work together to build and sustain them for future of all African children.

It will be a day when our political, religious, intellectual, and educational leaders will care for our environment. I have a vision of an African educational system that values, maintains, and incorporates, as an integral part of the curriculum, local cultures. This system will activate individual talent and use it for the production of valuable goods and services. It will be a day when all African institutions and the departments within them value, maintain, and practice cultural and ethnic diversity. I have a vision of a day when our intellectuals do not condemn African leaders and when they are not seen as a threat in our society. Instead they will put their knowledge, skills, and experience into positive practice for the development of the entire continent. I have a vision of a day when recent secondary and college graduates, the unemployed, both white- and blue-collar workers, intellectuals, and community and religious leaders all refrain from disparaging our cities, towns, institutions, and leaders, but instead, put their knowledge, skills, and experience into positive practice for the development of our African continent. This is a vision of a day in which Africans of all religions, races, genders, and classes will work together for the common good of all of our children who will become the future leaders of our continent. I have a vision of a day when we will value our own products, have our own market and control our own resources so that we will share and trade fairly among ourselves. I have a vision of a day when all Africans will say no to Western aid and its sanctions, which oppress, suppress, discriminate, divide, and control us. I have a vision of an Africa where physical and mental slavery has been eliminated and our people work together to build a better continent. I see a day in which Africans unite with all African descendants around the globe, from Asia to the Americas, to work for the common good of our children who will become the future leaders of the human race. I see a bright future day when we will have a United States of Africa with a single currency for the entire continent.

When all this has been achieved and maintained, I will be able to say we have true democracy, equality, liberty, freedom, and justice in our African institutions, communities, and nations. On this day, all Africans will be able to proclaim that we are in charge and control of our own continent and that this is a society ruled by all of its people for the benefit of all who live within it. I challenge all Africans today to join with all people in Africa, to unite with a common vision for a united, nonviolent, independently sustainable Africa that is a safe and productive society because we owe it to our children, our ancestors, and ourselves. The guiding principles that support this vision and commitment are a united, peaceful society where all humans, regardless of race, gender, religion, or class, are valued and treated with equal dignity, respect, and fairness. However far down the tunnel the source of light of my vision seems to be at this moment, I am hopeful with its presence down there and so I can say, "At least there is light at the end of the tunnel." Africa, from North to South, East to West and Central, I therefore declare, we can do it!

Notes

Chapter 3

1. R. R. Greene and H. P. I. Ephross, *Human Behavior and Social Work Practice* (Hawthorne, N.Y.: Aldine De Gruyter, 1991), 203–59.

2. R. R. Greene and H. P. I. Ephross, *Human Behavior*, 203–59.

3. R. R. Greene and H. P. I. Ephross, *Human Behavior*, 203–59.

4. Monica McGoldrick, K. J. Pearce, and J. Giodano, J., *Ethnicity and Family Therapy* (New York: The Guilford Press, 1982); R. R. Greene and H. P. I. Ephross, *Human Behavior*, 3–28, 187–228, 203–59.

5. Monica McGoldrick, K. J. Pearce, and J. Giodano, J., *Ethnicity*, 3–28, 187–228.

6. Monica McGoldrick, K. J. Pearce, and J. Giodano, J., *Ethnicity*, 3–28, 187–228.

7. Asma El Dareer and Raqiya Haji Dualeh Abdalla, *Woman, Why Do You Weep?* (London: Zed Press of London, 1982); Monica McGoldrick, K. J. Pearce, and J. Giodano, J., *Ethnicity*, 3–28, 187–228.

8. Hanny Lightfoot-Klein, "The Sexual Experience and Marital Adjustment of Genitally Circumcised and Infibulated Females in The Sudan," *Journal of Sex Research* 26, no. 3 (August, 1989): 375–92.

9. Hanny Lightfoot-Klein, "The Sexual Experience," 375–92.

10. Allison Slack, "The Status of Women in Sudan," *Human Rights Quarterly 10*, no. 4 (November, 1988): 437–86.

11. Allison Slack, "The Status," 437–486.

12. Robert, Myers, Francisa Omorodion, Anthony Isenalumhe, and Gregory Akenzua, "Circumcision: Its Nature and Practice Among Some Ethnic Groups in Southern Nigeria," *Journal of Social Science and Medicine 21*, no. 5 (May 21, 1985): 581–88.

13. Maria Assad, "Female Circumcision in Egypt," *Studies in Family Planning 11*, no. 1 (January 11, 1980), 3–16.

14. El Asma Dareer and Raqiya Haji Dualeh Abdalla, *Woman*, 15–116.

15. William House, "The Status of Women in Sudan," *Journal of Modern African Studies 26*, no. 2 (June 26, 1988), 277–302.

Chapter 4

1. Colin Rosser, *Urbanization in Tropical Africa* (New York: Ford Foundation, 1972) 10–74.

2. Nathan Keyfitz, *Population Change and Social Policy* (Cambridge, Mass., 1982), 125–61.

3. Ali A. Mazrui, *The African Condition*. (London: Cambridge University Press, 1980), 9–65.

4. Salah El-Shakhs and Robert Obudho, "Urbanization, National Development, and Regional Planning in Africa," 13–88.

5. Colin Rosser, *Urbanization,* 10–74.

6. Ali A. Mazrui, *African Condition,* 9–65.

7. Nathan Keyfitz, *Population Change,* 125–61.

8. Nathan Keyfitz, *Population Change,* 125–61.

9. Nathan Keyfitz, *Population Change,* 125–61.

10. Colin Rosser, *Urbanization,* 10–74.

11. Anthony O'Connor, *The African City.* (New York: Africana Publishing Company, 1983), 4–60.

12. Colin Rosser, *Urbanization,* 10–74.

13. Salah El-Shakhs and Robert Obudho, 13–88.

14. P. O. Sada and J. S. Oguntoyinbo, "Urbanization Processes and Problems in Nigeria." *Urbanization Problems in Africa.* (Ibadan, Nigeria: Ibadan University Press, 1981), 7–40.

15. Alfred A. Jarrett, "The Encroachment of Rural-urban Migration in Sierra Leone," *International Social Work 5,* no. 33 (Fall 1990): 49–72.

16. Salah El-Shakhs and Robert Obudho, "Urbanization, National Development, and Regional Planning in Africa," 13–88.

17. Alfred A. Jarrett, "Encroachment," 49–72.

18. Alfred A. Jarrett, "Encroachment," 49–72.

19. David Drakakis-Smith. *The Third World City.* (New York: Routledge, 1990), 15–85.

20. Nathan Keyfitz, *Population Change,* 125–61.

21. Alfred A. Jarrett, "Encroachment," 49–72.

22. Salah El-Shakhs and Robert Obudho, "Urbanization, National Development, and Regional Planning in Africa," 13–88.

23. J. A. Jackson, *Migration.* (London: Cambridge University Press, 1969), 14–156.

24. J. A. Jackson, *Migration,* 14–156.

25. Ali A. Mazrui, *African Condition,* 9–65.

26. Ali A. Mazrui, *African Condition,* 9–65.

27. Ali A. Mazrui, *African Condition,* 9–65.

28. Samir Amin, *Modern Migrations in Western Africa.* (London: Oxford University Press, 1974), 325–58.

29. Ali A. Mazrui, *African Condition,* 9–65.

30. Samir Amin, *Modern Migrations in Western Africa,* 325–58.

31. Ali A. Mazrui, *African Condition,* 9–65.

32. Alfred A. Jarrett, "Encroachment," 49–72.

33. Alfred A. Jarrett, "Encroachment," 49–72.

34. Samir Amin, *Modern Migrations in Western Africa,* 325–58.

35. J. A. Jackson, *Migration,* 14–156.

Chapter 5

1. Colin Rosser, *Urbanization,* 10–74.
2. David Drakakis-Smith, *The Third World City,* 15–85
3. Alfred A. Jarrett, "Encroachment," 49–72.
4. Alfred A. Jarrett, "Encroachment," 49–72.
5. Colin Rosser, *Urbanization,* 10–74.
6. Salah El-Shakhs and Robert Obudho, "Urbanization, National Development, and Regional Planning in Africa," 13–88.
7. Alfred A. Jarrett, "Encroachment," 49–72.
8. Nolan Zavoral, "Has House Puts the Jock in Jocularity," *Star Tribune,* 15 November 1992, 2.
9. Nolan Zavoral, "Has House," 2.
10. Alfred A. Jarrett, "Encroachment," 49–72.
11. P. O. Olusanya, P. O., *Socio-Economic Aspects of Rural-Urban Migration in Western Nigeria.* Lagos, Nigeria: Nigerian Institute of and Economic Research, 1969, 127–31.
12. Ecoculture, Etc., "Africa-Caribbean-Pacific Community," *UNESCO Courier,* no. 131 (January–February, 1992): 49–77.
13. Alfred A. Jarrett, "Encroachment," 49–72.
14. P. O. Olusanya, *Socio-Economic Aspects of Rural-Urban Migration in Western Nigeria.,* 127–31.
15. Alfred A. Jarrett, "Encroachment," 49–72.
16. Salah El-Shakhs and Robert Obudho, "Urbanization, National Development, and Regional Planning in Africa," 13–88.

Chapter 6

1. Colin Rosser, *Urbanization,* 10–74.
2. Alfred A. Jarrett, "Encroachment," 49–72.
3. Alfred A. Jarrett, "Encroachment," 49–72.

Chapter 7

1. P. O. Sada and J. S. Oguntoyinbo, "Urbanization Processes and Problems in Nigeria," 7–40.
2. Salah El-Shakhs and Robert Obudho, "Urbanization," 13–88.
3. P. O. Sada and J. S. Oguntoyinbo, "Urbanization Processes," 7–40.
4. P. O. Sada and J. S. Oguntoyinbo, "Urbanization Processes," 7–40.
5. Julius Nyerere, *Freedom and Socialism: A Selection from Writings and Speeches, 1965–1967* (Dar es Salaam: Oxford University Press, 1968), 79–85. This book includes The Arusha Declaration, Education for Self-reliance, The Varied Paths to Socialism, The Purpose Is Man, and Socialism and Development.
6. Julius Nyerere, *Freedom,* 79–85.
7. Julius Nyerere, *Freedom,* 79–85.
8. Shepard, Jack, "Drought of the Century," *Atlantic Monthly 4,* no. 2 (February, 1985): 32–7.
9. Shepard, Jack, "Drought," 32–7.
10. P. D. Collins, "The State and Industrial Capitalism in West Africa," Development and Change, *ECA Report 14,* no. 3 (July, 1983): 18–74.

Chapter 8

1. Ali A. Mazrui, *African Condition,* 9–65.

2. Henry Kamm, "New Gulf War Issue: Chemical Arms," *UN Chronicle 21*, no. 14 (March, 1984): 16–29.

3. Nathan Keyfitz, *Population Change,* 125–61.

4. James O'Connor, *The Fiscal Crises of the State* (New York: St. Martin's, 1973), 43–98.

5. C. Offe, *Contradictions of the Welfare State* (Cambridge, Mass.: MIT Press, 1984), 35–123

6. N. Poulantzas, *Political Power and Social Classes* (New York: Routledge, 1973), 13–89.

7. N. Poulantzas, *Political Power,* 13–89.

8. N. Poulantzas, *Political Power,* 13–89.

9. N. Poulantzas, *Political Power,* 13–89.

10. N. Poulantzas, *Political Power,* 13–89.

11. N. Poulantzas, *Political Power,* 13–89.

12. N. Poulantzas, *Political Power,* 13–89.

Chapter 9

1. Rosabeth Moss Kantor, *Commitment and Community: Communes and Utopias in Sociological Perspective* (Boston, Mass.: Harvard University Press, 1972), 1–85.

Chapter 10

1. Edgar H. Schein, "Organizational Culture and Leadership," Second Edition (San Francisco: Jossey-Bass Publishers, 1992), 13–113.

2. Martin Luther King, Jr., "The Words of Martin Luther King, Jr." (New York: Newmarket Press, 1987), 17–67.

3. Norman R. F. Maier, *Problem-solving Discussions and Conferences: Leadership Methods and Skills* (New York: McGraw-Hill Book Company Inc., 1963), 12–200.

4. Mark J. Splain, "Negotiations: Using a Weapon as a Way Out," in Lee Staples (Ed.), *Roots to Power* (New York: Praeger, 1984), 164–70.

5. Burton Gummer, Burton. *The Politics of Social Administration* (Englewood Cliffs, N. J.: Prentice Hall, 1990), 1–199.

6. Anonymous, *Among the Black Civil Rights in America.*

7. *The Kitab-i-aqdas*, section 40 (Wilmette, Ill.: Bahai Publishing Trust, 1992), 21–247.

8. *The Qur'an*, Surah IX, Section 38 (Elmhurst, N.Y.: Tahrike Tarsile Quran, Inc. 1990), 14–405.

9. *The Holy Bible*, John 4, verse 35. (Iowa Falls, Ia.: World Bible Publishers, 1992), 144–84.

Chapter 11

1. Martin Luther King, Jr., *The Words of,* New Market Press New York, New York, 1967, 17–67.

2. Marx, Karl, *Classical Sociological Theory,* 17–59.

3. Max Weber, *The Protestant Ethic and the Spirit of Capitalism* (New York: Charles Scribner's Sons, 1976), 3–154.

4. Max Weber, *The Protestant Ethic*, 3–154.

5. Marx, Karl. 1964. Selected Writings in Sociology and Social Philosophy. Translated by T.B. Bottomore. (London: McGraw-Hill, 1964).

6. Max Weber, *The Protestant Ethic*, 3–154.

7. Karl Marx, *Classical Sociological Theory*, 17–59.

8. Max Weber, *The Protestant Ethic*, 3–154.

9. Karl Marx, *Classical Sociological Theory*, 17–59.

10. *The Kitáb-I-Aqdas*, 21–247.

11. *The Holy Bible*, Jesus of Nazareth, Matthew, vrs. 24–7, 144–84.

12. *The Qurán*, Surah LVII, vrs. 11, 12, 14–405.

13. Janice M. Beyer and Harrison M. Trice, "Cultural Leadership in Organizations," *Organizational Science 2*, no. 2 (May, 1991): 149–66.

14. Janice M. Beyer and Harrison M. Trice, "Cultural Leadership," 149–66.

15. Janice M. Beyer and Harrison M. Trice, "Cultural Leadership," 149–66.

16. Edgar H. Schein, *Organizational Culture and Leadership*, Second Edition (San Francisco: Jossey-Bass Publishers, 1992), 13–113.

17. Philip R. Harris and Robert T. Moran, *Managing Cultural Differences*, Third Edition (Houston, Tex.: Gulf Publishing, 1993), 5–194.

18. David A. Kolb, Irwin M. Rubin, and Joyce S. Osland, *The Organizational Behavior Reader*, Fifth Edition (Englewood Cliffs, N.J.: Prentice Hall, 1991), 371–417.

19. Schein, Edgar H., *Organizational Culture*, 13–113.

20. Peter M. Senge, "The Leader's New Work: Building Learning Organizations," *Sloan Management Review 32*, no. 1 (Fall, 1990): 7–23.

21. Janice M Beyer and Harrison M. Trice, "Cultural Leadership," 149–66.

22. Max Weber, *The Protestant Ethic*, 3–154.

23. Max Weber, *The Protestant Ethic*, 3–154.

24. Janice M Beyer and Harrison M. Trice, "Cultural Leadership," 149–66.

25. Jay A. Conger, "The Dark Side of Leadership," *Organizational Dynamics 19*, no. 2 (Fall, 1990): 44–55.

26. Jay A. Conger, "The Dark Side," 44–55.

27. Jay A. Conger, "The Dark Side," 44–55.

28. Jay A. Conger, "The Dark Side," 44–55.

29. Peter F. Drucker, "Leadership: More Doing Than Dash," *Wall Street Journal*, 6 January 1988, 1–4.

30. John P. Kotter, "What Leaders Really Do," *Harvard Business Review 90*, no. 33 May–June, 1990): 103–11.

31. John P. Kotter, "What Leaders," 103–11.

32. John P. Kotter, "What Leaders," 103–11.

33. Edwin A. Locke, *The Essence of Leadership* (Lanham, Md.: Lexington Books, 1991), 1–9.

34. Peter F. Drucker, "Leadership," 1–4.

35. Philip R. Harris and Robert T. Moran, *Managing Cultural Differences*, 5–194.

36. Janice M. Beyer and Harrison M. Trice, "Cultural Leadership," 149–66.

37. Peter F. Drucker, "Leadership," 1–4.

38. Schein, Edgar H., *Organizational Culture*, 13–113.

39. Schein, Edgar H., *Organizational Culture*, 13–113.

40. Schein, Edgar H., *Organizational Culture*, 13–113.

41. Schein, Edgar H., *Organizational Culture*, 13–113.

42. Schein, Edgar H., *Organizational Culture*, 13–113.

43. Schein, Edgar H., *Organizational Culture*, 13–113.

44. Jean Bartunek, "Changing Interpretive Schemes and Organizational Restructuring: The Example of a Religious Order," *Administrative Science Quarterly,* no. 29 (September, 1984): 355–72.

45. Jean Bartunek, "Changing Interpretive Schemes," 355–72.

46. Schein, Edgar H., *Organizational Culture*, 13–113.

47. H. Mintzberg, Duru Raisinghai, and Andre Theoret, "The Structure of 'Unstructured' Decision Process," *Administrative Science Quarterly 21,* no. 2 (June 1976): 146–274.

48. Jean Bartunek, "Changing Interpretive Schemes," 355–72.

49. Schein, Edgar H., *Organizational Culture*, 13–113.

50. Schein, Edgar H., *Organizational Culture*, 13–113.

51. Schein, Edgar H., *Organizational Culture*, 13–113.

52. Schein, Edgar H., *Organizational Culture*, 13–113.

53. Louise Wilby, Knight, "Jane Adams and Hull House: Historical Lessons on Nonprofit Leadership," (San Francisco, Calif.: Nonprofit Management and Leadership, 1991), 125–41.

54. Kenneth Kaunda, *Zambia Shall Be Free* (London: Heinemann Educational Books, 1962), 1–154.

55. Jay A. Conger, "The Dark Side," 44–55.

56. Note: (50 reels 35 mm. Microfilm. Originals in the Edward R. Murrow Center of Public Diplomacy in the Tufts University Library), *Edward R. Murrow Papers, 1927–1965: A Guide to the Microfilm Edition.* (Sanford, N.C.: Microfilming Corp. of America, 1982).

57. James M. Kouzes and Barry Z. Posner, *The Leadership Challenge* (San Francisco, Calif.: Jossey-Bass, 1987), 35–276.

58. Max DePree, *Leadership Is an Art* (East Lansing: Michigan State University Press, 1987), 15–89.

59. Peter F. Drucker, "Leadership," 1–4.

60. Kwame Arhin, "The Life and Work of Kwame Nkrumah" (Trenton, N.J.: Africa World Press, Inc.), 177–204.

61. Peter M. Senge, "The Leader's New Work," 7–23.

62. Peter M. Senge, "The Leader's New Work," 7–23.

63. John P. Kotter, "What Leaders," 103–11.

64. John P. Kotter, "What Leaders," 103–11.

65. Lao Tsu, quoted by Peter M. Senge, "The Leader's New Work: Building Learning Organizations," *Sloan Management Review 32,* no. 1 (Fall, 1990): 7–23.

66. Suresh Srivastva and David L. Cooperrider, *Appreciative Management and Leadership* (San Francisco: Jossey-Bass, 1990), 34–204.

67. Suresh Srivastva and David L. Cooperrider, *Appreciative Management,* 34–204.

68. James D. Thompson, *Organizations in Action* (New York: McGraw-Hill, 1967), 1–157.

69. Parsons, P., J. Belcher, and J. Jackson. (1998). "A Labor-Management Approach to Health Care Cost Savings: The Peoria Experience." *Public Personnel Management 27,* no. 1 (Spring): 23–37.

70. James D. Thompson, *Organizations,* 1–157.

71. James D. Thompson, *Organizations,* 1–157.

72. James D. Thompson, *Organizations,* 1–157.

73. James D. Thompson, *Organizations,* 1–157.

74. James D. Thompson, *Organizations,* 1–157.

75. James D. Thompson, *Organizations,* 1–157.

76. James D. Thompson, *Organizations,* 1–157.

77. James D. Thompson, *Organizations,* 1–157.

78. James D. Thompson, *Organizations,* 1–157.

79. James D. Thompson, *Organizations,* 1–157.

80. Julius Nyerere, *Freedom,* 79–85.

81. Samantha Anderson, *Thomas Sankara Speaks,* (New York: Pathfinder Press, 1988), 111–44.

Bibliography

Amin, Samir. *Modern Migrations in Western Africa*. London: Oxford University Press, 1974.

Arhin, Kwame. *The Life and Work of Kwame Nkrumah*. Trenton, N. J.: Africa World Press, 1993.

Bartunek, Jean M. "Changing Interpretive Schemes and Organizational Restructuring: The Example of a Religious Order." *Administrative Science Quarterly, 29* (1984): 355–72.

Beeghley, L., Powers, H. Charles and Turner, Jonathan H. *The Emergence of Sociological Theory*. New York-: Wadsworth Publishing Company, 1995.

Beyer, Janice M., and Harrision M. Trice. "Cultural Leadership In Organizations." *Organizational Science 2*, no. 2 (May 1991): 149–69.

Collins, Randall, and Michael Makowsky. *The Discovery of Society*. New York: McGraw-Hill, Inc., 1993.

Conger, Jay A. "The Dark Side of Leadership." *Organizational Dynamics* (Fall 1990): 44–55.

Drakakis-Smith, David. *The Third World City*. New York, New York: Routledge, 1990.

Drucker, Peter F. "Leadership: More Doing Than Dash." *Wall Street Journal,* January 6, 1988.

Elster, Jon. *An Introduction to Karl Marx.* New York: Cambridge University Press, 1994.

Harris, Philip R. and Robert T Moran. *Managing Cultural Differences.* 3d ed. Houston, Tx.: Gulf Publishing, 1993.

Imoagene Oshomha., Salah El-Shakhs., and Robert Obudho. "Urbanization, National Development, and Regional Planning in Africa." In Salah El-Shakhs and Robert Obudho, *Sociological Aspects of Modern Migration in West Africa.* Lagos, Nigeria: Praeger Publishers, 1974.

Jackson, J. A. *Migration.* London, UK: Cambridge University Press. 1969.

Jarrett, Alfred A. "The Encroachment of Rural-urban Migration in Sierra Leone." *International Social Work v*, no. 33 (October 1990): 49–72.

Kanter, Rosabeth Moss. *Commitment and Community.* Boston: Harvard University Press, 1972.

Kaunda, Kenneth. *Zambia Shall Be Free.* London: Heinemann Educational Books, 1962.

Keyfitz, Nathan. *Population Change and Social Policy.* Cambridge, Mass.: Abt Books, 1982.

Knight, Louise Wilby. "Jane Addams and Hull House: Historical Lessons on Nonprofit Leadership." *Nonprofit Management and Leadership, 2.* no. 2, (Winter 1991): 125–41.

Kolb, David A., Irwin M. Rubin, and Joyce S. Osland. *The Organizational Behavior Reader.* 5th ed. Englewood Cliffs, N. J.: Prentice Hall, 1991.

Kotter, John P. "What Leaders Really Do." *Harvard Business Review 90*, no. 3, (May–June , 1990): 104–11.

Kouzes, James M., and Barry Z. Posner, *The Leadership Challenge.* San Francisco: Jossey-Bass, 1987.

Locke, Edwin A. *The Essence of Leadership.* Lanham, Md.: Lexington Books, 1991.

Mabogunje, Akin L. *Towards an Urban Policy in Nigeria.* New York: Africana, 1962.

Mabogunje, Akin L., E. P. O. Sada, and J. S. Oguntoyinbo. "Urbanization Processes and Problems in Nigeria." *Urbanization Problems in Africa.* Ibadan, Nigeria: Ibadan University Press, 1981.

Mazrui, Ali A. *The African Condition*. London: Cambridge University Press, 1980.

Meyer, John, John Boli, George Thomas, and Francisco Ramirez. "World Society and the Nation State." *American Journal of Sociology 103*, no. 1 (July 1997): 144–81.

O'Connor, Anthony. *The African City*. New York: Africana Publishing, 1983.

Olusanya, R. P. O. *Socio-Economic Aspects of Rural-Urban Migration in Western Nigeria*. Lagos, Nigeria: Nigerian Institute of and Economic Research, 1969.

Rosser, Colin. *Urbanization in Tropical Africa*. New York: Ford Foundation, 1973.

Schein, Edgar H. *Organizational Culture and Leadership*. 2nd ed. San Francisco: Jossey-Bass, 1992.

Senge, Peter M. "The Leader's New Work: Building Learning Organizations." *Sloan Management Review 32*, no. 1 (Fall, 1990): 7-23.

Srivastva, Suresh, and David L. Cooperrider. *Appreciative Management and Leadership*. San Francisco: Jossey-Bass, 1990.

Thompson, James D., *Organizations in Action*. New York: McGraw-Hill, 1967.

Trice, Harrison M., and Janice M. Beyer. *The Cultures of Work Organizations*. Englewood Cliffs, N.J.: Prentice Hall, 1993.

Weber, Max. *The Protestant Ethic and the Spirit of Capitalism*. New York: Charles Scribner's Sons, 1958.

Weber, Max and Henderson A. Parsons (trans.) *The Theory of Social and Economic Organization*. London, Edinburgh, Glasgow: William Hodge and Co., 1947.

UN Chronicle, March 1984

Financial Times, 26 October 1989

UNESCO Courier, January 1992

Index

About the Author

Michael Ba Banutu-Gomez was born in the early 1960s, in Bakalar Village, in the North Bank Division of The Gambia, West Africa. His father was Bisenty Cau Banutu-Gomez, and his mother was Nyima Bamba Joku-Mendy. His parents were of the Manjako ethnic group, speaking the Manjako language, originally from Guinea-Bissau, West Africa. Michael came from a family of twelve children. His parents were farmers and palm tree tappers. His father was also a blacksmith (*bahak*). Because there was no elementary school in his village, he and his brothers and sister went to stay with Pa Joof of the Serer ethnic group, in Mbollet-Ba Village so they could walk to St. Michael's elementary school in Njongon Village, two miles away. Michael attended Catholic elementary and secondary school in his country.

Michael Ba received his Qualified Teacher Certificate from the Gambia Teacher Training College. He has received his bachelor in Sociology and Applied Social Relations at Eastern Connecticut State University. He received his Masters in Social Work, with concentration in Management from Boston University. He received his doctorate at Case Western Reserve University Wetherhead School of Management, Department of Organizational Behavior. Michael Ba has presented his research work at professional conferences here in the U.S. While in The Gambia, he taught at Saint Theresa's Elementary School in Kanifing as well as Malfa Elementary School in Banjul. He also worked for Ministry of Education, Youth Sport and Culture. He served as the Assistant Organizing Executive Scout Commissioner for The Gambia National Scout Association. He helped build relationships between The Gambia Scout Association and the Danish Scout Association in which they started an exchange visit scout program. He worked for Fleet Bank of Massachusetts as well as the Massachusetts Department of Social Services. He also worked for Oxfam America where he was the Coordinator for the West Africa and Horn of Africa Programs. Michael Ba is an organizational development consultant. He and his wife, Shandra, have their own consulting firm called Banutu Consulting Firm, Inc. He has consulted for the U.S., Africa, and India. Michael Ba has consulted for Global Excellence in Management (GEM) Innovation and has conducted leadership and certificate training program for chief executive officers and government officers worldwide. He has also conducted training on sustainable development. Michael Ba taught at Illinois Institute of Technology, Stuart School of Business in Chicago. He also taught at Robert Morris College, Business Administration School in Chicago.

While he was in graduate school in Boston, he started the African Student Organization, which won an award as the best programming student organization in the school for three consecutive years. The organization was reviewed by the Boston Globe newspaper. He also started The Gambian Association of Massachusetts. He pioneered fundraising activities for the organization, which sent 9,704 classroom materials to The Gambia elementary schools.

Michael Ba has published his work in academic journals as well as in the *Daily Observer* newspaper in The Gambia. He helped to develop the constitution for the worldwide Gambian Education Support Organization (GESO). He is a member of The Gambian Education Support Organization, The Gambian Association of Massachusetts, The Gambian Association of Chicago, The Academy of Management, The New England Sociological Association, The National Association of Social Work, and The African Initiative for Community Development Board Member. Above all, his research interest is Africa. Michael Ba Banutu-Gomez was the main speaker at a conference organized by Gambians in the Midwest on September 4, 1999. He spoke about Leadership and African Unity. Presently, Michael Ba Banutu-Gomez is Assistant Professor at Rowan University, College of Business in Glassboro, New Jersey.